SUBVERSION AND SCURRILITY: POPULAR DISCOURSE IN EUROPE FROM 1500 TO THE PRESENT

In memory of Gareth Roberts

Subversion and Scurrility:
Popular Discourse in Europe
from 1500 to the Present

Edited by
Dermot Cavanagh
and
Tim Kirk

Ashgate

Aldershot • Burlington USA• Singapore• Sydney

Published by
Ashgate Publishing Limited
Gower House
Croft Road
Aldershot
Hants GU11 3HR
England

Ashgate Publishing Company
131 Main Street
Burlington
Vermont 05401–5600
USA

Ashgate website: http://www.ashgate.com

British Library Cataloguing-in-Publication data

Subversion and scurrility: popular discourse in Europe from 1500 to the present
  1.Subversive activities in literature 2.Libel and slander in literature 3.Literature and society – Europe 4.European literature – History and criticism. I.Cavanagh, Dermot II.Kirk, Tim
  809.9'3353'094

Library of Congress Cataloging-in-Publication data

Subversion and scurrility : popular discourse in Europe from 1500 to the present / edited by Dermot Cavanagh and Tim Kirk.
  1.Satire, English–History and criticism–Congresses. 2.Political satire, English–History and criticism–Congresses. 3.Popular culture–Great Britain –History–Congresses. 4.Popular culture–Europe–History–Congresses. 5. Satire–History and criticism–Congresses. 6.Invective in literature– Congresses. 7.Invective–Congresses. I.Cavanagh, Dermot. II.Kirk, Tim
  PR931.S75 2000
  827.009–dc21   99–055006

ISBN 1 84014 643 5

Typeset in Times by Pat FitzGerald and printed on acid-free paper and bound in Great Britain by Athenaeum Press, Ltd.,

Contents

List of Figures

Contributors

Gerhard Ammerer teaches history at the University of Salzburg. He is author of *Funktionen, Finanzen und Fortschritt. Zur Regionalverwaltung im Spätabsolutismus am Beispiel des geistlichen Fürstentums Salzburg* (Salzburg, 1987) and co-editor (with Hanns Haas) of *Ambivalenzen der Aufklärung. Festschrift für Ernst Wangermann* (Vienna and Munich, 1997). He is currently working on *Vaganten ohne Lyrik. Studien zu den Ursachen der Nichtshaftigkeit und den (Über-)Lebensformen auf der Strasse im Österreich des Aufgeklärten Absolutismus.*

Dermot Cavanagh teaches English at the University of Northumbria. He is currently completing a book on *'Dangerous Words': Language, Disorder and Ideology in the Tudor History Play.*

Alexander Cowan teaches history at the University of Northumbria. He is author of *The Urban Patriciate: Lübeck and Venice 1580–1700* (Böhlau, 1986) and *Urban Europe, 1500–1700* (Arnold, 1998). He is currently working on social distinction in early modern Venice.

Nick Cox teaches English at Leeds Metropolitan University and is working on Shakespeare and the representation of resistance.

Neil Durkin works for Amnesty International. His doctoral thesis was 'Cankered Country: Cultural Debates in the English Revolution' (Lancaster University, 1994), and he is currently working on contributions to the *Encyclopaedia on Censorship* (Fitzroy Dearborn, 1999)

Lynn Forest-Hill is a member of the Wessex Medieval Centre at Southampton University and co-edits the Centre's biannual newsletter. She works on representations of women's networks and on the structural significance of playful gender relationships, in the medieval mystery cycles. Her book *Transgressive Language in Medieval English Drama: Signs of Challenge and Change* is published by Ashgate.

Malcolm Gee teaches art history at the University of Northumbria. He specialises in modern French art and its market institutions in the period c.1900–39. He edited the collection *Art Criticism since 1900* (Manchester University Press, 1993) and *The City in Central Europe: Culture and Society 1800–the Present* (Ashgate, 1999) with Tim Kirk and Jill Steward.

Tim Kirk teaches history at the University of Northumbria. He is the author of *Nazism and the Working Class in Austria* (Cambridge, 1996) and editor, with Anthony McElligott, of *Opposing Fascism* (Cambridge, 1999). He is currently working on a book on the Nazi new order in Europe.

James Knowles teaches English at the University of Stirling. He has co-edited *Shakespeare's Late Plays: New Readings* (Edinburgh, 1999) with Jennifer Richards and is currently writing a book, *The Theatrical Closet*, and editing Ben Jonson's *Entertainments* for the Cambridge edition of the *Complete Works of Jonson*.

Willy Maley teaches English at the University of Glasgow. He is the author of *Salvaging Spenser* (1997) and *A Spenser Chronology* (1994) and has written articles on several contemporary Scottish authors.

Andrew McRae teaches English at the University of Exeter. He is the author of *God Speed the Plough: The Representation of Agrarian England, 1500–1600* (Cambridge, 1996) and is now working on a book on early Stuart political satire.

James Rigney teaches English at Hughes Hall, Cambridge University and is an Honorary Research Fellow at Roehampton Institute, London. He is currently editing *Timon of Athens* for the third edition of the Arden Shakespeare.

Preface

This book had its origins in an interdisciplinary conference at the University of Northumbria at Newcastle in 1996, and most of the contributions to the book were presented as papers there. We should like to thank all those who attended for their helpful comments and criticisms during discussion and afterwards, especially those who spoke at the conference but chose not to contribute to this volume: David Gray, Michael Pincombe and Paul Usherwood. We should also like to thank those of our colleagues who agreed to chair sessions and act as discussants. Thanks are also due to the British Academy, the Austrian Institute and, at the University of Northumbria, the European Office and the Department of Historical and Critical Studies for their financial support. The editors would also like to thank the conference participants for their patience with the editing process, and for the efficiency with which they delivered their contributions. We should also like to thank a number of people for their help and advice: Jeremy Gregory, David Kaufmann, Liz Harvey, Roger Newbrook, Jennifer Richards, Stephen Salter, Michael Wildt. Not least we should like to thank Rachel Lynch at Ashgate for her enthusiasm and patience.

The collection is dedicated to the memory of Gareth Roberts, friend and colleague, who delivered an outstanding paper at the conference but died before this project came to completion.

Introduction:
Subversion and scurrility in the politics of popular discourses

Dermot Cavanagh and Tim Kirk

I

There is another side to every story. Every public celebration of a coronation, of a victory, of the achievement of nationhood, is accompanied by dissenting or excluded voices, which are frequently overlooked, and subsequently presented as marginal in the received histories which form our understanding of the past. In recent years historians and cultural critics have paid increasing attention to the significance of such voices and what they tell us of the unexpected breadth and diversity of political opinion. Their work has demonstrated the possibility of revealing another side to every story; an alternative discourse, whether this is the reasoned critique of a political opposition, or merely a scurrilous denunciation born of prejudice or the desire for material gain. The focus of this interest has more often than not been in the construction of a political history from below, an historical sociology of dissent, and this volume seeks to build upon that perspective.

In order to discover this alternative account of the past – what James C. Scott has termed the 'hidden transcript' of society – scholars have looked both for new material and for new ways of interpreting familiar documents.[1] In the case of many sources, a seditious intent is clear: for example in heretical expression, satirical broadsides, and propaganda. In others, not least police and court records, their intended purpose – the documentation of criminality and the judicial process – is often less interesting than the incidental revelation they provide of a system of values and perspectives at odds with the dominant ideology. Indeed, as we shall see below, many regimes have found precisely this sort of information interesting enough to consider surveillance of popular opinion an important function of the police and judicial systems. Contributors to this collection have used both kinds of source in order to construct a cultural history of subversion and scurrility in the broadest sense, drawing on different modes of expression (gossip, rumour, defamation) from across a range of cultural forms (literature, polemic, the visual arts, song).

Although much of the emphasis of the volume is on popular discourses, the perspective of dissent from within the elite has also been considered.

We have set out, then, to explore some instances of scurrilous discourses in particular historical contexts. The formative moment in the changing relationship between authority and dissent, however, is at the inception of modern state formation. The emphasis of this collection, therefore, is on the political culture of early modern Britain, where new relationships between state and society were pioneered. Other contributions then go on to consider ways in which such relationships were managed in other societies and in later periods. Striking similarities will be discernible between the registers of religious conflict in the Reformation, and the anticlericalism of the twentieth century artistic avant-garde; between the anxious eavesdropping of the early modern state and the policing of popular opinion in fascist Europe. In this introduction, therefore, we hope to establish a broader context within which the individual studies can be located.

II

Governments have always sought not only to prevent insurrection but insubordination too; they have tried to control what people say, for want of being unable to control what they think. From the semi-mythical figure of the prince mingling incognito with the multitude, to the focus group of the modern populist, rulers have always wanted to know what people are saying. But they have been preoccupied with popular opinion most of all when it threatens to slip out of their control, when it ceases to be led by the precepts of those in established authority and – worse – begins to express support for those who challenge the political order.

The relationship between the government and the people, then, has frequently been tense; civil society has tended to frustrate attempts to control it. This tension has been most forcefully expressed at the boundary between subversive politics and criminality. From the incipient centralisation of state authority in Europe during the late Middle Ages rulers have repeatedly sought 'to assert and extend their authority by creating . . . victimless crimes, offences against abstractions such as "the ruler", "the state", "society" or "morality" '.[2] Prohibitions against language that damaged the public integrity of office-holders or brought dominant values into disrepute, consolidated the idea of crimes against authority itself. In her study of the 'sins of the mouth' in the late Middle Ages, however, Lynn Forest-Hill reminds us that official standards are not always shared. Even within the homiletic address of religious theatre there are also unpredictable opportunities for the audience to empathise with displays of social truculence and expressions of social grievance. Such equivocal possibilities are comparable with the 'reversibility' detected by Michel Foucault in the spectacular punishments inflicted by the pre-modern judicial system: the capacity of the crowd to switch sympathies to the criminal and thereby to experience a solidarity – concealed or overt – with those who challenge the social order.[3]

The restriction of public expression has often been justified with reference to the ignorant and volatile character of the 'masses', whose coarse and rancorous temperament was supposedly manifested in their stridently expressed views and in their susceptibility to corrupt persuasion. In early modern Europe this self-serving understanding of plebeian instincts can also be seen in the frequent artistic representation of the 'many-headed multitude', and the literary depiction of their vulgar speech and its consequences. It was a truism that the common people were scurrilous in their criticisms of the powerful and fickle in their political loyalties, and hitherto popular public figures might suddenly find themselves objects of derision. This reflected not so much any real characteristics – after all members of the elites easily outdid their social inferiors in malleability and spite – so much as the real instability and dislocations of the times. In his analysis of 'rumours and risings', Nick Cox examines the powerful convergence (at least in the perceptions of the governing elite) between discontented speech and revolt in late-Elizabethan England. In the crisis-ridden years of the 1590s, Cox detects an important shift in patrician ideology in which the discourse of the propertyless identifies them as a potentially insubordinate class to be governed; this perception finds a simultaneous cultural ratification in Shakespeare's *Henry IV, Part 2*.

In early modern culture, such anxieties concerning the temperament of the multitude were increased as traditional strictures against political and religious heterodoxy were subjected to unprecedented degrees of critical scrutiny and challenge. Part of the disruptive impact of the Reformation, for example, was precisely to unsettle existing distinctions between licit and illicit speech and the adequacy of their existing definition by church and state. As Beat Hodler has pointed out, Luther's polemics sought to challenge, even invert, assumptions concerning corrupt speech: it was in the apparently debased or heretical word that the truth appeared. For Luther, scandalous words or actions were 'unavoidable in this world because the Word of God stands in opposition to human actions'.[4] Religious schism, then, made the distinctions between heresy and orthodoxy, legitimate and illegitimate authority, scandalous and righteous expression, matters of unprecedented public dispute. The very fact of the Reformation, in itself an opposition to established authority on an unprecedented scale, caused concern even to Protestant states.

This theme underpinned G.R. Elton's groundbreaking study of policy and police in Reformation England, which demonstrated the ways in which attempts to monitor public reactions to religious and social innovations became both more urgent and more integral to the rationale of government.[5] Elton also showed an unusual sensitivity to the range and variety of idioms in which popular discussion took place, including rumour, slander, and prophecy. Although instinctively sympathetic to the perspective of government, he also gave a penetrating account of the legislative strategies by which Tudor authority sought to identify and discipline those who expressed the belief that, as another historian of the period has put it, 'the very fabric of material and spiritual life was threatened by a predatory crown'.[6] In particular, *Policy and Police* analysed the development of treason legislation to encompass expression and the increasing attempts to control dissent by construing this as sedition.

Elton was working within a context of growing interest in the complexity of popular opinion, and of a wide-ranging inquiry into the degree of ideological consensus and social cohesion in the sixteenth century. Many historians now find a wide variety of views in early modern society, including a generous amount of scepticism and resentment on the part of subordinates. A number of resourceful studies have attempted to uncover how the 'simple, contented face of the common man or woman dutifully fulfilling his small role in society frequently gave way to the face of hunger, the face of despair, and the face of anger'.[7] Adam Fox, for example, has documented popular attitudes and values by examining ballads, libels, rumours and news-mongering – conventions which are animated by a spirit of derision, and which pose an irreverent challenge to the deferential tone of elite culture.[8] In such forms, the lower orders fashioned a counter-version of events which expressed animosity towards government policy. Through slander they sought to adulterate the reputation of their betters, criticise the unfairness of their public dealings, dispute prevailing religious policy, publicise the neglect of the commons, and expose other violations of community norms. The seriousness with which such speech was taken can be inferred from the measures implemented against it. The drive to expose and discipline expressions of popular antagonism towards authority made sedition and slander offences with a detectable social bias. Popular discourse was to become the subject of systematic policing.

Many of the earlier essays in this collection explore the subversive potential of popular scurrility to qualify or oppose officially sanctioned values. Dermot Cavanagh's study of John Skelton's anti-clerical poem *Collyn Clout* shows how an early Tudor writer could recognise the integrity of popular perceptions and dramatise the sectional motivations of elite discourses. Ironically, Skelton's engagement with scurrilous idioms has also led to an enduring (and revealing) cultural bias in the subsequent reception of his writing which sees his work itself as vulgar and undisciplined. Such criticism serves only to illustrate Skelton's point better by displaying the persistence of the same cultural prejudices his poem exposed. Skelton's adoption of 'vulgar' idioms still has the capacity to affront and is symptomatic of a more general separation between the popular voice and a genteel literary tradition. But even 'elevated' forms of satire have built on the popular. Andrew McRae considers ways in which this association between English plebeian culture and the development of literary satire has been suppressed. By examining practices of scurrilous invective at very local levels, McRae demonstrates how influential popular libels were on this emergent genre: the boundaries between popular and elite culture were permeable. Nevertheless, as John Skelton recognised, one must be attentive to the political motivations which inform any appropriation of the people's 'voice'. As McRae shows attempts to identify coherent subversive groups are often frustrated: 'while some [libels] might be linked to the alehouse, others can be traced to a disaffected gentleman's study'.[9] We cannot be schematic in separating a vigorous popular critique of social transgressions from the expression of factional resentments within the educated ruling classes. As James Knowles demonstrates, the scurrilous accusation of sodomy, for example, was as common in court circles as elsewhere; and at court it could even lend status and glamour to the figure against whom such charges were made. Moreover, if subversion need not always be popular, popular discourse is certainly not always scurrilous, and to understand popular culture wholly in terms of its subversive nature is to offer a diminished account of its complexity.

The equation between scurrilous expression and popular sentiment could be exploited by rival groups within the elite as a way of lending weight and forcefulness to their polemics. James Rigney's essay, for example, investigates the utility of popular and pre-literate slurs against members of the clergy for the Long Parliament in its propaganda against the Established church. The malleability of such discourses, however, is manifested in the Royalist conversion of defamatory gossip into printed 'news' concerning the hypocrisy and double standards of puritan moralists. Neil Durkin considers a similar Royalist appropriation of popular resentment. His account of disorder in the last days of the English republic explores the convergence between two quite discrete manifestations of opposition to the army and government. He shows how the hostility of London apprentices, especially towards the popular bogeyman Colonel Hewson, were exploited for their own purposes by proponents of restoration. Such satirical broadsides are also identified as an important political ingredient in the vogue for mock-heroic which emerged after the accession of Charles II.

Durkin's recovery of the popular snobbery directed against the low-born Hewson in the context of a more general support for the monarchy, also serves to remind us that defamatory irreverence could have equivocal implications. 'What!' exclaimed Margaret Dixon of Newcastle upon Tyne on hearing of the accession of Charles II. She continued:

> Can they finde noe other man to bring in then a Scotsman? What! is there not some Englishman more fit to make King then a Scott? There is none that loves him but drunk whores and whoremongers. I hope hee will never come into England, for that hee will sett on fire the three kingdomes as his father before him has done. God's curse light on him. I hope to see his bones hanged at a horse tayle, and the doggs runn through his puddins.[10]

Xenophobic and gender prejudices were far from unusual in popular feeling, and scurrilous attacks were frequent on Jews, social outsiders, unruly women and other figures perceived as deviant. Peter Stallybrass and Allon White have alerted us to the presence of 'displaced abjection' within carnivalesque practices: the tendency of subordinated groups to demonise and scapegoat those weaker than themselves.[11] Historians have vindicated this theoretical insight. Penny Roberts, for example, has noted how rumours concerning arson in early modern France were often directed at perceived enemies of the community (foreigners, Jews, vagrants, Huguenots) and Laura Gowing has explored the defamation of women's sexual reputation in accordance with a patriarchal vision of household order.[12] Slander reveals not only the personal vulnerability of the individual but the weaknesses of the community as well. Alex Cowan shows in his contribution to this volume how scurrilous charges brought against women who had married into the Venetian patriciate of the seventeenth century exploited the anxieties of a defensive elite for personal advantage. Such cases are a reminder that the expression of slander or scurrility tells us little in itself; it is only when we come to question the motives of the scurrilous that the real social meaning of the episode is disclosed.

As Europe emerged from the ideological conflicts of the seventeenth century, rulers were confronted increasingly with the problems of a recognisably modern society characterised by the establishment and development of new public institutions and social practices. Both public and private life was increasingly regulated. Norms of reasonable behaviour were established and policed; discipline was imposed through the agency of the emergent professions, and deviation was monitored and punished. Above all, however, in the eyes of 'respectable people', social and political order depended on the effectiveness of police surveillance of the urban 'crowd'. A Paris police official of the mid-eighteenth century fantasised about a city divided and sub-divided, numbered and catalogued, all its citizens documented and their details filed in a central bank of revolving filing cabinets: 'everything was to be regulated, known, counted'.[13]

Eighteenth-century Paris has been the focus of much of the most important work in this field. The absolutist ideology of the ancien regime, as Gerhard Sälter has argued, made public affairs a part of the extended private sphere of the ruler, rendering the free expression of political opinion difficult or impossible. What remained was rumour and gossip, transmitted along oral networks – which had existed in Paris since the beginning of the seventeenth century.[14] But even this informal talk was subject to surveillance: the police placed spies and informers all over the city, and as Arlette Farge has shown, the 'systematic reporting of opinions expressed among the common people was not a mere amusement: it was one of the grounding activities of a police system which was obsessed with the detail of what was said and articulated'.[15] Rumours, arguably, might become the basis for subversive thought and actions; drunken outbursts against the king, for example, might turn into treasonous intentions. But above all such rumours challenged the monopoly over public discourse claimed by the state, and reflected simultaneously the politics of an informal popular opinion which could not be expressed openly.[16] They could also be used actively by oppositional groups or movements to foment unrest, spread anxiety, and prompt demands for political change or other concessions from governments by disseminating disinformation, or spreading rumours of the restoration of (often fictitious or semi-fictitious) ancient privileges or rights.

This function of popular discourse, it has been argued, passed away in western Europe with the passing of the *ancien regime* itself, and the development of a 'civil society' in which anti-government opinion could be articulated.[17] With the growth of a politically conscious middle class came the development of a 'public sphere' independent of the state, and the emergence of social groups which articulated a new kind of 'public opinion'. They did so above all in the expanding newspaper and periodical press which, as Gerhard Ammerer argues here, could become the principal vehicle of a critical opposition. The Viennese public had sufficiently overcome its prejudices against the Turks to be in a position to question the crass attempts of the pro-government press to whip up xenophobic sentiment during the Habsburg empire's last war against the Turks. Instead both the educated elite and the general public expressed scepticism about the war itself and its motivation, and ridiculed the sycophancy of the government's supporters. In short the war promoted the growth of a particular kind of politicised culture which was to be characteristic of other political emergencies, above all the revolution in France and its repercussions in other parts of Europe.[18]

Critical opposition was more difficult in central Europe than in the west.[19] Both the French revolution and the events of 1848 prompted governments in Germany to develop systems of police surveillance which monitored the activities of dissident intellectuals and the emergent labour movement. Thus in late-nineteenth-century Hamburg, one of the most liberal states east of the Rhine, police kept the recently legalised Social Democrats under close surveillance by placing undercover policemen in public houses in working-class districts. In so far as the policemen were instructed merely to listen and report, supplying information on the popular mood rather than individual seditious statements, they anticipated the working practices of the SD (the security service of the SS) under Hitler. It was with the forcible repression of civil society by authoritarian regimes in the twentieth century that the policing of covert dissent acquired renewed importance.[21] As Tim Kirk suggests here, it was important for a populist régime like the Nazi dictatorship to know what people were saying even as it tried to silence them. The Nazis' strategy was to contain the outright opposition of a substantial minority, while confidently proclaiming national unity. Their own police files document the widespread popular scepticism prompted by such talk of a 'national community'.

The extreme circumstances of the Third Reich revealed among other things the ambivalent relationship between the churches and a repressive secular state. Some clergymen certainly proved to be turbulent priests, but many, along with other anti-democratic conservatives of the 1920s, felt that political power and constitutional authority had been usurped by republicans and that the events of 1933 constituted something of a restoration. In France the traditional establishment had been similarly dispossessed, but for much longer. Nevertheless the potential for the old elites to recapture power in a *coup d'état* was keenly felt by the French during the 1920s, and such anxieties were not without foundation during the general political and economic crisis of the following decade. As Malcolm Gee shows here, the virulent campaigns of the Surrealists between the wars were directed not just at the church, as an institution which might profit from such a restoration, but also against conservative values which the republic, in its liberal inclusiveness, purported to tolerate, such as 'fatherland' or 'family'. Indeed, in a liberal state the credentials of the artistic and political avant-garde as a force for dissent had to be established by provoking outrage. In order to attract attention to their argument in the context of a relatively tolerant society, the point had to be made in extreme terms, which challenged society's perceived complacency.

Dissident culture has continued to employ extreme forms of expression to make a critical point. The obscene language used in James Kelman's fiction has created a public furore and prompted some commentators to disqualify it from consideration as art. As Willy Maley argues here, however, Kelman's work is in many ways intensely moralistic; and more so than that of his commercially more successful contemporary Irvine Welsh. Whereas Kelman's social criticism presupposes a better alternative, Welsh refuses to judge even his most disorderly characters and thereby engage with the dominant discourse about social exclusion.

Welsh's work reveals one of the more disturbing truths about dissent: those who reject the established social order and its prevailing values do not necessarily offer something better or, indeed, any coherent alternative at all. Those who welcome the republican, anti-clerical and revolutionary sentiments evinced by dissidents opposing a tyrant, an oppressive morality, or an authoritarian state, will be dismayed by some of the attitudes in oppositional communities. Our contributors have shown that scurrilous expression has a variety of potentialities, not all of them progressive. Oppositional mentalities are revealed as complex and unstable; dissent is defined by its context. As these essays demonstrate, however, the ways in which opposition is expressed are infinitely variable, but the impulse to protest is a constant.

Notes

1   James C. Scott, *Domination and the Arts of Resistance: Hidden Transcripts* (New Haven: Yale University Press, 1990); see also his *Weapons of the Weak: Everyday Forms of Peasant Resistance* (New Haven: Yale University Press, 1985).
2   R.I. Moore, *The Formation of a Persecuting Society: Power and Deviance in Western Europe, 950–1250* (Oxford: Basil Blackwell, 1987), 110.
3   Michel Foucault, *Discipline and Punish. The Birth of the Prison*, trans. Alan Sheridan (Hardmondsworth: Penguin, 1977), 58–69.
4   Beat Hodler, 'Protestant Self-Perception and the Problem of Scandalum: a Sketch', in *Protestant History and Identity in Sixteenth-Century Europe*, Vol.1 *The Medieval Inheritance* (Aldershot: Scolar Press, 1996): 23–30, 25.
5   G.R Elton, *Policy and Police: The Enforcement of the Reformation in the Age of Thomas Cromwell* (Cambridge: Cambridge University Press, 1972).
6   C.S.L. Davies, 'The Cromwellian Decade: Authority and Consent', *Royal Historical Society Transactions*, 6th series, 7 (1997): 177–95, 192–3.
7   Barret L. Beer, *Rebellion and Riot: Popular Disorder in England during the Reign of Edward VI* (Kent State: Kent State University Press, 1982), 1.
8   Adam Fox, 'Libels and Popular Ridicule in Jacobean England', *Past and Present* 145 (1995), 47–53; 'Rumours, news and popular political opinion in Elizabethan and early Stuart England', *Historical Journal* 49 (1997), 597–620.
9   See below, p. 66.
10   J. Raine (ed.), *Depositions from the Castle of York, relating to offences committed in the Northern Counties in the seventeenth Century*, 40 (Durham: Surtees Society, 1861), 83.

10   Subversion and Scurrility

11 Peter Stallybrass and Allon White, *The Politics and Poetics of Transgression* (London: Methuen, 1986), 19.

12 Penny Roberts, 'Arson, conspiracy and rumour in early modern Europe', *Continuity and Change* 12 (1997), 9–29; Laura Gowing, 'Gender and the Language of Insult in Early Modern London', *History Workshop Journal* 35 (1993), 1–21 and see also her *Domestic Dangers: Women, Words, and Sex in Early Modern London* (Oxford: Clarendon Press, 1998).

13 Daniel Roche, *The People of Paris. An Essay in Popular Culture in the 18th Century* (Leamington Spa: Berg, 1987), 271.

14 Gerhard Sälter, 'Gerüchte als subversives Medium. Das Gespenst der öffentlichen Meinung und die Pariser Polizei zu Beginn des 18. Jahrhunderts', *Werkstattgeshichte* (15) 1996, 11–19.

15 Arlette Farges, *Subversive Words. Public Opinion in Eighteenth Century France* (Cambridge: Polity, 1994), 3.

16 Sälter, 'Grerüchte', 12–13.

17 Andreas Würgler, 'Fama und Rumor. Gerücht, Aufruhr und Presse im Ancien Regime', *Werkstattgeschichte* 15 (1996), 20–32.

18 See, for example, George Rudé, *The Crowd in the French Revolution* (Oxford: Clarendon Press, 1959); Helmut Reinalter, *Jakobiner in Mitteleuropa* (Innsbruck, 1977); Ernst Wangermann, *From Joseph II to the Jacobin Trials. Government and Public Policy in the Habsburg Dominions in the Period of the French Revolution* (Oxford, 1969) See also *Berliner Straßenecken-Literatur 1848/9. Humoristisch-Satirische Flugschriften aus der Revolutionszeit* (Stuttgart: Reclam, 1977)

19 See Wolfram Siemman, *"Deutschlands Ruhe, Sicherheit und Ordnung". Die Anfänge der politischen Polizei 1806–1866* (Tübingen: Niemeyer, 1985).

20 Richard Evans, (ed.) *Kneipengespräche im Kaiserreich. Die Stimmugsberichte der Hamburger Politischen Polizei 1892–1914* (Reinbek: Rowohlt, 1989); idem, 'Proletarian mentalities: pub conversations in Hamburg' in his *Proletarians and Politicans. Socialism, protest and the working class in Germany before the First World War* (New York and London: Harvester Wheatsheaf, 1990) 124–191.

21 See, for example, Ian Kershaw, *Popular Opinion and Political Dissent in the Third Reich: Bavaria 1933–1945* (Oxford: Oxford University Press, 1983); Robert Gellately, *The Gestapo and German Society: Enforcing Racial Policy* (Oxford: Clarendon Press, 1990); Reinhard Mann, *Protest und Kontrolle im Dritten Reich: Nationalsozialistische Herrschaft in Alltag einer rheinischen Großstadt* (Frankfurt and New York: Campus, 1987); Timothy Kirk, *Nazism and the Working Class in Austria: Industrial Unrest and Political Dissent in the 'National Community'* (Cambridge: Cambridge University Press, 1996); Sarah Davies, *Popular Opinion in Stalin's Russia: Terror, Propaganda and Dissent, 1934–1941* (Cambridge: Cambridge University Press, 1997).

1
Sins of the mouth: signs of subversion in medieval English cycle plays

Lynn Forest-Hill

All the forms of language which we in the late twentieth century define as scurrilous were known in the Middle Ages as sins of the mouth. In this essay I will argue that in plays from the medieval English biblical cycles[1] such sins of the mouth reveal the subversive attitudes of the characters who use them, and may have encouraged members of the audience to express similar attitudes. Thus scurrilous language in biblical drama is associated with two forms of subversive expression – diegetic and non-diegetic. Diegetic subversion is signalled when characters in performance use sins of the mouth; non-diegetic subversion is signalled when members of the audience respond in kind to the sinful language used by characters. This essay looks at the way sins of the mouth are used to subvert various forms of power and authority in the plays, primarily by low-status characters, and I will argue that, while sinful language in the plays may have provided an opportunity for non-diegetic subversion, the contexts and structure of the drama prevent this becoming a serious challenge to the medieval hierarchies of authority, although spectators may, nevertheless, have enjoyed the freedom to express themselves.

Both forms of subversion associated with the cycle plays have to be understood in the special contexts relating to medieval urban drama. The cycles are each a series of plays, written in the vernacular, based on biblical sources, and charting God's relationship to humanity from Creation to the Last Judgement. Records of performances show that they flourished from the last quarter of the fourteenth century until they were suppressed by the Reformation during the sixteenth. In York and Chester performances took place at Corpus Christi:[2] as an important liturgical feast, the day was a public holiday and an occasion for festivities which drew people from all levels of urban society, from the surrounding countryside, and from farther afield.[3]

Audiences for the plays were therefore heterogeneous and responses to the drama would reflect that heterogeneity.

Among the various purposes of the cycles, the most prominent were to entertain and, through the medium of entertainment, to instruct their audiences in Christian doctrine. They also provided a means of bonding an unstable population through an act of celebration which took the cultural form most familiar to both literate and illiterate spectators. Although dramatists were writing ostensibly in the service of theological doctrine, the growing confidence of urban communities seems to have prompted perceptive comments about the socio-political conditions which affected those communities, and sins of the mouth provide the means by which the dramatists reveal the presence of discord in their society.

The cycles probably represent the work of many authors, who, to varying degrees, use sins of the mouth to characterise sinful humanity and dramatise low-status subversion of the medieval hierarchy. This encompassed the spiritual hierarchy of the Christian Church, and the temporal hierarchies which recognised the authority of masters over their apprentices, and of husbands over their wives and children. All these forms of authority are challenged and subverted in the cycles, which depict resistance to ecclesiastical authority, conflicts between masters and men, and between husbands and wives. These are, however, represented in different ways by different playwrights. The dramatists named by modern critics the York Realist, and the Wakefield Master (who contributed to the Towneley cycle), together with the author of the Chester *Shepherds'* play, focus on specific forms of subversion as part of their dramatisation of biblical episodes, but all use sins of the mouth to dramatise these conflicts and often their use of such scurrility signals a special concern.

Many kinds of subversive speech are dramatised in the cycle plays as characters indulge in insults, abuse, oaths, and curses; these represent forms of language which broke the rules governing acceptable vocabulary in medieval society.[4] Sins of the mouth are listed and defined in many medieval sermons. The sermon cycle *Jacob's Well*, from 1440, warns 'if thou clepe another 'thefe', or suche an-other name . . . or shamyst hym . . . for malyce or for wretthe . . . it is dedly sinne'.[5] During the second quarter of the fifteenth century Richard Rolle declared 'Synnes of the mouth ben these . . . ' and he condemned among others 'to swere oft sithes [times] . . . cursynge' and 'scornynge',[6] while *Jacob's Well* adds to these 'speche of harlotrye and rybaldrye' (262).

Medieval court cases for defamation show that the misuse of language concerned ordinary people. For example, at the consistory court in York in 1381 John Greenhode was alleged to have called John Topcliffe 'false lurdan' [scoundrel],[7] while evidence from the Paston letters illustrates a common form of insulting language used against women. In 1448 Margaret Paston wrote to her husband that during an altercation a man 'called my moder and me strong hores'. The two women took the case to the Prior of Norwich.[8] The vocabulary of insults found in such court cases is commonly used as simple abuse in the cycles, but the court cases show that sins of the mouth are not used in drama simply as a dramatic convention but have a social significance which contributes to their effectiveness as a dramatic device.

Plays in which sins of the mouth are used extensively are characteristically confrontational. The liveliness of sinful language helps capture the attention of spectators and is in keeping with the festive context of the cycles. Furthermore, sinful language would be expected by an audience as part of its experience of watching certain plays, and particular characters. The familiarity of sinful language helps to situate the characters who use it, the action of the plays, and especially their tensions, in medieval, as well as biblical time. However, the entertainment value of sinful language in a festive and ludic context may have acted as a control on audience responses to those tensions. Moreover, diegetic representations of subversion, no matter how pertinent they were to medieval society, are commonly absorbed by the structure of individual plays, and controlled by the overall structure of Fall, Redemption, and Judgement which defines the cycles. This structure presents subversion as part of sinful temporal society, but also as a force which has no lasting power to disrupt the more doctrinally important progress towards Redemption. Nevertheless, any instance of sinful language would be received by spectators according to the skill of the dramatist, the degree of a spectator's faith, and his or her experiences. These could produce responses which did not accord with a play's ostensible purpose to instruct, but could be consistent with the dramatist's observations of social or political discord. Wherever sins of the mouth are used in the plays they indicate subversive attitudes towards authority which may speak to the discontent of spectators, providing a recognition of grievances without overtly demanding change.

The plays of Cain and Abel, and Noah, introduce subversion of authority early in the cycles and thus dramatise the discord which characterises post-lapsarian society; these diegetic challenges mirror common forms of social grievance. For example, in all four extant cycles Cain's evil nature is charac-terised by his foul-mouthed rejection of those social and religious norms which were familiar to medieval audiences. His disrespect for his father, for the obligation to make sacrifice, and for God's curse, dramatise subversive attitudes towards the domestic hierarchy, and to the practices of tithing and excommunication. His challenges are expressed in insulting and abusive language. In the N-Town *Cain and Abel* play Cain remarks 'Thow my fadyr I

nevyr se, / I gyf not therof an hawe!' [I don't give a damn][9] but his insolence
turns to violent abuse when he and Abel offer their sacrifices. Cain asks

> Herke, Abel, brother, what aray is this?
> Thy tythyng brennyth as fyre ful bryght!
> It is to me gret wondyr, iwys.
>
> (3: 131–3)

When Abel replies 'Goddys wyll, forsothe, it is / That my tythyng with fyre
is lyth' (3: 135–6), Cain rages at his brother:

> What! thou stynkyng losel, and is it so?   scoundrel
> Doth God thee love and hatyth me?
> Thou shalt be ded, I shall the slo!   slay
>
> (3: 144–6)

It is Cain's refusal to make proper sacrifice, named specifically as 'tythyng',
which leads to its mystical rejection symbolised by the poor fire. This incites
his anger, provoking the murder of Abel, and God's intervention.

In the York *Cain and Abel* play God sends an angel to pronounce His curse
on Cain after the murder. The angel tells Cain; 'God hais sent the his curse
downe, / Fro hevyn to hele, maledictio dei',[10] but Cain tells the angel
abusively:

> The same curse light on thy crowne,
> . . .
> For he that sent that gretyng downe
> The devyll myght speyd both hym and the,
> Fowll myght thowe fall!
>
> (7: 93; 95–7)

God's curse is excommunication, known as the Great Curse in the Middle
Ages. The abusive language, including a devil curse, through which Cain
expresses his rejection of God's judgement, challenges the language of
transcendent authority: it also reflects resistance in medieval society to the
Church's ultimate power to punish through excommunication.

Reluctant tithers like Cain could be excommunicated, as *Jacob's Well*
declares: 'we denouncyn . . . accursed, dampnyd, and departed fro god . . . all
false tytherys, and alle that . . . wrongfully wytholdyn it' (55–6). However,
court cases and historical records indicate reluctance among parishioners to
contribute tithes, and people did indeed reject the power of the Great Curse.
In 1524–5 Richard Dudley, prebendary of Masham in the diocese of York
brought actions against five men for non-payment of tithes[11] and at an
ecclesiastical court in London in 1493 Nan Hopper was accused of being a

scorner of the court for saying 'Cursse and blisse, I set not a straw by the cursing ther'.[12] Thus Cain's abusive rejection of the social obligation of tithing reflects attitudes existing in medieval society.

Cain is cast as the medieval bad tither in all the cycles, and the characterisation associates such actions with unregenerate, low-status villainy. Although the characterisation of Cain focuses on the readiness of some individuals to challenge authority, this is always linked to his murder of Abel, exceeding any subversion which could be approved by the audience. Nevertheless, if the scurrilous terms of his transgression are perceived as entertaining, the performance might prove more enjoyable than admonitory.

While Cain's abusive challenges are unique in the cycles in their resistance to the highest forms of spiritual authority recognised by medieval society, the subversion of other forms of authority is also dramatised through the use of sins of the mouth. Seasonal inversions of the hierarchy are represented in the Cain plays from the York and Towneley cycles, and in Shepherds' plays from Towneley and Chester. These acts mirror those inversions of authority which were a licensed and traditional part of medieval society. During the twelve days of Christmas in wealthy households and institutions such as the Inns of Court, Lords of Misrule challenged the status of their secular masters. At the same season, Boy Bishops challenged ecclesiastical authority. The inversion of the domestic hierarchy, when the ideal of subservient womanhood was temporarily reversed, is included in the Noah plays of the Chester, Towneley, and York cycles, and would have been familiar to audiences from Hock-tide festivities at Coventry and elsewhere.

Festive inversions of authority thus took various forms, although in all cases the festivities were of limited duration, and were clustered in the first half of the year.[13] The traditional forms and their containment limited the potential for serious disorder. Nevertheless, a tradition of licensed subversion existed in medieval society and is mirrored in the cycles, where all the forms which were individually licensed at specific times during the first half of the year are gathered together in one act of celebration framed by the themes of redemption and integration.[14] While the playwrights define the place of subversion within the redemptive process, and so contain it, they also exploit the freedom associated with festive license in order to enliven the biblical episodes, and to explore the extent of discord and dissent in medieval society.

The Towneley Murder of Abel recalls Christmas challenges to the hierarchy of authority as Cain's apprentice Pikeharnes confronts his master. Cain complains that his plough-horses will not work because the boy does not feed them. Pikeharnes replies insolently:

Thare prouand, syr, forthi,   food
I lay behind thare ars,
And tyes them fast bi the nekys.[15]

However, the challenge in the play is not only to Cain. Pikeharnes's most
scurrilous challenge is directed at the audience. He opens the play with a call
for silence which is conventional in cycle plays,[16] and he threatens the
spectators, saying '. . . who that ianglis [chatters] any more, / He must blaw
my blak hioll [hole] bore' (2: 6–7). Not content with this scatological insult,
the abusive apprentice goes on to mock the spectators by casting them as
Cain's men. He tells them:

A good yoman my master hat: is called
Full well ye all hym ken.
. . .
Bot I trow, bi god on life,   think
Som of you ar his men.
                (2: 15–16; 19–20)

The challenges would be entertaining, especially to apprentices in the
audience, while masters would recognise the harmlessness of the festive
game, and the implicit reassertion of the norms which are being transgressed.
However, the dramatist problematises the traditional festive challenge to
masters by questioning the degree to which they may themselves be unworthy
of respect. Cain is a known villain, therefore Pikeharnes's challenge to his
authority may be weighed against Cain's own transgression.

Subversion of the hierarchy thus becomes a more serious matter as the
apprentice's challenge could appear legitimate, but this interpretation is
controlled by dramatic and doctrinal conventions. Since both Cain and
Pikeharnes use sinful language they show themselves to be equals in sin and
their disputes carried on in the vernacular represent the discord which
characterises the condition of post-lapsarian humanity. This includes the
audience, particularly in the light of Pikeharnes's remarks to them. This
instructional point may, however, escape the spectators who simply enjoy the
performance of the cheeky apprentice.

The challenge by apprentices to their masters is also used by the author of
the Chester *Shepherds'* play, although the shepherds are not villains, but
kindly men. Nevertheless, the boy Trowle refuses the food they offer him,
telling the second shepherd rudely:

Nay, the dyrte is soe deepe,
stopped therin for to steepe;   soak
and the grubbes theron do creepe
at whom at thy howse.[17]   home

His challenge to their status as his masters continues until, in the wrestling match in which Trowle is the more aggressive and successful, he warns the shepherds,

. . . warre lest your golyons glent.	testicles vanish
That were little dole to our dame,	grief
though in the myddest of the daye yee were drent.	drowned
(7: 247–9)	

Having insulted their sexual prowess, he enjoys his success at wrestling warning them: 'Hould your arses and your hinder loynes, / then hope I to have as I have hadd' (7: 272–3).

These entertaining subversions of the hierarchies of age and labour mirror customary festive inversions of authority, but they also serve the didactic purpose of the plays. Pikeharnes indicates that challenges to the temporal hierarchy are symptomatic of a sinful society, and reflect its disobedience towards God. Trowle's insubordination prefigures the challenge Christ will present to the old, sinful, temporal *status quo*, a resolution presented later in the play when Trowle and the shepherds worship the infant Christ together, and he defers to their age. This re-establishes the hierarchy, emphasising its new, Christian, context. At the same time, these plays celebrate the subversion of age and authority which youth always represents, and license spectators to join in that celebration.

The audience is also encouraged to join in the gendered conflict which arises in the Noah plays of the Chester, Towneley and York cycles. Hock-tide inversions of the domestic hierarchy are reflected in, and enliven these plays, as Noah's wife's verbal abuse and physical violence dramatise her defiant attitude to her husband, and indirectly to God. The insulting exchanges between Noah and his wife in the Towneley *Noah* play provide lively entertainment. Noah returns home and greets his wife civilly saying 'God spede, dere wife! / How fare ye?' to which she replies insultingly: 'Now, as euer myght I thryfe / The wars I thee see' (3: 276–7) [The worse for seeing you]. She continues to complain until Noah loses patience and tells her 'We! hold thi tonge, ram-skyt [shit], / Or I shall the still' (3: 313–14).

While the diegetic conflict is set up through exchanged insults, it becomes non-diegetic as the Wife's direct address to the women in the audience encourages them to take her part and sympathise with her challenge to her husband's authority. The Wife declares:

We women may wary	curse
All ill husbandys;	
I haue oone, bi Mary,	
. . .	

Bot yit otherwhile,
What with game and with gyle,
I shall smyte and smyle,
And qwite hym his mede.   give him his reward
(3: 300–1; 309–12)

Such defiant language challenges the medieval ideal of the silent and
subservient woman, and would be received with pleasure and approval by
those women in the audience who did not accept that patriarchal ideal, or who
knew it to be unrealistic in the context of their own experiences. Historical
evidence of the economic realities of the Middle Ages shows that women had
responsibilities, and were active in the community, in ways which the cycles
largely choose to ignore.[18] Women in the audience might therefore be
encouraged and feel free to express their own complaints against the ideal of
the domestic hierarchy in the relative safety of the festive, ludic context.

On the other hand, men watching might find pleasure in the comic
representation of an arch-wife. They might appreciate the chance to criticise
(safely) the shrewish wife, or enjoy seeing domestic conflict projected and
distanced from them. Individual women might also criticise Noah's Wife, or
enjoy the representation of domestic violence, but the characterisation of the
Wife, acted by a man, could be so obviously a burlesque that both men and
women in the audience would enjoy the performance purely for its comedy.
The festive contexts which influence the performance would restrict the
interpretation of a serious challenge to the patriarchal hierarchy, while
permitting the pleasure, for both female and male spectators, of expressing
subversive attitudes.

Edgar Schell has suggested that the representation of conflict in the
Towneley Noah play is evenhanded.[19] However, while Noah has a speech to
the men in the audience about the hard life of married men, his Wife has
another speech to the women and, symbolically, ends up sitting on Noah at the
end of a fight. Although neither of them use gendered abuse in the play, she
also has the better of the reductive naming, calling him Wat Wynk (3: 554) and
Nicholl Nedy (3: 585). Although Noah's wife eventually becomes obedient,
the impression remains of a woman who is capable of mounting a vigorous
challenge to the ideal of a husband's domestic authority – a challenge which
could be enjoyed by wives in the audience whether or not they felt the need,
or the ability, to challenge their own husbands in similar ways.

The gendered conflict in the Noah plays is resolved through the
development of the story as the Wife assumes the ideal attitude of obedience
when the Flood begins to rise around her, and this limits the influence of her
behaviour on the audience. However, the conflict between Noah and his Wife
is not the only form of gendered conflict in the cycles which undermines male

dominance. In the plays of the Slaughter of the Innocents the mothers confront the knights who are killing their babies with a display of anger and physical violence in which the abusive language of the mothers attacks the knights' brutal abuse of power. The mothers' verbal and physical assaults on the knights, like that of Noah's wife on her husband, are comic both in their inversion of gender norms, and in their excess, but in these plays sins of the mouth take the form of gendered abuse, and, unlike the Noah plays, the conflict in the Slaughter plays is not resolved.

In the Chester *Innocents* the first woman objects to the first knight referring to her and her companion(s)[20] as 'these queanes'. She challenges this gendered insult with common insults to the knight himself and by casting doubt on the social status of his mother, asking:

> Whom callest thou 'queane,' scabde dogge?
> Thy dame, thou daystard, was never syche.
> Shee burned a kylne, eych stike;
> yet did I never non.
> (10: 297–300)

The allusion may be to the occupation of a 'common ale-wife',[21] although other low-status occupations, such as burning lime, or particularly burning charcoal, are possible, and are perhaps even more insulting as accusations of maternal low-status which reflect on the knight.

Although the first knight later insults the first woman calling her 'Dame Parnell' [slut] (10: 347), the women have the better of the abusive naming. Besides the conventional insults of 'theife', and 'stronge theiffe', others are unique to this play. The second knight is named 'rotten hunter with thy gode, / stytton stallion, styke tode' (10: 313–4). The knights are also beaten and mocked. The first woman tells the first knight and his companion:

> Have thou this, thou fowle harlott,
> And thou, knight, to make a knott!
> . . .
> And thou this, and thou this,
> though thou both shyte and pisse!
> (10: 353–4; 357–8)

The second woman is then confronted by the second knight who tells her sadistically

> Dame, shewe thou me thy child here;
> he must hopp uppon my speare.
> And it any pintell beare,   penis
> I must teach him a playe.
> (10: 361–4)

The woman responds, not with horror, but with a mocking and scatological challenge:

> my child shall thou not assayle.
> Hit hath two hooles under the tayle;
> kysse and thou may assaye.   prove it
> (10: 366–8)

The abuse and assaults of the mothers cannot, of course, prevent the killings, which the audience should already know are inevitable, but they lend a vernacular reality to the biblical material of the play, and also subvert the power and authority under which the killings are carried out. The plays of all the cycles except N-Town degrade that power, using abusive language and incongruous violence to set the horror of the murderous knights in the context of farce, and the subversion of their power is emphasised by being carried out by women.

Audience reaction to these plays is likely to have been very varied. Some people might have been distressed, but some might have reacted against the knights in the plays in spite of, or because of, the ludic context. An abundance of contemporary medieval complaints suggests that problems existed with the conduct of knights in society[22] and a real-life grievance against the violence of local knights could be safely expressed in the celebratory context surrounding the performance.

Plays in which spectators are encouraged to take pleasure in the diegetic criticism of authority and use the performance as an opportunity to express their own subversive attitudes commonly have a structure which defuses non-diegetic subversion. In the Slaughter plays, however, the subversion of martial power and violence is not always dispelled by the end of the play, and in the Towneley *Herod*, which includes the Slaughter episode, it is heightened.

The Towneley *Herod* includes scurrilous language in the form of Herod's abuse of his own knights when they confess to having lost the Magi. He rages:

> Fy, losels and lyars,
> Lurdans ilkon!   louts
> Tratoures and well wars!
> Knafys, bot knyghtys none!
> (16: 235–8)

Herod's wild abuse of his knights encourages spectators to laugh at both king and knights, thus undermining the structure of tyrannical power. The Slaughter episode follows and includes the mothers' abuse of the knights and physical assaults on them. When the knights return from the Slaughter, Herod promises to reward their efforts but they greet this in such a way that the allegiance between lords and vassals is exposed to mockery. Herod tells his knights:

> If I bere this crowne
> Ye shall haue a lady
>
> Ilkon to hym layd   each one
> And wed at his wyll.
> (16: 623–6)

But the first knight protests: 'So haue ye lang sayde — / Do somwhat thertyll!' [about it] (16: 627–8). Herod accedes to the demand promising 'Markys, ilkone, a thowsande' (16: 670), but adds artfully:

> I shall be full fayn   very happy
> To gyf that I sayn;   say
> Wate when I com agayn,
> And then may ye craue.   ask
> (16: 673–6)

The abusive and deceitful relationship in which the knights are involved with Herod parodies the ideal of fidelity between lords and vassals. The incremental process of the abuse, mockery and deception of these diegetic knights suggests the tenuousness of their power, and encourages the audience to question martial power, especially if they have experienced such abuses.

Herod's deceitful treatment of his knights is consistent with his evil nature, and their relationship is shown to be comically corrupt. Nevertheless, while this is contained by the ludic context, the audience may have felt that their laughter challenged familiar structures of temporal power which were capable of threatening the freedom of individuals and communities. Documentary evidence of such threats exists,[23] but evidence also exists of peaceful and beneficial relationships between lords and urban communities.[24] As the examination of the Noah plays has already shown, social discontent is mirrored in the plays as it serves the instructional purpose of the drama, and the cycles conventionally focus on those (potential) challenges to the ideals of medieval society which serve to dramatise resistance to the will of God in the biblical sources.

Power and authority which were a legitimate part of medieval society are challenged to some extent in every cycle, but in the Towneley cycle *The Second Shepherds' Play* includes the subversion of the pretentiousness of a low-status character. Mak the sheep-stealer is presented as a maintained man – one who supports a lord or magnate and is supported by him with money and gifts – a common source of medieval social discontent.[25] The first shepherd introduces the topic in his complaint:

| These men that ar lord-fest, | bound to a lord |
| Thay cause the ploghe tary; | plough |

. . .

Thus ar husbandys opprest,
In ponte to myscary
On lyfe.
. . .
For may he gett a paynt slefe
Or a broche now-on-dayes,
. . .

| Dar noman hym reprefe, | rebuke |
| What mastry he mays; | no matter what force he uses |

. . .

And all is thrugh mantenance
Of men that ar gretter.
(13: 29–30; 40–2; 44–5; 51–2)

When Mak enters the shepherds greet him civilly but he puts on airs, affecting a Southern dialect, and insulting the shepherds. He tells them:

Fy on you! Goyth hence
Out of my presence!
I must haue reuerence.
(13: 296–9)

Mak's pretensions are overtly foolish because the shepherds protest they know him, but he threatens:

I shall make complaynt,	
And make you all to thwang	be flogged
At a word	

(13: 306–8)

The shepherds now challenge his airs with scatological abuse and curses:

1 Pastor	Now take outt that Sothren tothe,	tooth
	And sett in a torde!	
2 Pastor	Mak, the dewill in youre ee!	

(13: 311–13)

In so far as Mak could be identified by the medieval audience as a maintained man and representative of many of the perversions of the law which plagued their society, they could join in condemning him, and thus express their own discontent. However, spectators might relish other subversive aspects of this character.

Mak is a sheep-stealer, but his language also suggests he is a sorcerer or black-magician, and while that language is not scurrilous in an ordinary sense, it may be regarded as sinful language in the context of the Christian faith and framework of the plays. The shepherds settle down to sleep, making Mak lie between them because they distrust him, but the stage directions indicate that when the shepherds are asleep Mak gets up and says[26]

> Now were tyme for a man
> That lakkys what he wold
> To stalk preuely than
> stealthily
> Vnto a fold.
> . . .
> Bot abowte you a serkyll
> As rownde as a moyn,   moon
> To I haue done that I wyll,
> . . .
> That ye lyg stone-styll   lie
> . . .
> And I shall say thertyll
> Of good wordys a foyne: few
> 'On hight,
> Ouer youre heydys, my hand I lyft.   heads
> Outt go youre een! Fordo youre syght!'   eyes
> (13: 367–90; 400–410)

This spell[27] seems incongruous in a play which will eventually depict the coming of the angel to announce the birth of Jesus and show the shepherds evolving into devout Christians, but it is part of Mak's entertaining opposition to more universal norms. As a maintained man Mak participates in a system much complained of in medieval society, as a sheep-stealer he is a criminal, and as a weaver of spells he excludes himself from Christian society; but his entertaining subversiveness is contained in the ludic context, and the audience may thus enjoy his misconduct even if they would disapprove of it in everyday life. More problematically, in the diegetic context, unlike other low-status subversive characters, Mak is neither condemned, like Cain, nor reintegrated like Noah's Wife. Mak's subversiveness demonstrates, rather, that some individuals, by their actions and choices, will never become integrated into Christian society, but will always remain at its margins.

While *The Second Shepherds' Play* is unique in its treatment of low-status subversion, this essay has shown that scurrilous language – sins of the mouth – in plays from all four biblical cycles, alludes to the presence of, or potential for, subversion in medieval society. Some forms of behaviour, such as Cain's challenges to tithing and excommunication reflect serious subversion, but others reflect festive inversions of authority which were licensed in medieval society. Socially significant forms of subversion are dramatised as they serve the instructional purposes of the plays, although individual dramatists may use them to highlight particular social problems.

Subversion in the plays is likely to have provoked the expression of non-diegetic sins of the mouth which were part of the common vernacular language. Non-diegetic sinful language was probably turned against diegetic villains such the knights, when it would contribute to the condemnation of abuses of martial power. It may, however, have been used in support of characters like Pikeharnes and Noah's wife, who have little or no connection with the biblical sources but are set up in the plays to provoke audience responses. If these are subversive, they are also absorbed into the process of redemption and judgement of which the play, and the audience, are a part. Dramatic sins of the mouth thus provide cues and encouragement for similar non-diegetic expression, but within limits controlled by the structure and theme of an individual play or the cycles. Nevertheless, spectators may have felt that they had indeed stretched the boundaries of control in their short-lived enjoyment of subversive expression.

Notes

1   These cycles of biblical plays have been called Corpus Christi plays, and mystery cycles. Only two of the extant collections of biblical plays, York and Chester, can be defined strictly as 'mystery cycles', i.e. perfomed by guilds or 'mysteries'. The N-Town and Towneley collections take the same cyclical form but it is not known by whom, oɼ where, they were performed. I shall, therefore, refer to all four as 'cycles', and thus 'cycle plays'.

2   The Chester performance moved to Whitsun by 1532 and to Midsummer from 1575. ◦

3   Sandford Brown Meech (ed.), *The Book of Margery Kempe*, Early English Text Society [hereafter EETS], old series, 212 (London: Oxford University Press, 1940), I, 23.

4   They are not concerned with rules of grammar.

5   Arthur Brandeis (ed.), *Jacob's Well*, EETS, old series, 115 (London: Kegan Paul, Trench, Trübner, 1900), part I, 99. Archaic forms of spelling have been modernised in all quotations.

6   S.J. Ogilvie-Thomson (ed.), *Richard Rolle: Prose and Verse*, EETS, 293 (Oxford: Oxford University Press, 1988), 11–12.

7   R.H. Helmholz (ed.), *Select Cases on Defamation to 1600* (London: Selden Society, 1985), 4.

8   Norman Davis (ed.), *Paston Letters and Papers of the Fifteenth Century* (Oxford: Clarendon Press, 1971), part 1, 224.

9   Stephen Spector (ed.), *The N-Town Play*, 2 vols., EETS, second series, 11 (Oxford: Oxford University Press, 1991), I, 3: 21–2. All quotations are from this edition.

10   Richard Beadle (ed.), *The York Plays* (London: Edward Arnold, 1982), 7: 86–7. All quotations are from this edition.
11   Katharine M. Longley (ed.), *Ecclesiastical Cause Papers at York: Dean and Chapter's Court 1350–1843*, Borthwick Texts and Calendars: Records of the Northern Province, 6 (York: University of York, 1980), 5.
12   Paul Hair (ed.), *Before the Bawdy Court* (London: Paul Elek, 1972), 45.
13   Charles Phythian-Adams, 'Ceremony and the Citizen: The Communal Year at Coventry, 1450-1550' in Richard Holt and Gervase Rosser (eds), *The Medieval Town: A Reader in English Urban History 1200–1540* (London: Longman, 1990), 238–65, 255–57. See also Ronald Hutton, *The Rise and Fall of Merry England: The Ritual Year 1400–1700* (Oxford: Oxford University Press, 1994).
14   Licensed inversions did not take place after midsummer, and Corpus Christi was the Christian festival closest to midsummer.
15   Martin Stevens and A.C. Cawley (eds), *The Towneley Plays*, 2 vols, EETS, second series, 13; 14 (Oxford: Oxford University Press, 1994), II: 46–8. All quotations are from this edition.
16   Although not to such low-status characters.
17   R.M. Lumiansky and David Mills (eds), *The Chester Mystery Cycle*, 2 vols, EETS, second series, 3; 9 (London: Oxford University Press, 1986), 7: 214–17. All quotations are from this edition.
18   See for example: P.J.P. Goldberg, 'Women in Fifteenth-Century Town Life' in J.A.F. Thomson (ed.), *Towns and Townspeople in the Fifteenth Century* (Gloucester: Alan Sutton, 1988), 107–28. Also Norman Davis (ed.), *Paston Letters and Papers of the Fifteenth Century*, 2 parts (Oxford: Clarendon Press, 1971), part I, 227.
19   Edgar Schell, 'The Limits of Typology and the Wakefield Master's Processus Noe', *Comparative Drama* 25 (1991), 168–87, 180.
20   Only two women and two knights have speaking parts but others could, of course, have been part of the action.
21   David Mills (ed.), *The Chester Mystery Cycle* (East Lansing: Colleagues Press, 1992), 186, n. 299.
22   See for instance *Jacob's Well*, 134; *The Paston Letters of the Fifteenth Century*, part II, 311; also Maurice Keen, *Chivalry* (New Haven: Yale University Press, 1984), esp. chapter XII.
23   See, for instance, the Duke of Buckingham's oppression of 12 local people recorded in Arthur F. Leach (ed.), *Beverley Town Documents*, Selden Society (London: Bernard Quaritch, 1900), lxix, n. 3. See also William Holdsworth, *A History of English Law*, 12 vols (London: Methuen, 1925), III, 503.
24   Michael Hicks, *Bastard Feudalism* (London: Longman, 1995), 81.
25   See John G. Bellamy, *Bastard Feudalism and the Law* (London: Routledge, 1989) and Michael Hicks, *Bastard Feudalism*.
26   l. 386, s.d. *Tunc surgit, pastoribus dormientibus, et dicit.*
27   David Mills, 'Approaches to Medieval Drama', in Peter Happé (ed.), *Medieval English Drama* (London: Macmillan, 1984), 35–53, 47.

2
Skelton and scurrility

Dermot Cavanagh

On 9 September 1513, the army of James IV of Scotland was destroyed at
Flodden Field by troops under the command of Thomas Howard, Earl of
Surrey. James's expedition had crossed the border earlier that month in
support of his French allies currently under attack by English forces led by
Henry VIII. At Flodden this campaign ended in an annihilation which
engulfed the Scots sovereign: 'O what a noble and triumphaunt courage was
thys for a kyng to fyghte in a battayl as a meane souldier,' the English
chronicler Edward Halle recorded in 1548, 'But what avayled hys stronge
harnes, the puyssaunce of hys myghte champions . . . how soever it happened,
God gave the stroke, and he was no more regarded then a poore souldier, for
al went one waye.'¹ A more immediate commentator, the poet John Skelton,
found less occasion for chivalric pathos in the defeat and death of the Scots
king. Using his newly assumed status as 'Orator Regius' at the Henrician
court, Skelton composed *Agaynst the Scottes*. Invoking the inspiration of
'Melpomone, O muse tragedyall' and, more convincingly, Thalia, the muse of
comedy, Skelton commingled jubilance with execration of the enemy in
addressing the vanquished monarch and his slaughtered countrymen:

> Kinge Jamy, Jemmy, Jocky my jo,
> . . .
> Thus fortune hath tourned you, I dare well say,
> Now from a kyng to a clot of clay.
> Out of your robes ye were shaked,
> And wretchedly ye lay starke naked.
> . . .
> The rude ranke Scottes, lyke dronken dranes,
> At Englysh bowes have fetched their banes.
> (91; 164–67; 172–3)²

Along with his xenophobia, there remains a disquieting aspect to Skelton's
relish for the degradation inflicted on the body of the king as it is stripped,
degraded and returned to its material condition as dirt. This conception of the
exalted national mood appears to have offended more refined temperaments.
Skelton had published a first, and equally vitriolic, version of the poem as *A*

Ballade of the Scottysshe Kynge early in September which was 'ill received in certain quarters. His raving over a corpse was considered as bad taste'.[3] However treacherous James IV may have appeared to English eyes, he was of royal blood and, moreover, the brother-in-law of the English king: James was buried at St Paul's in a solemn funeral service. Unabashed by any distaste which he had aroused, Skelton resumed work on the final version of *Agaynst the Scottes* and concluded the finished poem with an envoy defending his vituperation, a device to which he had frequent resort. To those, he conceded, '*dyvers* people that remord [rebuked] this rymyng agaynst the Scot Jemmy' (emphasis added), the poet retorts that it is precisely the magnitude of James's betrayal of a brother-king that merits the most 'shamefull rekenyng' (32), and the poem ends by impugning the lack of 'true Englysh blood' (23) in his critics.

The recognition that Skelton's 'literary gifts were inseparable from a bottomless and apparently free-floating aggression' has long informed critical responses to his work.[4] The poet's reputation has been affected powerfully by the scurrilous poetic abuse he directed against the reputation of others, whether living or dead: Sir Christopher Garnesche, George Dundas, the memory of two deceased parishioners traduced in his mock *Epitaphe*, the hawking cleric excoriated in *Ware the Hauke*, the heretical scholars Thomas Arthur and Thomas Bilney, and, most notoriously, Cardinal Wolsey in 'one of the most intriguing campaigns of character assassination ever undertaken'.[5] More pertinent for this essay is an enduring association between the poet's use of 'base' language and an assumed empathy for the insubordinate tendencies of popular culture. Certainly, Skelton's antipathy towards James IV leads him into a scurrilous lèse-majesté towards the office of kingship itself and, interestingly, both the hostile and, as we shall see, appreciative responses aroused by his writing define its popular status in terms of a predilection for uninhibited ridicule. Such a view, however, not only simplifies the character of popular culture but it also overlooks Skelton's use of scurrility for the dramatisation of social oppositions, rather than for mere invective.

This essay will begin by examining the critical reception of Skelton's work to reveal the social bias underlying issues of poetic taste. Hostility towards the poet's 'irresponsible' use of scurrilous language reveals an enduring cultural suspicion of the divisive character of popular expression. These reactions ignore, however, that Skelton's poetic treatment of plebeian speech is one of the most original and sophisticated aspects of his work. Correspondingly, this essay will contrast the angry social dialogue evoked in Skelton's long anticlerical poem *Collyn Clout* with the more uniform appropriation of the popular voice found in Thomas More's *Responsio ad Lutheram*. This comparison will establish an increasing concern with the dissident potential of plebeian feeling in early Tudor culture, especially its

anticlerical propensities. Such a comparison also demonstrates that Skelton's
response to the popular voice is more complex than subsequent critical
interpretation has allowed.

I

A socially charged criticism of Skelton's impropriety originates with the
immediate reactions provoked by his poetry. A contemporary and rival poet,
Alexander Barclay, distinguished the decorum of his own work from the wild
comedy of compositions such as Skelton's *Phyllyp Sparrow*, with, he implies,
its exploitation of social antagonisms: 'I wryte no Jest ne tale of Robyn hode,
/ Nor sawe no sparcles ne sede of vyciousnes; / Wyse men love vertue, wylde
people wantones.'[6] In his *Eclogues*, Barclay has the impoverished pastoral
poet Minalcas debunk the bloated pretensions of those, like Skelton, who
styled themselves Poet Laureates. Such figures are exposed as a
presumptuous rabble, squandering ignorant words: 'They laude their verses,
they boast, they vaunt and jet, / Though all their cunning be scantly worth a
pet. / Avoyde of pleasure, avoyde of eloquence, / With many wordes, and
fruitlesse of sentence.'[7] Similarly, the grammarian William Lily crushed
Skelton's poetic stature, in 1519, as vulgar and unlettered: 'Skelton, thou art,
let all men know it, / Neither learned, nor a Poet.'[8]

Such views were confirmed by the more positive afterlife of the poet's
reputation as a notorious prankster; a 'madbrayned knave' according to
Gabriel Harvey.[9] The most witty and carnivalesque of his feats were recorded
for posterity in a series of Tudor jest-books[10] and such popular notoriety
undoubtedly informed the most significant attack on Skelton's appetite for
scurrility in George Puttenham's *The Arte of English Poesie* (1589).
Puttenham makes frequent reference to Skelton whenever a particularly
strident example of artistic decrepitude is needed. For example, when
Puttenham inveighs against '*Cacemphaton* . . . the unshamefast or figure of
foule speech, which our courtly maker shall in any case shunne', his prize
example of such 'a Buffon or rayling companion' or 'Scurra' is Skelton.[11]
Although having the propensity to be 'a sharpe Satirist', Skelton debased his
gift 'with more rayling and scoffery then became a Poet Lawreat, such among
the Greeks were called *Pantomimi*, with us Buffons, altogether applying their
wits to Scurillities & other ridiculous matters' (50). Puttenham's animus is
directed especially towards the abject influence of popular life upon the poet,
a factor which affects the form of his verse, as well as its unbecoming content.
The poet's distinctive use of 'Skeltonics', sequential rhymes in a terse
strophic metre, is traced to his weakness for the minstrelsy of popular ballads:

made purposely for recreation of the common people at Christmasse diners & brideales, and in tavernes & alehouses and such other places of base resort . . . Such were the rimes of *Skelton* (usurping the name of a Poet Laureat) being in deede but a rude rayling rimer & all his doings ridiculous, he used both short distaunces and short measures pleasing onely the popular ear: in our courtly maker we banish them utterly. (69)

The antipathy aroused by Skelton's use of rough comedy and invective, his command of what one commentator terms 'the dictionary of thieves' lingo',[12] continued beyond the sixteenth century. In his *History of English Poetry* (1778), Thomas Warton observed

It is in vain to apologise for the coarseness, obscenity and scurrility of Skelton, by saying that his poetry is tinctured with the manners of his age. Skelton would have been a writer without decorum at any period . . . His festive levities are not only vulgar and indelicate, but frequently want truth and propriety. On the whole, his genius seems better suited to low burlesque, than to liberal and manly satire. It is supposed by Caxton, that he improved our language; but he sometimes affects obscurity, and sometimes adopts the most familiar phraseology of the common people.[13]

This same neo-classical distaste for the coarse and undisciplined nature of the poet's writing is epitomised in Pope's dismissal of 'beastly Skelton' and his 'Ribaldry, Obscenity, and Billingsgate language'.[14] Such a view was still influential upon twentieth-century evaluations: 'he writes verses like a buffoon . . . His verses might have been improvised by some untiring tavern poet . . . In this age of dull repetitions, Skelton pleases because he is brutal and coarse.'[15] Perhaps most influentially, C.S. Lewis, though not unsympathetic to the poet, described 'Skeltonics' as 'the form used by every clown scribbling on the wall in an inn yard'; in *Collyn Clout* these tendencies overwhelmed the poet's better judgement: 'Skelton has ceased to be a man and become a mob.'[16]

Not all critics agree, however, in disparaging Skelton's sympathy for the sentiments and vocabulary of the multitude. The poet's work is often stigmatised because of its composition during an assumed disintegration of medieval certitudes and before the sophistication of the Tudor 'courtly makers' demonstrated the subtle poetic wit which could 'transform apparent impropriety into propriety'.[17] Yet, his poetry has also prompted positive responses: Skelton's reputation as a festive usurper of courtly language and values has helped rehabilitate his status. More generous evaluations stress the range of his social sympathies in contrast to the increasing polarisation of post-Reformation society, characterised by the withdrawal of elites from the unseemly practices of the lower orders.[18] In an important if hyperbolic essay, Elizabeth Barrett Browning turned Pope's insulting epithet 'beastly Skelton' into a celebration of his 'wonderful dominion over language . . . he tears it, as with teeth and paws, ravenously, savagely: devastating rather than creating, dominant rather for liberty than for dignity. It is the very sans-culottism of eloquence.'[19] Here, Skelton's lack of restraint is interpreted as subversive of stifling poetic and social decorum. Barrett Browning implies that it is this incendiary spirit which has intimidated a gentrified critical tradition. Later critics informed by Bakhtinian ideas, have also admired Skelton's uninhibited relish for a variety of social discourses. In a subtle essay, Bernard Sharrat notes how Skelton's verse ranges from poems which use 'distinctly "low" language and vivid ventriloquism' to those which deploy 'ornate elegance'; the effect is to make us 'realise the range of social language Skelton could deploy within his verse, the potential for linguistic interanimation available to him'.[20]

Sharrat's emphasis on the practice of 'ventriloquism' and 'interanimation' between competing discourses, helps to address some useful questions to a critical tradition which has tended 'to identify Skelton with a comic, low world of popular culture'.[21] What is known of the poet's life and frustrated ambitions qualifies any sense of his popular status. Skelton pursued, and episodically enjoyed, a limited amount of court favour, including an appointment as tutor to the future Henry VIII. His pliability in the cause of his own advancement is manifested most strikingly by his eventual acceptance of patronage from the detested Cardinal Wolsey.[22] In an early attempt to secure place, the poet produced a solemn elegy *Upon the Dolorus Dethe . . . of the Mooste Honorable Erle of Northumberlande* (c. 1489), commemorating the assassination of the earl by Yorkshire rebels during a riot against taxation. Skelton excoriates as 'bestis', 'uncurteis karlis', the 'rude villayns' who have committed treason in slaughtering 'ther moste singlar goode lorde': 'Well may ye be cåld commons most unkynd.'[23] More recent research has explained these apparent contradictions as symptomatic of the poet's opportunism. In *John Skelton and the Politics of the 1520s* (1988), Greg Walker has invited us to see Skelton as a pragmatic figure, whose shifting attitudes are determined by his quest for patronage, popular acclaim and the furtherance of his own reputation. From such a perspective: 'Skelton appears to have endorsed a situation ethics: his poetry is reactive, responsive to specific historical situations which demanded idiosyncratic strategies.'[24] These interpretations would emphasise that there has been a substantial misunderstanding of Skelton's status and intentions. The poet is only popular insofar as he shares and defends common religious and social values, or exploits plebeian idioms in pursuit of personal advantage. Thus, the range of motives and attitudes in Skelton's poetry makes it difficult to interpret his use of scurrility as evidence for the constitution of popular culture. Yet, perhaps Skelton's intentions are not wholly careerist in nature; his works are those of a serious artist who sought to present a critical and inclusive social vision. Skelton's work is best seen not only as a contingent response to personal pressures, but as an attempt to explore the uncertainties produced by broader social divisions and conflicts. For example, as this chapter will show, *Collyn Clout*, is exceptionally resourceful in creating a social drama where the value of the popular voice is depicted in terms of the conflicting reactions it arouses.

Whatever its shifting intentions, the poetic complexity of Skelton's work has been recognised, increasingly, as exceptionally sophisticated rather than spontaneous or uncontrolled. The appearance of popular modes has to be interpreted within a body of work which demonstrates formidable learning and ambition: 'the only English poet' of the late-Medieval period, who 'wants something more than to *be* Chaucer'.[25] An aspect of this ambition is expressed in his use of diverse registers of speech and in the relations identified between them. In particular, Skelton uses scurrility to explore social tensions and to dramatise the often partial and self-interested manner in which social oppositions are defined. To this end, scurrilous invective has a mobile identity and address in his work and *Collyn Clout* is an especially clear example of how experimental and suggestive Skelton could be in its deployment. In this poem, scurrility is not perceived as intrinsic to the threatening disposition of a subordinate group; it is equally characteristic of the ecclesiastical and legal discourses that attempt to restrain the populace. Thus, oppositions between popular and elite break down when they use the same discourse for similar motives. Rather than construing Skelton's sympathies as providing a uniform and determining context for his work – whether devout, popular, or elite – *Collyn Clout*'s representation of a dialogue between voices works to explore problems in sympathy and political judgement. Skelton avoids both a stereotypical recognition of the unruly mob or a validation of the antipathy it arouses. While the poet's critical reception offers evidence of distaste for plebeian speech, his poetry exemplifies the capacity for critical social reflection in early modern representations of the popular voice. The subtlety of Skelton's location of popular speech in terms of a social dialogue can be highlighted by comparing this to a more coercive appropriation of such idioms in a contemporary text: Thomas More's *Responsio ad Lutheram*.

II

In a recent essay, Donald R. Kelley has observed that the religious and political conflicts that tore through early modern culture manifested themselves in 'a struggle over language and the values attached to particular sacred words'.[26] One might extend this to scurrilous words and detect an analogous struggle over the control of destructive expression. In broad terms, the increasing prosecution of slander and defamation in the period was animated by 'the general threat to good order inherent in insult, and the particular threat to authority inherent in sedition'.[27] In much legal and literary discourse the fickle and irrational nature of the early modern masses was often objectified through the threatening potential of their invective. Paul Slack has commented on 'the aura of dirt, pollution and peril which was firmly attached to the Tudor poor . . . It is as if social boundaries were being re-drawn and proper, respectable society being newly and more tightly defined'.[28] Such elite concerns were often expressed in relation to the intemperate invective associated with the masses; they appear, for example, in the critique of 'detraction' provided by Sir Thomas Elyot's *The Book named The Governor* (1531). Elyot admonishes those holding public office that their actions will affront someone and then those so offended, along with their 'favourers, abettors or adherents', will diminish legitimate reputation by insinuation and scurrilous rumour:

> forthwith they imagine some vice or default, be it never so little, whereby they may minish his credence, and craftily omitting to speak anything of his rigour in justice, they will note and touch something of his manners, wherein shall either seem to be lightness or lack of gravity, or too much sourness, or lack of civility, or that he is not benevolent to him in authority, or that he is not sufficient to receive any dignity, or to despatch matters of weighty importance, or that he is superfluous in words or else too scarce.[29]

Popular opinion is typified by the scandal it spreads concerning the arrogance and ineptitude of the governing class; such malicious gossip is a testimony to the ignorance and ingratitude of the populace. Elyot ignores, of course, that his own social views might equally be an example of the detraction they stigmatise. This is precisely the kind of insight found in Skelton's *Collyn Clout*; the poem discerns a relationship between pejorative reactions to the popular voice and the scurrilous nature imputed to it.

The controversy generated by the Reformation is, of course, an especially radical example of a struggle over language and both sides of the confessional divide sought to demonise the other by using a 'vocabulary of contamination'.[30] The impact of heresy upon popular opinion is crucial to the development of both Skelton and More's work, yet their dramatisations of the popular voice and its relation to heterodoxy are very distinct. More's appropriation of plebeian speech in *Responsio ad Lutheram* (1523), is a particularly stark example of an attempt to exploit its scurrilous appeal whilst disclosing its unregenerate nature. More accounts for Luther's writing in terms of the traffic between the latter's heretical imagination and the most degraded examples of popular utterance. Luther is envisaged as instructing his followers to 'hunt out the greatest possible matter of stupid brawls and scurrilous scoffs' as a material resource for the 'ornate mosaic of scurrility' that constitute his controversial writings.[31] Obediently, his disciples scour public spaces to record the most obscene, aggressive language they can find:

> they scatter among all the carts, carriages, boats, baths, brothels, barber shops, taverns, whorehouses, mills, privies, and stews. There they diligently observe and set down in their notebooks whatever a coachman spoke ribaldly, or a servant insolently, or a porter lewdly, or a parasite jeeringly, or a whore wantonly, or a pimp indecently, or a bath-keeper filthily, or a shitter obscenely. After hunting for several months, then, finally, all that they had collected from any place whatever, railings, brawlings, scurrilous scoffs, wantoness, obscentities, dirt, filth, muck, shit, all this sewage they stuff into the most foul sewer of Luther's breast. All this he vomited up through that foul mouth into that railers' book of his, like devoured dung. (60–61)

Here Luther's language and person is envisaged as waste matter, a text composed from the execrable, unlettered speech of the commons. In More's view, heresy is contaminated precisely because of its genesis in the most debased aspects of popular life, a world rife with profanity and social antagonism.

Even though More accuses Luther of hypocrisy in using abusive language against those who have abused him (79–81), it is difficult to conceive of a text more replete than *Responsio ad Lutheram* with the same language of scatological insult. More berates Luther as 'Reverend Father Tosspot', 'you pimp' and, in an extraordinary peroration, covers Luther in rhetorical excrement (683).[32] As has been noted, More's polemic appears uncomfortably similar to that which it demonises.[33] Such a contradiction is expressed in its ambivalent citation of popular scurrility with its ability to expose the material realities beneath impressive surfaces. In one sense, More adapts popular invective in this way as a persuasive resource which lends his text forcefulness and appeal; in another sense, such expression is, simultaneously, a waste-product of ignorance which threatens to defile his own discourse. In drawing on a dominant construction of the popular voice as ugly, irreverent and despoiling of reputation, one of the unforeseen (and destabilising) effects of More's polemic is to render the boundary between 'high' and 'low' surprisingly porous. The character of More's expression appears to share the origins and motivations of the discourse it opposes as adulterated and debased. More does acknowledge this troubling proximity – 'For I am ashamed even of this necessity, that while I clean out the fellow's shit-filled mouth I see my own fingers covered with shit' (312) – but perceives it is a risk worth taking as the faecal vocabulary of the mob helps both to make explicit and abhorrent the pollution of heresy. It is my argument that in Skelton's *Collyn Clout*, the responsibility for a decline in social and spiritual standards is attributed in a more complex manner, In particular, the poem is unusual in foregrounding the ironies and interrelationships that accompany antagonistic social dialogues. Far from being univocal in its use of scurrility, the poem dramatises the partiality with which opposing social groups define their opponents with a 'vocabulary of contamination'. Thus the *form* of the poem is far more socially inquiring than the partisan address offered by More or Elyot.

III

Collyn Clout, also printed in 1523 (although probably composed up to two years earlier), shares More's concern with the spectre of popular heresy although its interest is in the voices of the rural poor, rather than More's volatile town-dwellers. Skelton ventriloquises the views of that 'fourth sort or classe' the Elizabethan social theorist Sir Thomas Smith was later to define as 'day labourers, poore husbandmen . . . copiholders, and all artificers' who 'have no voice nor authorite in our common welth, and no account is made of them but onlie to be ruled'.[34] In *Collyn Clout*, such subjects are given the opportunity for extensive and 'unruly' anticlerical complaint in terms of 'a tenacious popular tradition' which coupled 'the social gospel with hostile criticism of the hierarchy'.[35] The outrage of the poem's speaker is rendered with special intensity through his shocking juxtapositions of the personal wealth of bishop-potentates and the commonwealth they have immiserated: 'Theyr moyles golde doth eate, / Theyr neyghbours dye for meate' (319–20). The poem's anger, however, is only partly defined by the traditional socio-economic concerns of medieval complaint with its detestation of covetousness and nostalgia for a social hierarchy bonded together in Christian charity.[36] Much more significant is its concern with the expression, rather than simply the experience, of social division: the poem dramatises the church's failure to provide an edifying and homiletic language which would ensure social consensus, and the consequent verbal conflict between the populace and the clergy. Scurrility, then, is not defined in *Collyn Clout* as a characteristic of a debased, volatile mass which can be exploited by the selfish and dissident; it is produced reciprocally during the social conflict expressed in the poem both as a popular expression of spiritual and social abandonment and as the self-defensive response of an elite that feels its privileges are threatened by critical scrutiny.

From the outset, the poem depicts a failure of community in terms of expression:

> For the temporalte
> Accuseth the spirytualte;
> The spirytualte agayne
> Dothe grudge and complayne
> Upon the temporall men.
> Thus eche of other blother
> The tone against the tother.
>   (61–7)

The divided England of *Collyn Clout* is a culture of complaint and mutual accusation, where the rival estates are quick to discredit each other and all reputations are vulnerable. This issue is embodied in its self-conscious opening, where the issue of a persuasive poetic style is debated in relation to a society prone to hostile interpretation. The question of how to find a language in which 'Vyce to revyle / And synne to exyle?' (11–12) is perceived as fraught with difficulty: learning and subtlety will be dismissed as pretension (15–25); plain speaking read as a sign 'he lacketh wytte' (32). The immediate rhetorical solution the poem finds is to adopt the persona of Colin Clout, the traditional honest plowman of Christian complaint, who reports the anger of the masses as a symptom of his shared distress at the church's increasing worldliness. In foregrounding this mediation, however, the poem also locates popular speech within a set of aggressive social exchanges that exposes its nature, as well as the responses it provokes, to inquiry. The persona expresses both identification with and recoil from the scurrilous quality of what he hears, an ambivalence which also accompanies his recording of the clergy's scabrous outrage at such plebeian assertiveness. This formal presentation of the persona's interactions with conflicting voices, again helps to indicate that within the poem scurrility has a complicated identity: it is conceived dynamically in relation to the conflicts between rival social estates and can either be used by the populace as a means to divest their betters of integrity, or used against them for the same ends. Like its narrator, the reader of *Collyn Clout* has to adjudicate the uses of scurrility, rather than render a phobic recognition of its popular character.

In the bulk of the poem, Collyn Clout orchestrates a chorus of lay protest at the degraded condition of Wolsey's church, especially the ostentation of its hierarchy:

> Some say ye sytte in trones,
> Lyke *princeps aquilonis*,
> And shryne your rotten bonys

> With perles and precyous stonys.
> But howe the commons gronys,
> And the people monys,
> For prestes and for lonys
> Lent and never payde,
> But from daye to daye delayde,
> The communewelth decayde.
>
> (344–53)

As the qualifying term 'some say' indicates (it is reiterated throughout the poem along with cognate phrases), popular opinion is undergoing powerful mediation. The speaker records the negligence attributed by the populace to those entrusted with their spiritual care; the shepherds of the flock are described as unlearned, avaricious and worldly: 'They gaspe and they gape / All to have promocyon: / There is theyr hole devocyon, / With money, yf it wyll happe / To catche the forked cappe' (85–9). The people accuse the clergy not simply of neglect, and a consequent pursuit of material advancement, but of an actively predatory disposition towards their flock. Significantly, the character attributed to the clergy is also that associated with a stereotype of popular culture. The poem reverses the association between disorder and the many-headed multitude by evoking a vagabond priesthood, 'bestyall and untaught,' who can only garble the liturgy and are addicted to drunkenness and fornication:

> Howe some synge *letabundus*
> At every ale stake,
> With, 'Welcome, hake and make!'
> By the breed that God brake,
> I am sory for your sake!
> I speke nat of the good wyfe,
> But of her apostels lyfe.
> *Cum ipsis vel illis*
> *Qui manent in villis*
> *Est uxor vel ancilla.*
> 'Welcom Jacke and Gylla!'
> 'My prety Petronylla,
> And you wyll be stylla,
> You shall have your wylla!'
> Of suche paternoster pekes
> All the worlde spekes.
>
> (248–63)[37]

The poem moves rapidly from detailing the ostentation of the clergy to their censoriousness with regard to popular criticism:

> How in matters they ben rawe,
> They lumber forth the lawe

To herken Jacke and Gyll
Whan they put up a byll;
And judge it as they wyll,
For other mens skyll,
Expoundynge out theyr clauses,
And leve theyr own causes.
                    (94–101)

It is central to the satiric representation of the church that it not only neglects
the responsibilities which attend its enormous communicative power, but it
exploits this position to repress the popular opinion it disparages as, ironically,
ignorant and unlearned. The commonalty do concede, grudgingly, that there
are some righteous clerics ('Almoost two or three'), but they are timorous,
'herted lyke an hen' and terrified to speak out with the courage Thomas
Becket once demonstrated, and as the common people dare to do (147–77).
Such criticisms are given more rhetorical force by the speaker's constant use
of statements which have the shape and content of the folk-wisdom condensed
in proverbs, so that we 'hear through him the echo of other voices which had
pronounced these old saws time after time, as men buckled under the morally
debilitating effects of organised systems of power'.[38] At its most extreme, the
populace's resentment of the church's abandonment of their spiritual welfare
leads to the latter being indicted, not only as exploitative – 'The money for
theyr masses, / Spent among wanton lasses' (423–4) – but as alien and
threatening as the 'Turke, Sarazyn or Jewe' (431).

Such quotations demonstrate the speaker's evident sympathy for the
outrage of the masses. Here Skelton's excessiveness has a tactical effect in
that during the vitriolic course of the poem's long verse-paragraphs, the
boundary between the persona's outrage and the attitudes he reports becomes
blurred. Yet, where the rhetorical expression of the poem becomes particularly
complex is when this distinction *is* reinstated in a forcible and surprising
manner. Popular criticism is not only marked out as issuing from the self-
interest of the clergy, but 'within' the poem as its own speaker feels obliged
to disavow it. Colin Clout expresses intermittent distaste for the scurrilous
mode and content of popular anger: 'The lay fee people rayles', the people
'talkes lyke tytyvylles', they 'Rayles lyke rebelles' (401–22). This alerts us to
an important component of the poem's composition: the abhorrence of the
speaker, expressed in insults and abuse, towards the verbal material he cites.
Early in the poem, Colin Clout describes the popular voice as crying 'Lyke
houndes of hell' (198), foreshadowing the more serious passages of retraction
where the populace is accused of 'sclaundrynge' the church and of
'shamfully' making false allegations (330–43). Later, he accuses the people of
rebellion in speech, a sinful misuse of language which demands correction.

This culminates in a lengthy passage where popular criticism of the church is marked out as conducive to heresy in ways analogous to More's *Responsio ad Lutheram*:

> With language thus poluted
> Holy churche is bruted
> And shamfully confuted.
> My penne nowe wyll I sharpe,
> And wrest up my harpe
> With sharp twynkyng trebelles
> Agayne all suche rebelles
> That laboure to confounde
> And brynge the churche to the grounde.
> As ye may dayly se
> Howe the lay fee
> Of one affynyte
> Consent and agre
> Agaynst the churche to be,
> And the dygnyte
> Of the bysshoppes see.
>
> (486–501)

Yet, in its desperate assertion of the bishop's 'dygnyte', a quality which has sustained such systematic detraction, questions are raised over the status of Colin's responses. As Stanley Fish observes the 'increasing length of Colin's reports tends to destroy the force of his sporadic disclaimers'.[39] Immediately such gestures of withdrawal are made, the speaker returns to an intense and sympathetic account of popular complaint. This pattern is repeated, conveying the confusion, even the prejudicial nature of Colin's outbursts, rather than their embodiment of a renewed sense of integrity.

Interpreting the persona's fluctuating reactions to the *vox populi* is further complicated by the negative depiction of censorious responses directed towards the scurrilous populace elsewhere in the text. As we have seen, the poem provides a vivid account of the clerical hierarchy's reactions to public criticism and the injustice which accompanies the forcible restraint of such views by the church courts. This concludes with a lengthy passage of hysterical abuse in the 'raging voice of an overweening bureaucrat'[40] against the 'losell prates / With a wyde wesaunt!' (1153–4) who taunt prelates. This pours invective upon the 'shamfull scorne' expressed by the 'vyllanne', 'lurdeyne', and 'daucocke' as a symptom of their being 'full of wylfulnes, / Shameles, and mercyles, / Incorrigible and insaciate' (1177–9). The poem depicts graphically the legal violence brought to bear upon those construed as rebels in speech:

Take him, wardeyn of the Flete,
Set hym fast by the fete!
I say, lieutenant of the Toure,
Make this lurdeyne for to loure;
Lodge hym in Lytell Ease,
Fede hym with beanes and pease!
The Kynges Benche or Marshalsy,
Have hym thyder by and by!
(1165–72)

This behaviour throws a disconcerting perspective on Colin Clout's own repugnance. Such compelling evidence of tyrannical will testifies both to the abuse of law and, subsequently, to its sacrilegious nature. The prelate cites, in a blasphemous mode, the scriptural precedent of prophets facing persecution to *legitimise* his own assault on pernicious speech:

Howe may we thus endure?
Wherfore we make you sure,
Ye prechers shall be yawde:
Some shall be sawde,
As noble Isaias,
The holy prophet, was;
And some of you shall dye
Lyke holy Jeremy;
Some hanged, some slayne,
Some beaten to the brayne;
And we wyll rule and rayne,
And our matters mayntayne,
Who dare say there agayne,
Or who dare dysdayne,
At our pleasure and wyll.
(1202–16)

In dramatising this voice of scandalised prelacy, normally associated with Wolsey, Skelton further explores how scurrility can be located in terms of hostility between the estates, rather than being a characteristic of insubordination from below.

Part of the interest commanded by *Collyn Clout* is in demonstrating that the critical character attributed to the popular voice in early Tudor writing is not necessarily prejudicial. A recognition of Skelton's willingness to enlist his poetic virtuosity in a variety of causes must also allow that his work can acknowledge and explore how social pressures and religious partisanship affected social expression. Many of his poems attend carefully to their dramatic situation; the reader is invited to consider the motivations and interests which are implicated in forceful displays of rhetoric. In *Collyn Clout*, Skelton dramatises a contest over the use of destructive speech, rather than attributing its expression to threatening or deviant groups. All of the estates have a dangerous potential which is embodied in their propensity for scurrility, a mode which has an appropriately divided nature as both a means for critical disclosure and for pursuing essentially self-interested and defamatory ends. As many of the essays in this volume demonstrate, scurrility is often used to apportion blame; to destroy the respect accorded to the language, values and reputations of individuals, groups, or institutions. *Collyn Clout* helps in documenting the fascination of early modern culture for the capacities of such language and its anxieties over who is permitted to use it and for what ends. As *Agaynst the Scottes* demonstrates, Skelton's poetry often draws on the power of scurrilous words in a uniform way. Yet *Collyn Clout* explores the mobility of such language, its use both for stigmatising the many-headed multitude and its potential to indict the corruption of social elites or the church's implication in creating the conditions for heresy. In dramatising scurrility as a language of antagonism and blame, the poem considers the potential for justice and inequity in both its expression and in its control.

Notes

1   Edward Halle, *The Union of the Two Noble and illustre Famelies of Lancastre & Yorke* (1550), fol. clii.
2   In John Scattergood (ed.), *John Skelton: The Complete English Poems* (Harmondsworth: Penguin, 1983). All subsequent reference to Skelton's poetry will be to this edition.
3   Maurice Pollet, *John Skelton: Poet of Tudor England*, trans. John Warrington (London: J.M. Dent, 1971), 74. The earlier version of the poem is printed in Scattergood's *John Skelton: The Complete English Poems*, 113–15.
4   Richard Halpern, *The Poetics of Primitive Accumulation: English Renaissance Culture and the Genealogy of Capital* (Ithaca and London: Cornell University Press, 1991), 103.
5   Greg Walker, *John Skelton and the Politics of the 1520s* (Cambridge: Cambridge University Press, 1988), 1.
6   Alexander Barclay, *The Ship of Fools*, 2 vols (Edinburgh: William Paterson, 1874), II, 331.
7   Beatrice White (ed.), *The Eclogues of Alexander Barclay*, Early English Text Society, old series, 175 (London: Oxford University Press, 1928), ls. 693–702. The rivalry between the two poets is analysed by David R. Carlson, 'Skelton and Barclay, Medieval and Modern', *Early Modern Literary Studies*, 1 (1995), 2.1–17.
8   'Et doctus fieri studes poeta / Doctrinam nec habes, nec es poeta', cited in Alexander Dyce (ed.), *The Poetical Works of John Skelton*, 2 vols. (1843), I, xxxviii. The translation is from Thomas Fuller's *Worthies* (Norfolk) (1662).

9   Cited in John Norton-Smith, 'The Origins of "Skeltonics"', *Essays in Criticism*, 23 (1973), 57–62, 58.
10   Culminating in *Merie Tales, Newly Imprinted & Made by Master Skelton Poet Laureat* (1567).
11   Puttenham, *The Arte of English Poesie* (1589), 212.
12   E.P. Hammond, *English Verse between Chaucer and Surrey* (Durham, North Carolina: Duke University Press, 1927), 339.
13   W. Carew Hazlitt (ed.), Thomas Warton, *History of English Poetry*, 4 vols (1871), III, 74.
14   From 'Imitations of Horace' (1737), cited in A.S.G. Edwards (ed.), *Skelton: The Critical Heritage* (London: Routledge & Kegan Paul, 1981), 15.
15   E. Legouis and L. Cazamian, *A History of English Literature*, 2 vols (London: J.M. Dent, 1926), I, 104.
16   C.S. Lewis, *English Literature in the Sixteenth Century, Excluding Drama* (Oxford: Oxford University Press, 1954), 136; 140. Perhaps the most extreme example of this tendency is G.R. Owst's comment on Skelton as an example of the cynical 'winter of discontent' which overwhelmed late medieval poetry: 'By the time that "beastly" Skelton is reached, the very backbone of moral purpose in satire seems at last to be breaking . . . The world of literature now seems at times wellnigh drowned in the peals of mocking, indecent laughter that betoken an inner bankruptcy and madness of soul', *Literature and Pulpit in England* (Cambridge: Cambridge University Press, 1933), 232–3.
17   Daniel Javitch, *Poetry and courtliness in Renaissance England* (Princeton, NJ: Princeton University Press, 1978), 52.
18   A thesis formulated influentially by Peter Burke, *Popular Culture in Early Modern Europe* (London: Temple Smith, 1978). For a critical account of Burke's work see, Tim Harris, 'Problematising Popular Culture', in Tim Harris (ed.), *Popular Culture in England, 1500–1800* (London: Macmillan, 1995), 1–27.
19   Elizabeth Barrett Browning, from 'The Athenaeum' (1842), cited in Edwards, *Skelton: The Critical Heritage*, 99.
20   Bernard Sharrat, 'John Skelton: Finding a Voice – Notes after Bakhtin', in David Aers (ed.), *Medieval Literature: Criticism, Ideology and History* (Brighton: Harvester, 1986), 192–222, 202.
21   A.S.G. Edwards, 'Introduction', in Edwards, *Skelton: The Critical Heritage*, 1–41, 13.
22   Walker details the vagaries of Skelton's career at court in *John Skelton and the Politics of the 1520s* (Cambridge: Cambridge University Press, 1988), 35–83.
23   These phrases occur at lines 83, 34, 46, 27, 56.
24   W. Scott Blanchard, 'Skelton: The Voice of the Mob in Sanctuary', in Peter C. Herman (ed.), *Rethinking the Henrician Era: Essays on Early Tudor Texts and Contexts* (Urbana and Chicago: University of Illinois Press, 1994), 123–44, 127. From a different perspective, Arthur Kinney perceives Skelton as a 'priest-poet', absorbed by the poetic potential of the liturgy and scurrilous only in attacking the sacrilegious: this would include the excommunicated, like James IV, or Wolsey, who threatened to discredit the church. See his *John Skelton, Priest as Poet – Seasons of Discovery* (Chapel Hill and London: The University of North Carolina Press, 1987).
25   A.C. Spearing, *Medieval to Renaissance in English Poetry* (Cambridge: Cambridge University Press, 1985), 234.

42	Subversion and Scurrility

26	Donald R. Kelley, 'Elizabethan political thought' in J.G.A. Pocock (ed.), *The varieties of British political thought, 1500–1800* (Cambridge University Press, 1993), 47–79, 48.
27	S.F.C. Milsom, *Historical Foundations of the Common Law* (London: Butterworths, 1969; rev. edn 1981), 379.
28	Paul Slack, *Poverty and Policy in Tudor and Stuart England* (London: Longman, 1988), 23–4.
29	S.E. Lemberg (ed.), *Sir Thomas Elyot, The Book named The Governor* (London: Everyman, 1962), 236–7.
30	Donald R. Kelley, 'Elizabethan political thought', 49.
31	More, 'Responsio ad Lutheram', in John M. Headley (ed.), *The Complete Works of St. Thomas More* (New Haven and London: Yale University Press, 1969), V: i, 60–1.
32	Ibid. These phrases and the concluding peroration occur at, respectively, 219, 311, 683.
33	See, Stephen Greenblatt, *Renaissance Self-Fashioning* (Chicago: University Press, 1980), 109–14.
34	Sir Thomas Smith, *De Republica Angolorum* (1583), 33.
35	A.G. Dickens, 'The Shape of Anti-clericalism and the English Reformation', in E.I. Kouri and Tom Scott (eds), *Politics and Society in Reformation Europe* (London: Macmillan, 1987), 379–410, 387.
36	The influence of this tradition upon Skelton's poem is detailed by A.R. Heiserman, *Skelton and Satire* (Chicago: Chicago University Press, 1961), 208–39. Its broader significance for Tudor culture is analysed by Andrew McRae, *God speed the plough: The representation of agrarian England, 1500–1660* (Cambridge: Cambridge University Press, 1996), 23–57.
37	Scattergood translates ls. 255–7 as 'With these or those who stay in towns there is a wife or a maid servant', 468.
38	Robert S. Kinsman, 'The Voices of Dissonance: Pattern in Skelton's *Collyn Clout*', *Huntington Library Quarterly*, 26 (1963), 291–313, 306.
39	Stanley Fish, *John Skelton's Poetry* (New Haven and London: Yale University Press, 1965), 184. The use of ambiguously reported popular speech, Annabel Patterson notes, is also adopted by Spenser in the *September* eclogue of his *Shepheardes Calender* (1579), where the 'ambiguity is intensified, thanks to the absence of a supervening authorial posture', in *Shakespeare and the Popular Voice* (Oxford: Blackwell, 1989), 45.
40	Robert S. Kinsman, 'The Voices of Dissonance', 309.

3
Rumours and risings: plebeian insurrection and the circulation of subversive discourse around 1597

Nick Cox

Enter Rumour, painted full of tongues
Open your ears, for which of you will stop
The vent of hearing when loud Rumour speaks?
I, from the orient to the drooping west,
Making the wind my post-horse, still unfold
The acts commenced on this ball of earth
(1. 0. 1-5)[1]

The stage direction which begins Shakespeare's *Henry IV, Part 2* carries onto the stage the portentous emblem for a discursive genre which, I will be arguing, was to carry a devastating political charge in the mid- and later-1590s. For Rumour's polyglot body, seething with tongues 'Upon' which 'continual slanders ride' (6), is the dramatic figure of that swarm of illegitimate discourses which the Elizabethan elite feared were generated and disseminated by their social inferiors. Whilst I take Shakespeare's Rumour as my starting point, this essay is not intended as a 'reading' of the play in which it appears, nor a conventional historical analysis of the popular discursive genre of which it is a trace. Rather my concern is to examine the connection between certain forms of subversive plebeian speech and more overt forms of popular resistance, such as riots. I will be concerned with the historical conjuncture around 1597 when rumour and riot were arguably more widespread and more feared than at any other time in the turbulent final decade of the sixteenth century. My deployment of the Shakespearean text here, then, is as one of a series of textual responses to this moment of crisis.

Rumour knows its tongues are most often attuned to a plebeian register for, although contemptuous of the use to which its 'well known body' (21) is put by 'the blunt monster with uncounted heads, / The still-discordant wavering multitude' (18–19), it must acknowledge that 'Rumour is a pipe / . . . of so easy and so plain a stop' that even they 'Can play upon it' (15–17). Joking at the audience's expense it renounces the 'need' to 'anatomise' its grotesque body before the carnivalesque gathering within the theatre, since this garrulous crowd, gathered as the auditors to enticing fictions, constitutes, it claims, 'my household'. Its 'office' is to 'noise abroad' (29) the news of successful insurrection against the legitimate and regally authorised Truth of monarchical inviolability. Whilst Rumour admits 'King Harry's victory' (22) and thus the 'falsity' of that which it reports, its discourse 'run[s] before' (22), overruns and displaces the 'true' account. Whilst Rumour knows what used to be called 'the facts': that Henry has 'beaten down young Hotspur and his troops, / Quenching the flame of bold rebellion / Even with the rebels' blood' (25–7), its own discourse works to fan the flames of further insurrection by disseminating 'through the peasant towns' (33) the news of successful rebellion. Rumour is thus a counter-discourse that disrupts the sovereignty of stable truth and its avowed availability to the 'many headed monster', the early modern plebs, makes it a dangerous instrument for those who sought to raise 'the flame of bold rebellion'. In the crisis years of the mid-1590s rumour and rebellion were to be conjoined in the minds of the elite as the despair and discontent of a famished populace spilled over into acts of popular resistance around which circulated the subversive discourse of plebeian dissent.

Northumberland's first speech, in the play, locates the text in a moment of crisis in which the seditious seeds scattered by Rumour are likely to fall on fertile terrain for, he claims, 'Every minute' promises to 'be the father of some stratagem' (1.1.8). The havoc which rumour insists it has played with the proper order of meaning and authority is, moreover, quickly manifest as Lord Bardolph's claim to be the bearer of the truth conveyed to him by 'A gentleman well bred, and of good name' is overturned by the tidings of a 'servant' sent 'to listen after news' (28–9). The uncertain space of the stage, traversed by rival accounts of the outcome of the struggle 'in a bloody field by Shrewsbury' (1.0.24) provides a suitably confused beginning to a play whose first audience would perhaps have found a parallel for their own recent history in Northumberland's assertion that 'The times are wild' and 'contention, like a horse / Full of high feeding, madly hath broke loose / And bears down all before him' (1.1.9–11). For although the text records the crushing of one rebellion, the recent memories of Shakespeare's audience would have given them proof, if any were needed, that political insurrection was hydra-headed and the innumerable mouths which made up rumours garrulous body could not easily be silenced.

In the period around 1597, when the text was probably written, fear of rebellion haunted the discussions of the elite as reports of rumoured uprisings came in from anxious regional justices and provincial gentry. What was at stake in these communications was not simply the fear of insurrection itself but also anxieties about the circulation of discourse: seditious or incendiary threats, mutterings which gave voice to class hostility against the gentry and the discursive traces of planned or promised insurrection.

A letter of 25 September 1596 sent by the Somerset Justice of the Peace Edward Hext to Burghley provides a peculiarly vivid insight into this kind of anxiety amongst the elite. 'In this tyme of dearthe' there were, he had heard, 'those' amongst 'the poore Cuntrymen' 'that styke not to say boldlye they must not starve, they will not starve'. These threats of autonomous political action by the poor were the more ominous, Hext implied, for, already 'this yere there [had] assembled 130 in a Companye and tooke a whole loade of Cheese from one dryvinge yt to a fayre and dispersed it amongest them'. For Hext this act of *taxacion populaire* was the work of desperate men and women 'imboldened', as he put it, by 'the Infynytt numbers of the wicked wandrynge Idell people of the land'. He feared that unless the state intervened to discipline the masterless and relieve the poor the impoverished labourers 'may grow dangerous by the ayde of suche numbers as are abroade, . . . who no dowpt anymate them to all contempte bothe of noble men and gentlemen, contynially Bussynge into there eares that the ritche men have gotten all into ther hands and will starve the poore'.[2]

Hext was writing in the wake of the riots in London in the summer of 1595, when a crowd of a thousand apprentices and disbanded soldiers had threatened to break open the armouries of the Tower of London, kill the Lord Mayor and burn down his house. Several days of rioting were followed by a crackdown on vagabonds in and around the capital. The imposition of martial law in the days that followed the riot was designed to prevent further outbreaks of violence by inhibiting the movement of disorderly individuals but also the circulation of dangerous rumours. It was, as one proclamation put it, those men and women, without 'any certain place of abode nor any good or lawful cause of business' who 'lie privily in corners of bad houses' and spent their idle hours, 'listening after news and stirs, and spreading rumours and tales', who were always the most 'ready to lay hold of any occasion to enter into any tumult or disorder'.[3]

The five alleged 'ringleaders' of the Tower Hill riots were hanged, drawn and quartered. It was, according to Peter Clark, 'virtually the only occasion in the century before 1640 when such a ferocious punishment was meted out to ordinary rioters'.[4] Part, at least, of the purpose of this exemplary use of sovereign force was to reaffirm the relations of power which had been threatened by the plebeian insurrection in the capital. Yet, in the months that followed the Tower Hill riots, seditious rumours and the prospect of plebeian insurrection they carried, continued to circulate within the metropolis.

In September of 1595 the Mayor and aldermen of London had written to the Privy Council calling for 'the suppressing of . . . Stage Plaies'. It was an old complaint, oft repeated in the turbulent last decade of the century, but their case that plays were intolerable 'in a Christian Common wealthe' was supported in this instance by the 'disorders and lewd demeanors which appear of late . . . as of the late stirr and mutinous attempt of those fiew apprentices and other servantes, who wee doubt not driew their infection from these and like places'. The theatres, they insisted, afforded opportunities for 'the refuse sort of evill disposed and vngodly people about this Cytie . . . to assemble togetherr'. The 'maisterless men and vagabond persons that haunt the high waies' had, they claimed, 'within these fiew daies', since the suspension of Marshal law, 'now retorned to their old haunt and frequent the Plaies (as their manner is) that ar daily shewed at the Theator and the Bankside'. Elizabethan theatrical companies were always only precariously differentiated from itinerant peddlers, street entertainers, rogues and vagabonds. In the eyes of the civic authorities, in the wake of plebeian insurrection, theatricality appears as an agent of riotous contagion. So the respectable entrepreneur, who would sign his name 'William Shakespeare, gent.', must have understood all too clearly the difficulty the City governors had in being 'able to keepe the people of this Cytie' in 'good order and due obedience'.[5]

It is for this reason, perhaps, that the plays that Shakespeare's company were to perform in the mid and late 1590s, when the theatres reopened, are, for all their seeming eloquence on the subject of rebellion, anxious to hold at bay the spectre of plebeian revolt. Tainted by their resort to rebellion the aristocratic traitors in *Henry IV, Part 2* seek, nevertheless, to enforce a separation between their actions and those of the supposedly fickle and purposeless multitude. 'An habitation giddy and unsure / Hath he that buildeth on the vulgar heart' rasps the Archbishop of York, castigating the 'fond many' who, at Bolingbroke's return from exile, with 'loud applause' had 'beat heaven' with 'blessing him' (1.3.90–2). The crowd that cheered Henry's accession is condemned as the 'beastly feeder' now 'so full of him / That thou provokest thyself to cast him up'.

> So, so, thou common dog, didst thou disgorge
> Thy glutton bosom of the royal Richard
> And now thou wouldst eat thy dead vomit up,
> And howlest to find it.
> (95–100)

The speech, like so many in the Shakespearean canon, insists that the 'vulgar' have no real political objectives or purpose. This figuration of the lower orders as, in Christopher Hill's words, 'fickle, unstable, incapable of rational thought: the headless multitude, the many-headed monster', which the Shakespearean text works to perpetuate and legitimate, may well have been an ideologically motivated misrepresentation of popular political interests.[6] For an elite whose comprehension of the needs, the interests and even the movements of their social subordinates was limited, the ideological concept of a plebeian class without the capacity for consistent and meaningful political action was, to an extent, reassuring.

At the same time, however, this notion exacerbated existing anxieties about the unpredictability of the masses. If the multitude was as unstable as this elite discourse about them implied, then it was all but impossible to know where or when some rising might occur. This perhaps explains the tone of combined contempt and fear with which rumours of impending risings were reported amongst the elite. It also helps to explain the appalled sense of shock which followed acts of popular resistance whose clear, specific objectives refuted the myth of the many-headed multitude. The popular insurrections of the mid-1590s induced, I would suggest, an important shift in patrician ideology with respect to the lower classes. Rather than viewing them as a mass who were ungovernable, the propertied came to see their subordinates as a class who must be governed at all costs. Since rumour was understood to be the instrument for the dissemination of subversive intent it too would become a subject for examination, regulation and control.

Shakespeare's play envisages the aftermath of rebellion in terms of a triumphant return to order and the elimination of all threats of resistance. The rebels 'all / Are brought to the correction of' the monarch's 'law' (4.4.84–5), with an ease symbolised by Falstaff's arrest of Coleville who 'with his confederates' is conveyed 'To York, to present execution' (4.3.72–3). 'There is not now a rebel's sword unsheathed' (4.4.86), claims Westmoreland, and his words are followed by the news that those who 'stand against' (94) the monarch are all 'overthrown' (99). In 1595 however the putting down of rebellion had not been succeeded by a return to order and obedience. The Mayor and aldermen, as we have seen, were quick to draw the Privy Council's attention to the fact that, with the lifting of Martial Law, the perceived perpetrators of disorder had returned and, as John Walter notes, the executions 'did little to stem the litter of libels and ballads which exposed a dangerous vein of popular discontent'.[7] If the Shakespearean text's triumphalism about the defeat of rebellion seems to obscure the relative inefficacy of the Elizabethan state's response to actual insurrection there is, none the less, an indication of the relative weakness of the Tudor regime in the figure of Henry IV who, in punishing rebellion had, like Elizabeth 'wasted all his rods / On late offenders' making explicit his 'lack' of any other 'instruments of chastisement' (4.1.412–14). In the image of the Shakespearean monarch, whose 'power, like to a fangless lion, / May offer, but not hold' (216–17) there is a perfect figuration of sovereign power weakened in the wake of its brutal but inefficient display of force.

When rioters had torn down the pillories on 27 June, as an overture to the violence on Tower Hill two days later, Edward Flower, a Knightsbridge husbandman, had reportedly claimed that the rioters' acts were a work of popular justice 'for the good of the Commonwealth'. One of his seditious claims was the reiteration of a rumour that '3,000 were lying in the fields, with bills and clubs to rescue' the riotous apprentices 'if anything were done to them'.[8] The threat was to find an echo in the words of an anonymous letter sent to the magistrates of Norfolk a few months later which 'spoke of 60,000 craftsmen in London and elsewhere ready to rise' and threatened the gentry that 'some barbarous and unmerciful soldier shall lay open your hedges, reap your fields, rifle your coffers and level your houses to the ground' ending with the legitimating slogan: 'Necessity hath no law'. The threats contained in the letter are no random list of menaces but rather statements about a popular will to address the specific grievances of the poor during the middle 1590s: enclosure and the hoarding of grain, along with class antagonism towards the gentry. These subversive words, like other incendiary utterances and texts which circulated in the latter part of 1595 and throughout 1596, were – it seems – prompted, in part, by the London riots, news of which, according to Peter Clark, 'spread quickly to the provinces' to be combined with rumours of planned insurrections across the south of England.[9] In 1596 an Essex weaver reportedly told a large crowd 'that it would never be better untill men did rise and seeke thereby an amendment and wished in his harte that a hundred men would rise and he would be their captain to cut the throats of the rich Churles'.[10]

This kind of class antagonism was the basis of periodic outbursts of popular resentment throughout the late sixteenth century and Shakespeare's history plays occasionally give representation to these sentiments, most notably of course in the words of Jack Cade in *Henry VI, Part 2*. Cade's followers insist that the commonwealth is 'threadbare' and that 'it was never merry world in England since gentlemen came up' (4.2.7–9) and Cade calls for 'you that love the commons' to 'follow me' with the pledge 'We will not leave one lord, one gentleman; / Spare none but such as go in clouted shoon' (4.2.172–5).[11] Cade's brutish and singular malevolence isolates and marginalises the combination of utopian communism and class antagonism that his discourse contains. Yet the hatred of the gentry and desire for popular liberty that Cade voices appear, from the fragmentary records that survive, to have been, if not commonplace, at least a significant strand of popular discourse in the mid-1590s. By 1596 the hardship resulting from another poor harvest and the subsequent rise in the price of grain brought renewed fears of insurrection. In October the Earl of Bath felt compelled, as John Walter notes, to call for the gentry to return to their estates 'to be at hand to stay the fury of the inferior multitude if they should happen to break out in sudden outcry for want of relief, as without good circumspection many suspect they may and will do'.[12]

If the Shakespearean text is able to demonise and mock the voices of plebeian unrest in the first years of the decade in the first part of *Henry VI*, by 1597, when *Henry IV, Part 2* was probably first performed, even a caricature like Cade carried too heavy a potential political charge to be admitted into the text. Popular protest is inscribed within the later play only as part of a rhetoric of legitimation through which the aristocratic rebels seek to ennoble their struggle with the King. 'Rebellion', according to Westmorland, does not appear 'like itself', with those 'base and abject routs' (4.1.32–3) which the ideology of the Tudor elite associated with popular protest. Nonetheless the Archbishop and the 'noble lords' who seek to 'dress the ugly form / Of base and bloody insurrection' with their 'fair honours' (39–41) cannot banish entirely from their resort to 'ill-beseeming arms' (84) the spectre of 'damned commotion' they associate with plebeian riot 'Led on by boys and beggary' (34–6). Moreover, in weighing 'in equal balance' the 'wrongs our arms may do' with 'what wrongs we suffer' the aristocratic rebels come to the conclusion that their supposed inferiors had reached in the dearth-ridden England of the *fin de siècle* and 'find our griefs heavier than our offences' (67–9). Yet the text never allows the notion of plebeian insurrection to become anything more than a shadow traced by the easily contained treason of the nobility. The text is, indeed, eloquent about the possibility of such aristocratic dissidence, when 'That man that sits within the monarch's heart / And ripens in the sunshine of his favour' (4.2.11–12) turns like 'an iron man' to 'Cheering a rout of rebels with [his] drum' (4.2.8–9). The absolutist state had, of course, emerged through the successful elimination of aristocratic dissent and it is the nobility's willingness to 'Stoop tamely to the foot of majesty' (42) when the monarch promises to see their 'griefs . . . with speed redressed' (59) that allows Prince John to entrap the rebels with such ease. What the text does not and cannot, given the context of its inscription, acknowledge is that the impulse for rebellion might come from below.

This circumspection is comprehensible given the horrific proportions which the spectre of plebeian revolt had come to assume in the minds of the late-Tudor ruling class by the time Shakespeare wrote the play. By late 1596 the worst fears of the Earl of Bath and the Privy Council had been realised. On 14 December 1596 news came from Sir William Spencer, deputy lieutenant of Oxfordshire, that

there was a rising planned at Enslow Hill of 200 or 300 seditious
people, from various towns of that shire, with the design of raising a
rebellion. They were to spoil the neighbouring gentlemen's houses of
arms and horses, and go towards London, where they expected to be
joined by the apprentices.

The man later identified as the 'leader' of the rising, in probability one of
three or four primary activists, Bartholomew Steere, was reported to have told
his poor neighbours that 'it would never be well until the gentry were knocked
down' and so 'he would cut off all the gentlemen's heads and spoil the[ir]
houses'.[13] This class antagonism was combined, as in Shakespeare's Cade,
with the promise of a utopian future. When one poor neighbour had told him
he could barely find work to support his family 'this hard year', Steere had
responded: 'Work? Care not for work, for we shall have a meryer world
shortly; there be lusty fellows abroad, and I will gett more, and I will worke
one dai and plai an other, ffor I know ere yt be long wee shall have a meryer
world.' In the meantime they would reverse the hierarchy of privilege and
wealth that set the gentry above the labouring men by organising a rising of
the people to 'pulle downe the enclosures whereby waies were stopped up,
and arrable landes inclosed, and to laie the same open againe'.[14]

Steere's smouldering discontent had clearly been translated into active
resistance by the news of the riots in London the previous summer. In his
efforts to draw workers and servants into rising against their masters he
repeatedly mentioned 'the late insurrection in London, when certain
apprentices were hanged'.[15] The fate of the 'apprentices' seems to have
interlocked in Steere's mind with local folk memory to make him all the more
indomitable in his purpose for, he is reported to have said, 'there was once a
rising at Enslow Hill' but 'the risers were persuaded to go home, and were
hanged like dogs; but now, if they were once up they would never yield, but
go through with it'.[16] Even on the eve of the rising, when support seemed to
be waning and the prospect of Steere and his companions being 'hanged like
dogs' seemed all but inevitable he had said 'he could die but once and . . . he
would not allwaies live like a slave'.[17]

Quite how Steere could have learned of the events in London remains a
matter for conjecture, for contemporary historians as it was for the judicial
authorities who later sought to extract the full narrative from the conspirators
on the rack. It may have been that, as a servant in the household of Lord
Norris of Rycott, Steere had heard from those who had been in London to
witness the tumultuous events of the previous June.[18] In any case Steere's
knowledge of the London insurrection reveals a substratum of discursive
exchanges which could relay the news of popular protest from the capital to
an isolated village in rural England. For Steere the London riots provided not

only a precedent for popular resistance but also the promise of class solidarity for, he had told his companions Roger Symonds and James Bradshaw, 'that after they had risen, if they found themselves weak, they should go towards London, as he thought the apprentices there would take their part'.[19] Rumour, that 'pipe' on which the 'still-discordant wavering multitude, / Can play upon', appears here not as the isolated, extra-dramatic device of Shakespeare's play but as the instrument through which potentially revolutionary alliances between rural and urban plebeian revolt could be formed. This can seem fantastic but Steere had claimed that 'there would be somewhat adoe shortlie in this Countrie, more then had been seen a great while, ffor that manie would Rise'.[20] It was in the context of this national uprising that Steere saw the Oxfordshire rising for, after rising and having 'cut off all the gentlemen's heads; thence they were to go to Lord Norris's of Rycott who has two pieces of brass ordnance, which they were to take' along with 'arms for a hundred men which he had, and his horses . . . Thence they were to go to London'[21] 'and when the prentices heare that wee bee upp, they will Come and Joine with us'. 'After that', he promised, 'yt was but a months work to overrun the realm' adding that 'the poore did once rise in Spaine and Cutte down the gentlemen and sithens that tyme they have lyved merily there'.[22]

Steere's awareness of and ambitions to combine in a network of resistance well beyond his own locality seems to me to contradict John Walter's assertion, in the most thorough historical investigation of the rising to date, that it had a purely 'localist orientation'. Certainly the rising never came anywhere near to fulfilling Steere's ambitions, only four men turned up on the appointed day at Enslow Hill where, according to Walter, they waited for two hours before disbanding, only later to be arrested by the authorities.[23] Yet it was the wider network of proffered and promised support for the rising that seems to have worried the authorities most. 'They speak of hundreds who were to join them', wrote Spencer and Sir Anthony Cope to Lord Norris of the conspirators they had examined, 'We have laboured night and day, but cannot get confessions to make up 20 of the number. Their practice', they acknowledged, 'will very hardly be discovered unless it be on the rack.'[24]

Part, at least, of the reason for the horrified response of both the local landowners and the Privy council to the discovery of the rising was the potential it demonstrated for the circulation of discourses that carried the contagion of insurrection along lines of communication invisible to them. The innumerable murmured conversations the agitators had engaged in months in advance of the abortive rising: at markets and fairs, in the alehouses and lanes of Oxfordshire and the neighbouring counties, always hearing and speaking of discontent and planned disorder, reveal the existence of a huge infrastructure of potential resistance. The thirty names the Privy Council were able to torture out of the 'ringleaders' were, it seems, the nucleus of a broad range of encounters and discursive exchanges and the silence that evidently closed over the county after the rising was discovered should not be read as an indication of widespread indifference to its goals. Thomas Powell of Yarnton, a figure at the extreme fringes of those who lent their support to the rising had 'refused at first' but when James Bradshaw, the local miller, had said 'the whole county would rise' he had answered 'that if all [did] rise, he must needs be one'. It was this sentiment that was almost as disturbing for the inquisitors as the more militant stance of Steere. It implied that discontent was widespread and required only the spark provided by seditious rumours to ignite further insubordination. Even after the arrest of Steere and the other supposed 'ringleaders', Roger Ibill and James and Richard Bradshaw, the Privy Council were so cautious of the danger of further conspiracy that they commanded Lord Norris to see that they were sent to London 'under guard, their hands pinioned, and their legs bound under their horses' bellies'. 'And allow them no conference on their way', they went on 'if needful, they should be watched at night , at the inns where they lodge'. At the same time 'the justices and other gentlemen and officers' in Oxfordshire were to 'take special care to suppress any tumult or gathering of people'. 'Those gentlemen whose houses were threatened', they warned, 'should look to their safety, and have their servants, retainers and tenants ready in their defence.'[25]

When, days later, the mason Robert Burton, one of the men who had joined Steere on Enslow Hill on the day of the rising, was apprehended in London, the inquisition headed by Bacon and Coke, presumably fearing that there was some basis to Steere's claims that the apprentices would offer support to the rising, began to trace the lines of possible communication between the capital and the seat of the rising. A band of 80 gypsies who had been seen moving on the borders of Northamptonshire and Oxfordshire were arrested and tortured by order of the Council on suspicion that they might have had some connection with the events on Enslow Hill. The Oxfordshire conspirators, meanwhile, were questioned about their knowledge of 'Certen persons Calling themselves Egipcians' and, according to Walter, whether they had planned an alliance with ex-soldiers.[26] Steere's words had established a discursive alignment between landless rural artisans and the urban poor. The council now sought to trace the chain of plebeian exchanges which might have brought about that tumultuous alliance.

The Oxfordshire rising was punished with a severity designed to re-establish the relations of subjection which Steere and his companions had sought to overturn. Those of the ringleaders who survived torture and gaol fever were hanged, drawn and quartered on Enslow Hill, after a trial before a jury and bench stacked with the local gentry they had threatened to decapitate and 'in sight', as Walter puts it, 'of the enclosures' they had threatened to level. Their 'miserable end', Walter goes on to say, 'was doubtless made to serve as a macabre example of the fate accorded to those who had the temerity to challenge the gentry's hegemony.'[27]

Walter suggests that the panic-stricken response of the gentry and the government may well have been an over-reaction since, with a smart reversal in attitudes towards enclosure and a revival of paternalistic relations between the elites and their social subordinates, the crisis of the 1590s was substantially averted. He acknowledges that 'if the crisis was less than the government believed, this matters little when examining their response', but he marshals as 'evidence' of the absence of any real threat the fact that 'risings were mooted in several counties in the 1590s, but none of these came to fruition'.[28] An unexamined and, I would argue, anachronistic separation is at work in this assertion which divides subversive words and deeds. What concerned the Privy Council was not only full scale riots but also rumours, sedition, a whole universe of discourse about whose dimensions and political significance they were uncertain.

Having averted rebellion in Oxfordshire, the council had to counteract the effect of what Buchanan Sharp has called 'exaggerated reports' of it which began to circulate within popular discourse. In April 1597 there were claims in Norfolk 'that the poor had risen in the west and would be in Norfolk in a week'. The rumour was carried by one Thomas Welles who claimed, according to Sharp, that '4,000 persons would meet with him, go to a justice and ask him "that they might have corne cheape for ther monye and yf they could not gett anye reasonably for ther money then they wolde aryse and gett it with strength and that if they did arise they wold knocke downe the best first" '.[29] Within weeks of these reports the council were writing to Justices in Kent to warn them of the danger posed by 'certaine dysordered and lewde dysposed persons' who 'doe carry them selves in very tumultuous sorte'. They were concerned not simply about these individuals but with the danger that they would 'incyt with lewde words others to comytt the same dysorder and outrage' they had committed. In May they were still anxious about the 'very many ill disposed persons of the vulgare sorte' who were 'very apt to move trouble and commit great disorders under the pretense of the great want and scarcity that is at this present in this realme'.[30]

Disorder appears in these pronouncements as a form of contagion, spread by word of mouth, with the declaration of seditious intent only precariously differentiated, if at all, from the occurrence of riot itself. Francis Bacon, whose *Essays* were first published the year after the Oxfordshire rising and whose 'Of Seditions and Troubles' must have been shaped by his participation in the commission that oversaw the interrogation of the Oxfordshire agitators, claimed that 'seditious tumults and seditious fames differ no more but as brother and sister, masculine and feminine'. He thought 'libels and licentious discourses against the state, . . . and (in like sort) false news, often running up and down to the disadvantage of the state, and hastily embraced are signs of troubles'. The 'matter of seditions', which Bacon thought consisted of 'much poverty and much discontentment' had been established in the conjuncture of 1595–7 and the lesson Bacon's text records from his involvement in the interrogation of the Oxfordshire conspirators was that 'if there be fuel prepared' for rebellion 'it is hard to tell whence the spark shall come that shall set it on fire'.[31]

In the parliament of 1597–8 Bacon would be joined on a Commons committee to examine the condition of the poor by Edward Hext, whose warnings of apocalyptic disorder had perhaps struck a chord with the Privy Council in the wake of the Oxfordshire rising. The legislation they proposed had as its objective the relief of the 'deserving' poor and the re-subjection of the masterless through a regime of labour discipline and enforced settlement at the centre of which would be that novel institution of coercive power: the bridewell. In the society instituted by these acts there would be no room for Steere's otiose vision of 'a merry world' in which he would 'work one day and play another'. Rather such regulations sought to establish a binary separation between what Paul Slack has called 'the deserving and the undeserving poor, between the respectable pauper and the dangerous vagabond'.[32]

Tied to the parish by fear of bridewell and the need for relief, the poor were, theoretically, prevented from wandering and thus from finding opportunities for idle gossip, or worse, beyond the watchful eyes of their masters. It was this objective of fixity, I would suggest, that was one of the central concerns of the poor regulations drawn up by Bacon, Hext and their gentry allies on the committee. Nowhere in Europe was 'the rigour and precision of the English settlement laws' equalled, according to Paul Slack and the logic of confinement they sought to establish should be understood, perhaps, as the weapon with which the governing strata hoped to prevent the contagion of rebellion spreading throughout the social body.[33]

> Do nothing but eat, and make good cheer,
> And praise God for the merry year,
> When flesh is cheap and females dear,
> And lusty lads roam here and there,
> So merrily,
> And ever among so merrily.
>   (5.3.17–22)

The song that Silence sings in Act Five provides a striking recollection of the 'meryer world' that Bartholomew Steere had promised his poor neighbours they should have 'shortly'. Even the 'lusty fellowes' Steere had claimed were 'abroade' to usher in his vision of Cockaigne, seem to be hinted at in the 'lusty lads' who 'roam here and there' in the words of the song. Yet it is appropriate that it should be Silence who sings of this 'merry year' for although his song urges 'welcome merry Shrovetide! Be merry, be merry' (35) it is the Lenten regime of austerity and censorship that follows in the wake of Shrovetide that is ushered in by the new King Henry. Whilst Falstaff takes the news of the Prince's accession as a license to 'take any man's horse' since 'the laws of England are' now 'at [his] command' (5.3.134–6), the prospect of 'pleasant days' (139) he and Pistol imagine under Hal's misrule is sharply curtailed by the first actions of the new monarch. No merry world is ushered in by the reign of Henry V, rather the disorderly are promised 'whipping-cheer' (5.4.5) as the Bridewell Beadles range the streets and although Doll insists that the 'bluebottle rogue' who apprehends her will be 'soundly swinged' for his pains it is this 'filthy famished corrrectioner' who is the most appropriate harbinger of the new regime (19–20).

'Presume not that I am the thing I was': the madcap prince is himself the model for that process by which the subject in whom 'headstrong riot hath no curb' and whose 'counsellors' are 'rage and hot blood' (4.4.62–3) 'Cast[s] off' his idle companions and makes of 'their memory / A pattern or a measure' in relation to which he can construct a chastened, disciplined identity by 'Turning past evils to advantages' (75–8). Yet this reformation, by which he 'turn[s] away from my former self' (5. 5.61) also involves the regulation and correction of 'those that kept me company' (62) in idleness. The severe regimen imposed on Falstaff is a sentence passed not only on the 'surfeit-swelled, profane' (53) delinquent but on 'the rest' of his supposed 'misleaders' (67) and the regime that will transform 'the feeder of my riots' is strikingly similar to the strategy of the 1598 poor laws.

The King's dispensation involves the provision of the means of subsistence, in order to obviate the recourse to illegality or violence: 'For competence of life I will allow you', he proclaims, 'That lack of means enforce you not to evils' (69–70). In this the text discloses the political function of Elizabethan 'regulation and relief of the poor' which , as Paul Slack has demonstrated, formed part of a range of 'measures intended to reform the manners and the behaviour of the lower orders'. The Acts of 1598 sprung from the recognition by the elites 'that the poor were getting poorer and potentially more disorderly' and that a means 'to relieve their wants and make them respectable' was imperative. Thus 'the machinery of the poor law' was constituted, Slack's analysis reveals, not so much 'as an economic regulator, but as a moral, social and political one'.[34] So whilst the Lord Chief Justice orders his officers to 'Go, carry Sir John Falstaff' to prison and 'Take all his company along with him' (94–5), this, according to Prince John, is a 'fair proceeding of the King's' for 'He hath intent his wonted followers / Shall all be very well provided for'. Their incarceration is to be a condition of the transformative practice by which 'their conversations' will be rendered 'more wise and modest to the world' (100–4).

In keeping with this discursive reformation the place of the subversive figure of Rumour at the play's beginning is filled at its close by an obsequious Epilogue who speaks 'First' of 'fear' (Epilogue, 1). In tortured sentences it ducks the 'displeasure' (2) of an audience of 'gentlemen' and 'gentlewomen' (22–3) before whom it kneels to 'pray your patience' (9) and to whose 'mercies' it 'commit[s its] body' (13) in defence of 'a displeasing play' (8–9). Here, perhaps, the play positions itself within the 'dialectics of deference' which, according to John Walter, the poor were forced to accept as a condition of existence in early modern England.[35] For in its catechism: 'First, my fear; then, my curtsy; last, my speech' (1) there is a trace of the mode of subjection through which the gentry sought to shackle the poor with bonds of duty and obedience. In making his Epilogue beg for mercy, Shakespeare seemed already to understand that, for those in his audience who recognised themselves as his 'gentle creditors' (12), the 'spirit of consent and submission', as Douglas Hay has called it, was an ideological effect to be secured through practices like literary representation as much as in the bridewells of Tudor England.[36] In playhouses and poorhouses the work of banishing subversive words was renewed and on Shakespeare's stage at least, Rumour's swarm of dissenting mouths is replaced by the solitary 'tongue' of an Epilogue made 'weary' by the perfunctory iteration of the language of subjection. Yet we need only recall the quiet heroism of Bartholomew Steere who said 'he could die but once and . . . he would not allwaies live like a slave'[37] to recognise that the resistance of working people could not be so easily extinguished and that even those fragmentary traces of subversive speech recorded in the archives of their oppressors are a mark of the possibility, the necessity, of resistance.

Notes

1   All references are to P.H. Davison (ed.), *Henry IV, Part 2* (Harmondsworth: Penguin, 1977).

2   R.H. Tawney and Eileen Power (eds), *Tudor Economic Documents*, 3 vols (London: Longmans, 1924), III, 341.

3   Paul L. Hughes and F. Larkin (eds), *Tudor Royal Proclamations*, 3 vols (New Haven and London: Yale University Press, 1969), II, 232.

4   Peter Clark, 'A Crisis Contained? The Condition of English Towns in the 1590s', in Peter Clark (ed.), *The European Crisis of the 1590s: Essays in Comparative History* (London: Routledge, 1985), 54.
5   E.K. Chambers, *The Elizabethan Stage*, 4 vols (Oxford: Clarendon Press, 1951), IV, 318.
6   Christopher Hill, 'The Many-Headed Monster in Late Tudor and Early Stuart Thought', in C.H. Carter (ed.), *From the Renaissance to the Counter Reformation: Essays in Honour of Garrett Mattingley* (London: Macmillan, 1968), 296–324, 301.
7   John Walter, 'A "Rising of the People"? The Oxfordshire Rising of 1596', *Past and Present*, 107 (1985), 91.
8   *Calendar of State Papers Domestic of the Reign of Elizabeth I, 1595–7* (London, 1869), 63. Hereafter, *CSPD*.
9   Clark, 'A Crisis Contained?', 54.
10   Cited in Walter, 'A "Rising of the People"?, 91.
11   Norman Sanders (ed.), *Henry VI, Part 2* (Harmondsworth: Penguin, 1981).
12   Walter, 'A "Rising of the People"?, 91.
13   *CSPD*, 316; 342.
14   Walter 'A "Rising of the People"?', 100.
15   *CSPD*, 324.
16   *CSPD*, 342.
17   Walter, 'A "Rising of the People"?', 101.
18   Ibid., 107–8.
19   *CSPD*, 324.
20   Walter, 'A "Rising of the People"?', 108.
21   *CSPD*, 317
22   Walter, 'A "Rising of the People"?', 107–8.
23   Ibid., 95; 102.
24   CSPD, 319.
25   Ibid., 319; 318.
26   Walter, 'A "Rising of the People"?', 126–7.
27   Ibid., 128–9.
28   Ibid., 138–9.
29   Buchanan Sharp, *In Contempt of All Authority: Rural Artisans and Riot in the West of England* (Berkeley and London: University of California Press, 1980), 22.
30   Cited in *Acts of the Privy Council of England*, ed. John R. Dasent, new series, vol. 27 (London, 1903), 55–6; 92.
31   Francis Bacon, *Essays*, ed. John Pitcher (Harmondsworth: Penguin, 1985), 101–6.
32   Paul Slack, Poverty and Policy in Tudor and Stuart England (London: Longman, 1988), 61.
33   Ibid., 11.
34   Ibid., 130–31.
35   Walter, 'A "Rising of the People"?', 142.
36   Douglas Hay, 'Property, Authority and the Criminal Law', in *Albion's Fatal Tree: Crime and Society in Eighteenth Century England*, ed. Douglas Hay, Peter Linebaugh, John G. Rule, E.P. Thompson, and Cal Winslow (London : Allen Lane, 1975), 49.
37   Walter, 'A "Rising of the People"?', 101.

4

The verse libel: popular satire in early modern England

Andrew McRae

John Dryden's *Discourse on the Original and Progress of Satire* (1693) provides a narrative of generic refinement, as it traces the genre from classical times to the close of the seventeenth century. When Dryden looks for the origins of Roman satire, he imagines a crude 'company of clowns on a holiday, dancing lubberly, and upbraiding one another, in *ex tempore* doggerel, with their defects and vices'.[1] By the time the genre emerges in England, however, it is purportedly loosed from popular influences, instead springing solely from the neo-classicism of the Renaissance. Dryden represents English writers from the 1590s single-mindedly adopting the models of Juvenal, Horace and Persius, and thereby fashioning an urbane mode of satire for an educated elite. This narrative is generally compelling, and has remained dominant over the centuries since Dryden wrote. One of its less fortunate effects, however, has been to suppress the consideration of links between English popular culture and the development of satire. By contrast, my initial contention is that surviving evidence of indigenous practices of invective, as revealed by recent historical research, might prompt a reassessment of Renaissance satire.[2] An examination of such sources may indeed lead to a broadened appreciation of the origins and progress of satire in England.

This chapter will examine native practices of scurrility which involved the composition and transmission of libellous verse. 'Libel' was a term used to describe any piece of writing seen as 'politically controversial or socially scandalous'. The form could include pamphlets, speeches and political declarations; however, libels were most commonly in verse, and could stretch from a pithy epigram to a lengthy ballad.[3] Historians of political culture have demonstrated the prevalence of libelling in the early decades of the seventeenth century, and literary historians are beginning to follow their lead into this body of poetry.[4] I am concerned here, however, with libels produced in provincial contexts and concerned with fundamentally local tensions. Such poems were not transmitted into the manuscript sources of an elite literary culture, but rather survive only when a matter was brought to court in a libel action. The work of Adam Fox has revealed a wealth of such texts in Jacobean Star Chamber records, and my essay represents the work of a literary scholar asking a new set of questions of this material.[5] In particular, I want to consider the cultural functions and textual qualities of the poems, and to explore the extent to which they represent a popular poetic tradition which may be interrelated with the contemporary vogue for neo-classical satire.

The evidence of the Star Chamber cases leads Fox to conclude that libels powerfully articulate 'popular opinions and sensibilities'.[6] As he points out, the writers and distributors of the texts were typically of a lower rank than their victims, while bills of information consistently stress the social dangers of exposing the better sort to the ridicule of the commons.[7] Consequently, the texts hold the promise of access to the world of carnival, with its rituals of popular justice and its displays of verbal aggression.[8] A carnivalesque mode, in Mikhail Bakhtin's conception, sets the laughter of the populace against 'all that [is] immortalised and completed', and thus subverts hierarchical social structures and their associated ideologies.[9] My investigation of libelling will begin within this context, by exploring connections between surviving libellous poems and contemporary practices of popular unrest. As my analysis develops, however, I will equally consider the textual characteristics of the poems, and their interrelation with other literary types. In the process, I will explore the interaction between popular and elite cultures, and suggest that a hypostasised approach to 'popular opinions and sensibilities' threatens to suppress much of the complexity and sophistication of the verse libel.

Practices of libelling were commonly interwoven with rituals of shaming and social protest. Historians such as E.P. Thompson and Martin Ingram have demonstrated the significance of 'rough music' for the 'ritualised expression of hostility', and it is clear that many libellous poems were involved in such practices.[10] One bill of complaint, for example, describes the public singing of a ballad as part of a riotous gathering at night in a village churchyard which adjoined the house of the plaintiff, a recusant gentleman. The poem begins with a taunt to the man's four daughters:

> Gallantes of the hall,
> Come forth and show your faces,
> knowne it is to us all
> that you have greasy Arses,
> and the scall.[11]

Those involved in the rough music in this case might well have been motivated by a sense of a community disciplining moral transgressors, and they might have derived support for this view from the presence of their parson of forty-eight years. In another case, by comparison, poems were linked with a practice of humiliation at once more surreptitious and more divisive:

> the said libelling and seditious persons . . . in the Consistorie of the now Lord Bishop of Peterborowe scituate within the parish church of All Saints in Northampton (being a place used for publique administracion of justice in causes ecclesiastical within that dioces) did in most obscene beastly and filthie manner with their ordure & excrementes of nature defile the table standing in the middest of the said consistorie about which the Judge and other officers of the said Court doe use to sitt.

The main libel in the case methodically works its way through the failings of those who would sit at the defiled consistory table. It presents an anonymous and ostensibly populist assault on the hypocrisy of 'diverse and soundry honourable Lords knightes Justices of peace [and] Magistrates'.[12]

Beyond evidence of such carefully contrived carnivalesque practices, almost all libels were disseminated in ways which link them to popular culture. Bills of information repeatedly stress the reading and singing of libels in forums such as 'dyvers alehouses tavernes and other open and publique places'.[13] Some libellers also achieved notoriety by subversively appropriating for their purposes sites associated with orthodoxy; one defendant, for example, did 'unlawfullye and malliciouslye by waye of a Jeste and merimente scoffinglye singe, devulge, reade and publishe [his] libell in the Tower Lofte or Belfrye within the parishe Churche'.[14] In other cases, as Fox has noted, libellers 'employed performers, town waits, minstrels and ballad-singers to set their tunes to music and render them at civic gatherings or disseminate them over several counties as they travelled the circuit of alehouses and fairs'.[15] Such people were themselves routinely stigmatised as dissolute and masterless; one plaintiff described itinerant musicians as 'persons of . . . lewd behaviour professing of pipeinge & fidlinge runninge & rangeinge upp & downe the countie from place to place to get their livings at ffayres markettes & at Idle meetings & merrimements'. The description betrays the anxiety of a gentleman at having his reputation manipulated by 'men of base quallitie & of lewd & dissolute life'.[16]

Some of the poems in fact play on such anxieties for socially subversive effect. A verse circulated in Elizabethan London, for example, refers to 'a secrett / whispering' to be heard 'emongst the meanest sort / as tiplers apple sellers & such lyke'.[17] Others are fashioned as dialogues between relatively lowly figures, thereby locating authority in the very commonness of the speaking voices. In one piece, a traveller and a shepherd meet outside a village, and talk about the loose sexual morality of a local widow.[18] In another, designed to denigrate the reputation of a Staffordshire woman and thus prevent her marriage to a yeoman, the speakers are figured as weavers (though none of the defendants were in fact weavers):

> Solomon & Peter you may call our name
> me care not who doth know the same
> to let any more time we are very loth
> for this hath hindred us the weaving of an elne of cloth.[19]

A similar strategy is the construction of elusive speakers; as one piece taunts, 'Seeke not for me out of doubt / You will never finde me out'.[20] Within a confined social context, this is designed specifically to undermine authority, as the speaker pinpoints the corruption of local governors, then effectively merges into a mass of the disgruntled populace. Anonymity therefore becomes a condition of authorship that informs and determines the libel's distinctive poetic voice.

From these positions, identified with a community rather than an individual, libels commonly purport to serve the same function as 'rough music': directing 'mockery or hostility against individuals who have offended against certain community norms'.[21] The strength of such assumed values is apparent in a 1616 libel on the chief constable of a wapentake near Leeds:

> Who ever hearde of any soe madd,
> To stabbe themselves and laugh and bee glad,
> And him extoll was always false lad,
> What witt is in this good neighbours
> What nowe becomes of all idle talke,
> In Alehouse and taverne and as you doe walke,
> where some payed money and some did but chalke,
> what wise mirth is this good neighbours.[22]

The poem performs a simple shaming strategy, as it sets an oral culture of 'talke' and 'mirth' which binds all 'good neighbours' against the aberrant behaviour of Harrison. (The precise nature of his faults is not entirely clear, but he is compared unfavourably with 'th'old knight whome wee did prove, / did us protect and defend with love'.) The transgressor is counselled:

> Thoughe nowe somethinge late take counsell by mee,
> love vertue hate vice, lett all lovers bee,
> what's past it's past lett's all nowe agree,
> And love one another good neighbours.

Hence neighbourliness is figured as a levelling force, implicitly underset at the close by Christ's injunction to 'love thy neighbour as thyself'.[23]

Within this model of unity in the face of a threat to common values, a libel's author becomes roughly identifiable with an entire community. The logical extension of such an identification is apparent in the closing words of another piece, in which communal values give way to an argument for communal authorship:

> thus making my leave I take an end
> but if I have left any thing behind
> do you sett it downe at the nether end
> and I will take you for my freind.[24]

The concept of an ever-extendable poem, compiled by an anonymous community of 'friends', sets this form apart from the overwhelming momentum of Renaissance literary practice, with its tendency to isolate and valorise the individual author.[25] Furthermore, certain cases provide evidence of a levelling effect in the process of composition, which might also erase indices of individual learning. A Chelmsford schoolmaster who claimed to have been tricked and bullied into writing a libel in 1602, for example, described how a barber had 'given him the substance' of the libellous allegations. When he supplied the poem, the barber 'said he liked them very well', but he could not understand an allusion to Leviathan and a description of England as 'Albion'. The barber subsequently wrote another poem himself, stripped of any literary pretensions, which the schoolmaster described as 'lascivious, villainous and beastly'.[26] Poems composed in groups, often by illiterate men and women, must similarly have been levelled of distinction, and thus tuned for the ears of a popular audience.[27]

This popular location of libelling is furthered by connections with other textual forms and cultural practices. One case, for example, revolved around the significance of the following verse, which was alleged to have been sung in a festive gathering at the manor house of Claverton, Wiltshire:

> Goor Mistress Toord at one bare worde, Your best parte stinkethe, yf stincke be the best what then doth the resst as each man thinketh A poxe in your Arse, yow have burnt a good tarse, A verie filthie lott, and that was all I gotte.[28]

One of the defendants claimed that he recalled singing and dancing with old friends at the local manor house:

> and then occasion being geven to remember manie old songs and rymes which they had oftentimes heard to be song and repeated . . . did to his remembrance fyrst in dauncing the daunce called the Jewe of Malta and therunto singing one ditty or twoe, secondly dauncing the Irish daunce, singing to that another with diverse such like and other

daunces and songes of mirth did sing or recyte some certaine rymes or
songes somwhat like the rymes mencioned in the said bill but not the
same rymes.[29]

However cynical this response might appear, the defendants vigorously
pursued the matter, asking witnesses about 'dyvers old songes and Rymes,
made of Auntient & many yeares before'. Moreover, their claims may contain
at least a grain of truth. A 'ballad intituled the murtherous life and terrible
death of the riche jew of Malta' was entered in the Stationers' Register in
1594, the year of the first edition of Christopher Marlowe's play of the same
name.[30] Closer to the mark in terms of bawdy content is 'The Irish Jig: Or, the
Night Ramble', extant from at least the early years of the seventeenth
century.[31] It is obviously unclear in such cases whether print culture is
reflecting a pre-existent oral culture, or whether popular culture is rather
appropriating printed texts for its own purposes. In the current context,
however, the more important point is the extent to which libellers manipulate
other accepted popular forms and texts for their own local interests.

Indeed the jig, a form which appears to have been at issue in the Claverton
gathering, is cited frequently in Star Chamber libel actions. According to the
historian of this form, 'jig' was 'a generic term for popular song with dance'.
It had strong popular roots in sixteenth-century England, and was widely
recognised as a satiric form, before it was translated onto the stage as an
afterpiece to plays in the first few decades of London's professional theatre.[32]
In the provinces, there is ample evidence that amateur writers were producing
their own jigs. A Yorkshire case, for instance, documents one gentleman's
servant approaching another, and 'intreat[ing]' him 'to make a Jyge or songe'
on two of their neighbours, 'to be merrie withal, which he saide was a trewe
jeste and he could prove it'.[33] Another defendant attempted to turn the link
between libel and jig to his advantage. George James, a servant to a gentleman
and his wife, was alleged to have published a libel as part of a dispute about
his conditions of employment and his rights to a livery cloak. The verse
begins, 'Roysters give Roome, for here comes a Lass: / Thoughe shee never
solde Broome, nor had a good face', and depicts a woman of low degree and
morals, but without ever naming the plaintiff. In response, James claimed that
there was no case to answer, because the verse was in fact

a songe or Jygge and comedians which the Servauntes to the late highe
and mightie prince Henrie Prince of Wales did often in the presence of
his highnes . . . act daunce and singe as a Jygge in the end of their
enterludes and plaies beinge a generall songe without particuler
nominacion or alusion to anie, which said songe or Jygge hath beene
seene approved and allowed by the right worshipfull the Maister of the
Revelles.[34]

While this claim appears more than a little disingenuous, especially in the light of the plaintiff's explanation of various coded references in the offending text, it remains possible that James may have adapted an existing jig for his own purposes. Interestingly, he claims that his performance is sanctioned not merely by local custom, but by the Master of the Revels, one of the most important cultural authorities in the land.

If the jig occupied a shadowy position between popular and elite cultures, so too could plays themselves. Indeed players provided an obvious medium for the dissemination of libellous material, and there is ample evidence to suggest that people saw dramatic texts as manipulable rather than fixed. Thus, just as Hamlet saw the performance of 'The Mousetrap' as an opportunity to jostle Claudius's conscience, so too those involved in a stage play at Kendal in 1621 saw a play as an opportunity to attack various landlords seeking to extinguish the custom of tenant right.[35] The play was written by a local schoolmaster, and included a general complaint about 'greedy landlordes'; the performance at Kendal Castle, however, was far more pointed. It was alleged that the players made 'a representacion of Hell and in the same did personate and acte manie Lordes of the Mannors of the said Countie which they did libellouslie and disgracefullie then and there represent to be in hell'.[36] Similarly, the same year in Shropshire a group of men defamed a woman by writing a play, performed to 'a great multytude', in which 'it was devysed that one of the actors should be apparelled in womens apparell & bolstered & sett forth as though shee were great with Child & should apparsonatt' the defendant.[37] Although it is impossible to estimate how frequently such satire was attempted in early modern England, it is clear that many other libellers were equally aware of the mimetic resources of the play. One poem simply gestures threateningly towards those resources, as it suggests that a man's actions might well 'yeild matter to make a stage playe'.[38]

A similar sense of the manipulability of a textual form is apparent in the relation between libels and ballads. The ballad had established roots in popular culture, and many ballad texts indicate local origins and oral practices of transmission. By the early seventeenth century it was a staple of professional authors operating within an urban print culture, yet it continued to arouse anxiety for its associations with popular immorality.[39] The Star Chamber records demonstrate that libellers drew not only upon local oral traditions, but equally upon the resources and conventions of print. Several texts proclaim a title and a tune, in a manner that mimics the printed page of contemporary ballads. One piece is headed: 'A pleasant new history declaring of a misterie of Richard Nightingale by name & Anne Ballanie of dods lane you may sing it to a merry new tune'.[40] Another proclaims in its introduction that it is 'better to be sung than to be redd, to the tune of Bonny Nell' (a ballad which itself had a reputation as 'obscene and scurrilous').[41] A third invokes the serialising convention of the broadsheet ballad, as it claims to be just 'the first parte of pryde and lecherie'. Interestingly, the libellers in this case appear to have seen printed ballads as things they could write as well as things they could imitate. They were alleged to have 'most wickedlie endeavoured practized and laboured to putt the same wicked and infamous Libell in printe, And to that end and purpose sent the same Libell to a printer in London to have been printed'.[42]

These examples demonstrate that the libel was by no means quarantined from the practices of an emergent national literary culture. Moreover, although libels were by nature localised in their concerns, their authors and readers alike clearly valued certain literary qualities. According to one plaintiff, the libellers 'did very many tymes and to many severall persons unlawfully extoll applaud & comend protest and sweare that [their libels] were excellently penned, and well and scholler like written'.[43] The excellence of a libel, as that of a printed satire or epigram, might involve qualities of wit and verbal dexterity. In one instance, the libellers read the poem with meaningful 'wincking or nodding of the head', and 'did interprett the said libell with greate jollitie and laughter'.[44] Furthermore, although it is often difficult to credit claims by defendants that they disseminated a poem 'not knowing nor conceiving who the same did in any way touch or concerne', it is certainly conceivable that particularly artful libels could appeal to readers who had no direct knowledge of the intended target.[45] For example, as David Hey has recently demonstrated, a ballad well known in the late seventeenth and early eighteenth centuries as *The Dragon of Wantley*, was in fact written in the early sixteenth century as part of a campaign against a Yorkshire gentleman trying to create a deer park.[46] Like some of the best verse satire, the poem originated as a personal attack, but survived beyond any memory of its local function.

There is also evidence that at least some of the provincial libellers specifically considered their work in relation to satire. One long poem from Dorchester, titled 'To the Counterfett Companie and packe of Puritans', resembles many printed satires in its focus on hypocrisy and dissimulation. Its opening lines combine local detail with an explosion of indignation characteristic of the neo-classical satirist:

> Haveing my selfe heard a sermon newe of late
> preached in the Church by a puritan prelate
> I could not well containe nor hold my pen still
> least I should participate in the same ill.[47]

Another, also concerned with religious innovation, contains the satirist's characteristic note of literary self-consciousness:

> but soft my sater be not too free,
> for thou will make them spourne at thee,
> for rubb a horse where scabbes be thicke,
> and thou will make him wince and kicke.[48]

Elizabethan theory held that satire originated in Greek satyr plays, and satirists shaped their own satiric personae in accordance with this mythological figure. The vitriolic John Marston, for example, refers to a 'Satyre' which 'rub[s] our gauled skinnes'.[49] The Stratford libeller, who might well have been familiar with Marston's work, filters the same image through a markedly rustic vision.

It is possible that pieces such as these were in fact commissioned from hack writers, who had no other role in the local disputes. Indeed poets and statesmen, as well as local figures of authority, commonly depicted libels as statements 'sow'd / Among the vulgar' for political ends.[50] While such an argument runs counter to the weight of evidence considered up to this point, there are admittedly some indications that practices of popular culture might equally be employed by those of higher degree. One poem, for example, is signed 'Thomas unhedgeall', and invokes a discourse of populist menace in its closing reference to a local landlord: 'yet thus muche I woulde wishe him / to bee A poor mans friende / Or else wee muste unhedge him, / and soe I make an ende'.[51] The text emanated out of a dispute linked to the Midlands Revolt of 1607, yet it was in fact circulated by a major landowner, who was incensed that his enclosures, rather than those of neighbouring freeholders, had been targeted in riots.[52] The Dorchester libel cited above had a similarly strategic purpose. As David Underdown has shown, the series of attacks on 'the packe of Puritans' were part of a struggle for power over the town. The most prominent of the libellers fashioned for himself an identity as a defender of neighbourhood and hospitality, but was none the less one of the richest and most powerful men in the town, remembered after his death as 'Matthew Chubb the usurer'.[53]

The libels therefore frustrate attempts to identify coherent subordinate groups: while some might be linked to the alehouse, others can be traced to a disaffected gentleman's study. Moreover, while some might be taken as consistent with a carnivalesque affirmation of community values, others are more clearly exercises in social splintering. Like verse satires, many libels employ an art of discrimination and individuation. In the words of one plaintiff, libelling 'is a growing dangerous and enormous offence in this age and doth directlie tend to the sowing and increasing of debate strife and hatred betwixt neighbour and neighbour'.[54] The court records probably provide a misleading image of libels in this respect, since they only preserve cases in which the victim was sufficiently offended (and sufficiently wealthy) to take legal action. Many targets of jigs, crude ballads and rough music may rather have accepted the social shaming, and perhaps modified their behaviour accordingly. None the less, the impression that libels increasingly became acts of social division is supported by the documented rise in defamation actions from the mid-sixteenth century.[55] For whatever reason, railing words were frequently received in this period as damaging and socially divisive, rather than as the 'songes of mirth' one defendant described.[56]

This impression is compounded by the significance of religious dissension in the records of libelling. In libels dealing with national politics, as Alastair Bellany has observed, accusations of popery or puritanism were a standard form of stigmatisation.[57] Similarly, in the provinces religion was always a potent force of differentiation, especially after the rise of puritanism in the reign of Elizabeth. M.S. Byford's illuminating case-study of Elizabethan Colchester, for example, reveals an especially fractured and fractious civic society. In 1575, a Calvinist minister orchestrated a severe shaming ritual to punish two parishioners for adultery. The ritual in turn sparked a concerted and long-running libelling campaign, principally directed against reformist elements in the town, and involving a wide range of townspeople.[58] Significantly, each side in the vitriolic campaign employed cultural forms often associated with an inclusive mode of popular culture, and each side appealed to malleable notions of communal morality. The records of the dispute, however, indicate that each was as much concerned with stigmatising an enemy as with defending a community and its values. The multiple mobilisations of the carnivalesque were here anything but integrative in their effects.

Star Chamber records from the following decades document similarly divisive uses of libelling in the cause of religious controversy. Several pieces set values of neighbourhood and mirth against the spectre of the puritan. One appeals to all who 'love the King and common weale', to support an attack on secret 'conventicklers', while another claims reading in the works of William Perkins as evidence of a radically individualist form of religious observance.[59] But other pieces promote divergent views. Many reformist preachers, perhaps influenced by the example of the Marprelate tracts, 'spread mocking libels against the sermons of their conformist opponents'.[60] For example, another Colchester libel, written around 1604, appeals to 'well mynded people all' to recognise the local minister's transgressions of 'our saviour Christe his dissiplene'. The lengthy poem is embellished in the margins of written copies with citations of over forty biblical texts, yet like other libels it was disseminated orally, and one defendant was said to have learned it by heart.[61] Elsewhere puritans employed the libel as a weapon in the reformation of manners. One action brought against a preacher 'of a turbulent spiritt' cites a poem which attacks the sexual morality of local parishioners, and notes in passing the minister's diligent labours towards reform. Of a local woman the libel claims: 'Although by the minister she hath often been admonished, / yet the whores face for all that, is never a whitt blemished'.[62]

The extant evidence of libelling therefore provides a varied spectrum of material. Libels were written from any number of different viewpoints, for any number of different reasons, and range from simplistic invective to sophisticated satire. Yet almost all texts reveal an appreciation of the libel as a distinctive mode, and a mode which appeals to a notion of local community, even as it threatens to divide that community. Hence the libel may clearly be labelled a 'popular' form, even though closer investigation serves only to demonstrate the notorious hybridity of popular literature. It thus represents a form of satire which pre-existed the vogue for neo-classical verse satire in the 1590s, and which was a more vital presence within early modern culture than Dryden's concept of a Roman 'company of clowns on a holiday . . . upbraiding one another, in *ex tempore* doggerel'.[63] One might safely propose, therefore, that the popular influence on satire that Dryden tried to relegate to classical Rome was felt at least as urgently by writers within his own native culture.

By way of conclusion, I wish to suggest a few ways in which one might begin to trace the influence of this popular culture of invective on the development of Renaissance satire.[64] Before the consolidation of neo-classical verse satire in the 1590s, certainly, generic borders were loose. Sir John Harington, for instance, was both a writer and collector of scandalous verse. A note in his *Diary* records his intention to 'write a damnable storie and put it in goodlie verse about Lord A. He hath done me some ill turnes.'[65] An Elizabethan poem preserved by Harington, the anonymous 'Libel on Bashe', gives some indication of what he might have had in mind. It concludes with a consideration of poetic 'decorum', and claims Chaucer as authority for his practice of fitting 'bawdie words' to his subject's 'bawdie deeds'.[66] Skelton's satire is another influence on the poem; but so too is the scatology of popular culture:

> if his bodie were set upright
> & his necke were cut of quite
> a man that had good list to shite
> might sitt at ease upon his necke
> & down his throate without all checke
> The durt would fall in to his gutts

& then it might be tried by cutts
whether the durt that down did fall
or that which was there first of all
be putrified the best of twayne. (p. 229)

The libeller defines his purpose in a manner which conflates the popular and the elite: he wants 'to blaze [his enemy's] name in ryding ryme' (p. 226). While the blazon was a central strategy of Petrarchan poetry of praise, the rough riding was equally important to local practices of shaming. At a time when neo-classical satirists were making their first tentative steps in England, this apparently educated poet freely embraces the vitality of native traditions.

Renaissance satiric theory consistently worked to suppress such links with popular culture. Libel was encoded as satire's other: nurtured by popular traditions rather than classical authority, employing indigenous forms rather than satire's iambic pentameter couplet, attacking individuals rather than generalised types of vice, steeped in ephemeral topical issues rather than enduring moral struggles, and concerned with undermining authority rather than purging evil in the interests of authority.[67] None the less, there were obvious ways in which writers could justify scurrility, particularly when they looked to the example of classical literature. Satirists were instructed to observe the decorum of a base style, defined by one scholar as 'a low familiar way of talking'.[68] Moreover, while Renaissance writers were generally advised not to use identifiable names in their work, they were aware that numerous classical satirists did not observe this rule. Among the Greeks, Archilochus and Hipponax were known for their 'bitter rimes & biting libels', while Lucilius was recognised as one Roman writer who named his subjects.[69] In the face of England's censorship regime, feigned names provided one way in which writers might incorporate the vitriolic strain of such sources into their work. Although it is now impossible to determine the extent to which this strategy was employed, there can be little doubt that many libellous assaults lie behind the host of nonce names in any book of satires or epigrams from the period.

Attention to the context of popular culture might also cause readers of Renaissance satire to reassess the centrality of the satyr figure. The 'idea that poetic satire had its origin in a dramatic form distinguished for its viciousness of attack and spoken by rough satyrs' underpinned Elizabethan theories of satire, and was preserved by satirists even after scholars had demolished the theory.[70] According to the poets, the satyr was 'rude, lassivious and wanton of behavior', and he was specifically uneducated and rustic, 'Bred in Woods and Desert places'.[71] In the light of my analysis of libelling, it is worth considering the convenience of this piece of pseudo-classicism. At a time when satirists were struggling to defend the neo-classical foundations of their genre, they could hardly afford to admit links between their works and the scurrility of popular culture. The theory and figure of the satyr, however, authorised their use of strategies remarkably similar to those evident in contemporary libels. While such strategies could conveniently be justified by the history of wild satyrs or Roman 'clowns . . . dancing lubberly', a freshly historicising critical practice might equally align them with the documentable practices of countless anonymous English men and women. Such an approach might then see the borders between popular and elite literary practice – the very borders that Dryden was so keen to police – as more porous than any neo-classical satirist is ever likely to admit.

Notes

1   *Essays of John Dryden*, ed. W.P. Ker, 2 vols (New York: Russell & Russell, 1961), II, 56.
2   See especially Adam Fox, 'Ballads, Libels and Popular Ridicule in Jacobean England', *Past and Present*, 145 (1994), 47–83 [hereafter, Fox, 'Ballads']; Martin Ingram, 'Ridings, Rough Music and Mocking Rhymes in Early Modern England', in Barry Reay (ed.), *Popular Culture in Seventeenth-Century England* (London and Sydney, 1985), 166–97; and E.P. Thompson, 'Rough Music', in his *Customs in Common* (New York: The New Press, 1993), 467–538.
3   Pauline Croft, 'Libels, Popular Literacy and Public Opinion in Early Modern England', *Historical Research*, 68 (1995), 266–85, 266; 284.
4   See especially my 'The Literary Culture of Early Stuart Libelling' (forthcoming, *Modern Philology*, 2000); Arthur F. Marotti, *Manuscript, Print, and the English Renaissance Lyric* (Ithaca and London, 1995), ch. 2; James Holstun, ' "God Bless Thee, Little David!": John Felton and his Allies', *English Literary History*, 59 (1992), 513–52; and Kirk Combe, 'The New Voice of Political Dissent: The Transition from Complaint to Satire', in Kirk Combe and Brian A. Connery (eds), *Theorizing Satire: Essays in Literary Criticism* (Macmillan: Basingstoke and London, 1995), 73–94.
5   As well as reviewing the sources Fox identified in Star Chamber records, I will also consider similar material from other sources where appropriate. Fox's focus on the Jacobean period is due to the existence of thorough catalogues for these Star Chamber papers, and does not indicate a sudden explosion of libelling in these years. For an earlier attempt to situate similar material within a literary context, see C.J. Sisson, *Lost Plays of Shakespeare's Age* (Cambridge: Cambridge University Press, 1936), 186–203.
6   Fox, 'Ballads', 78.
7   Fox, 'Ballads', 56–7; Public Record Office (PRO), STAC 8/153/5.
8   Peter Burke, *Popular Culture in Early Modern Europe* (London: Temple Smith, 1979), ch. 7.
9   *Rabelais and his World*, trans. Helene Iswolsky (Bloomington: Indiana University Press, 1984), 10.

10   *Customs in Common*, 467–538, 469; Ingram, 'Ridings Rough Music and Mocking Rhymes in Early Modern England'.

11   PRO, STAC 8/288/12; 'scall' is a scabby disease of the skin. (My transcriptions will not change original spelling, but will expand conventional scribal contractions. While the legal documents rarely indicate line breaks in libellous poems, I will print them as verse where appropriate.)

12   PRO, STAC 8/205/20, f. 137.

13   PRO, STAC 8/153/5.

14   PRO, STAC 8/164/18, f. 2.

15   Fox, 'Ballads', 66.

16   PRO, STAC 8/275/22, f. 2.

17   British Library, Lansdowne MS 26/68.

18   PRO, STAC 8/153/5, f. 14.

19   PRO, STAC 8/220/31, f. 16.

20   PRO, STAC 8/205/20, f. 137.

21   Thompson, *Customs in Common*, 466.

22   PRO, STAC 8/167/27, f. 2.

23   Matthew 23.39.

24   PRO, STAC 8/220/31, f. 15.

25   See especially Robert Weimann, *Authority and Representation in Early Modern Discourse*, ed. David Hillman (Baltimore and London: Johns Hopkins University Press, 1996), 11–19.

26   F.W. Emmison, *Elizabethan Life: Disorder. Mainly from Essex Sessions and Assize Records* (Chelmsford: Essex County Council, 1970), 71–5.

27   For an example of group-composition, see Fox, 'Ballads', 49–51.

28   PRO, STAC 8/98/20, f. 28.

29   PRO, STAC 8/98/20.

30   T.W. Craik, introduction to the New Mermaid edition of *The Jew of Malta* (London: A & C Black, 1966), ix.

31   *Wit and Mirth: Or Pills to Purge Melancholy*, 5 vols (London, 1719), V, 108–9.

32   Charles Read Baskervill, *The Elizabethan Jig and Related Song Drama*, reprint edn (New York: Dover Publications, 1965), 16; 40, and ch. 1.

33   PRO, STAC 8/276/26, f. 2.

34   PRO, STAC 8/59/4.

35   *Hamlet*, III ii; *Records of Early English Drama: Cumberland, Westmorland, Gloucestershire*, ed. Audrey Douglas and Peter Greenfield (Toronto: University of Toronto Press, 1986), 188–98. (I wish to thank Steve Hindle for assistance with this reference.)

36   *Records of Early English Drama: Cumberland, Westmorland, Gloucestershire*, 197; 188.

37   *Records of Early English Drama: Shropshire*, ed. J. Alan B. Somerset, 2 vols. (Toronto: University of Toronto Press, 1994), I, 23–39; quoted passages at 26 and 33. (I am grateful to Denise Ryan for this reference.)

38   PRO, STAC 8/167/27, f. 2.

39   See Sharon Achinstein, 'Audiences and Authors: Ballads and the Making of English Renaissance Literary Culture', *Journal of Medieval and Renaissance Studies*, 22 (1992), 311–326.

40   PRO, STAC 8/220/31, f. 15.

41   Sisson, *Lost Plays*, 201; Baskervill, *Elizabethan Jig*, 35.

42   PRO, STAC 8/36/6, f. 8.
43   PRO, STAC 8/288/12, f. 51.
44   PRO, STAC 8/285/27, ff. 6, 8.
45   PRO, STAC 8/285/27, f. 6.
46   'The Dragon of Wantley: Rural Popular Culture and Local Legend', *Rural History: Economy, Society, Culture* 4 (1993), 23–40.
47   PRO, STAC 8/94/17, f. 12.
48   Sisson, *Lost Plays*, p. 201.
49   *Poems*, ed. Arnold Davenport (Liverpool: Liverpool University Press, 1961), 76.
50   Samuel Daniel, *The Civil Wars*, ed. Laurence Michel (New Haven: Yale University Press, 1958), bk. 2, st. 98.
51   PRO, STAC 8/159/6.
52   John E. Martin, *Feudalism to Capitalism: Peasant and Landlord in English Agrarian Development* (London: Macmillan, 1983), 168–70.
53   David Underdown, *Fire from Heaven: Life in an English Town in the Seventeenth Century* (New Haven: Yale University Press, 1993), 27–33.
54   PRO, STAC 8/92/10.
55   J.A. Sharpe, *Defamation and Sexual Slander in Early Modern England: The Church Courts at York*, Borthwick Papers no. 58 (York: University of York, 1980), 9.
56   PRO, STAC 8/98/20.
57   '"Raylinge Rymes and Vaunting Verse": Libellous Politics in Early Stuart England, 1603–1628', in Kevin Sharpe and Peter Lake (eds), *Culture and Politics in Early Stuart England* (Basingstoke: Macmillan, 1994), 295.
58   'The Price of Protestantism: Assessing the Impact of Religious Change on Elizabethan Essex: The Cases of Heydon and Colchester' (unpublished DPhil dissertation, University of Oxford, 1988), ch. 3.
59   PRO, STAC 8/27/7; Sisson, *Lost Plays*, 193.
60   Patrick Collinson, 'Ecclesiastical Vitriol: Religious Satire in the 1590s and the Invention of Puritanism', in John Guy (ed.), *The Reign of Elizabeth: Court Culture in the Last Decade* (Cambridge: Cambridge University Press, 1995), 161.
61   PRO, STAC 8/177/5, f. 9.
62   PRO, STAC 8/53/7.
63   *Essays*, II, 56.
64   I intend to explore this area more fully in a book on social satire, 1590–1640.
65   Quoted in Sisson, *Lost Plays*, 187–8.
66   *The Arundel Harington Manuscript of Tudor Poetry*, ed. Ruth Hughey, 2 vols (Columbus: Ohio State University Press, 1960), I, 232–3.
67   Dryden himself laboured over these distinctions; see, for example, *Essays*, II, 19–20.
68   Daniel Heinsius, *De Satyra Horatiana* (1627); quoted in Dustin Griffin, *Satire: A Critical Reintroduction* (Lexington: University Press of Kentucky, 1994), 14. On the base style, see also Alvin Kernan, *The Cankered Muse: Satire of the English Renaissance* (New Haven: Yale University Press, 1959), 58–60.
69   The quote is from a Renaissance translation of Pliny; quoted in Robert C. Elliott, *The Power of Satire: Magic, Ritual, Art* (Princeton: Princeton University Press), 13. On Renaissance debates over naming in satire, see A.L. Soens, Jr, 'Criticism of Formal Satire in the Renaissance' (unpublished PhD dissertation, Princeton University, 1957), 235–41, 308–12, 405–6.

70 Kernan, *Cankered Muse*, 55; on the seventeenth-century dismantling of this theory, Griffin, *Satire: A Critical Reintroduction*, 12–13.

71 Thomas Langley, *An Abridgements of the Notable Works of Polidore Vergile* (1570); George Wither, 'Vices Executioner: or the Satyrs Selfe-description of Himselfe' (both quoted in Kernan, *Cankered Muse*, 55, 57.

5

To 'scourge the arse / Jove's marrow so had wasted': scurrility and the subversion of sodomy

James Knowles

Treatments of political libel in the seventeenth century have largely concentrated on how libels fostered a 'systematic debasement' of the leading figures of the regime, contributing to a more fissiparous political culture, involving a widespread, popular, participation in politics.[1] Controversial statesmen, such as Bacon, Buckingham, Laud and Strafford all suffered libellous attack, often recording those assaults in detail, and some, such as Buckingham, undertook considerable measures to trace the sources and transmission routes of libels and issue counter propaganda.[2] These political libels, often scandalous poems, provide one of the richest resources for the study of early modern political culture, but also, because of the peculiarly sexual nature of many of the accusations, they provide an equally significant and as yet untapped source for historians of sexuality.

In this essay, I wish to move away from the political implications of such libels to consider how they might also have shaped sexual consciousness in the period. In particular I want to argue that the use of 'sodomy' and the description of the apparently sodomitical behaviour of the elite often subverted their condemnatory purpose, especially in the way they were transmitted and performed. The complex transmission and reception processes of political libels helps illustrate the interlocking processes of repression and 'tacit permission' which characterised discourses around sodomy.[3] For the early modern period 'sodomy' derived its utility as a political tool precisely because, as an 'utterly confused category', the 'term remain[ed] incapable of exact definition', retaining enough definition for menace yet not enough for complete regulation.[4] Yet 'sodomy' also allowed many other kinds of affective, potentially sexual bonds between men (especially those embedded in patronage) to flourish unobserved. Indeed, this 'permission' was not simply the avoidance of categorisation and accusation but, more positively, permitted the articulation of counter-narratives. The connections between the two topics of this chapter, sodomy and political libel, emerge most clearly in Simonds D'Ewes's account of Bacon's household after his loss of office which provides a useful model of the issues and processes around political sodomy:

> His most abhominable and darling sinne I should rather burie in silence then mencion it; were it not a most admirable instance how men are enflamed by wickednes and held captiue by the deuill . . .

> [Bacon] would not relinquish the practice of his most horrible & secret sinne of sodomie, keeping still one Godrick a verie effeminate faced youth to bee his catamite & bedfellow, although hee had discharged the most of his other household servants: which was the moore to bee admired because men generallie after his fall begann to discourse of that vnnattural crime which hee had practiced manie yeares; deserting the bedd of his Ladie; which hee accounted as the Italians & Turkes doe, a poore and meane pleasure in respect of the other; & it was thought by some that hee should haue been tried at the barre of iustice for it, & haue satisfied the law most seuere against that horrible villanie with the price of his bloud . . . [5]

The diary entry resounds with the rhetoric of political sodomy (linking horror, bestiality, foreignness and effeminacy), illustrating the process of the sodomy accusation, whereby the 'cry' of the sodomites generates God's judgement on their sins. The biblical Sodom narrative raised issues of judgement and discipline, creating a crucial exemplar of national judgement which politicised sodomy as a barometer of the moral health of the nation.[6] It is a sense of moral pollution which is marked in D'Ewes's evocation of the 'bloud' price which should have been exacted from Bacon for this 'horrible villanie'.

D'Ewes's account is, however, shot through with the contradictions which surrounded early modern sodomy. Although Bacon's 'secret sinne of sodomie' had continued for years it only emerges from the shadows after Bacon's fall and although there is a strong implication in the account that this information has previously circulated, it only becomes 'generallie' articulated after his impeachment. Thus far the D'Ewes account follows the pattern whereby sodomy accusations (in which sexual acts were only a minor constituent), levelled as adjuncts to other charges, symbolised how far individuals had transgressed the law.[7] Yet, the second part of the diary account explains how the general 'discourse . . . of his unnatural crime' prompted

> some bolde & forward man to write these verses following in a whole sheete of paper, & to cast it downe in some part of Yorkehowse in the strand . . .

Within this sty a hogg* doth lie   * Alluding   both   to   his
That must bee hang'd for Sodomy   surname of Bacon & to that
                                          swinish abominable sinne.[8]

Despite this

[Bacon] neuer came to any publicke triall for his crime; nor did euer,
that I could here, forbeare his old custome of making his servants his
bedfellows, soe to avoid the scandall was raised of him . . . [9]

The precise meanings of these gestures are both fascinating and elusive,
raising important issues about the significance of the public, performative and
spatial elements in libelling. The account reveals a transitional moment as
gossip and spoken accusation shift into libel, moving between one kind of
public sphere into another. This publication carries complex implications
because the placing of the libel within York House re-enacts the Biblical
process of the self-generating 'cry' of the sin, while it also represents a
symbolic penetration of Bacon's house and household (his private domain). It
is, indeed, as if the secrecy around sodomy, once broached, dissolves the
boundaries of public and private, while the emergence of the libel from within
the house further diffuses the secrecy, and makes the sin public not only
within the household, but outside, leading to another level of publication, the
'public trial'. Libels, thus, provide evidence of a very complex layering of
public and private spheres with fluid, transformational boundaries which
considerably complicate how we read the 'secrecy' around sodomy.

The most striking element of D'Ewes's account, Bacon's apparent public
insouciance, hints at more complex attitudes while its main stance often
eschews direct condemnation, with potentially critical comments hedged in
the language of reportage ('men . . . began to discourse', 'it was thought by
some', 'some bold and forward man' and the final admittance that 'nor did
ever, that I could here'). Indeed, D'Ewes even admits that Bacon's behaviour
was 'the moore to be admired', although such admiration was presumably not
for the 'most horrible and secret sine' which he frequently condemned
elsewhere in the diary but, perhaps, for Bacon's open continuation of his
"unnatural" practices despite his imperilled position. Strikingly, embedded in
the reportage lies the remarkable admission that Bacon regarded (or at least
was reported as regarding) 'his unnatural crime' as a 'pleasure'.

Libels, with their heavily sexualised rhetoric, reveal a much more complex
typology of sodomy, as well as a more nuanced, possibly even permissive
attitude than we have recognised. The dynamics of knowledge described by
D'Ewes, with a 'secret sinne' known 'generally' to have been 'practised many
years' yet remaining unspoken while known, recalls the 'open secret' which

conditioned nineteenth-century sexual attitudes, whereby 'the secret keeps a topic like homosexuality [sodomy] in the private sphere, but under surveillance, hovering on the edge of public visibility'.[10] It is precisely the nature of such 'public visibility', achieved through the 'scurrilous' verses, the semi-licensed, semi-illicit forms of discourse, which the rest of this essay considers.

Buckingham and porno-political rhetoric

The most extensive body of political libel concerns the omni-pervasive, all-powerful royal favourite, George Villiers, Duke of Buckingham, who inspired a vast corpus of verse, both during and after his lifetime.[11] Key events in his career prompted major outpourings (the Spanish trip, the Ile de Rhé expedition) while the associated rise of his family led to accusations centred upon their extravagance, dissoluteness and, especially, their base origins and crypto-Catholicism.[12] Thus probably the most widely circulated of the political libels of the period, 'Heaven Bless King James Our Joy' , imagines the whole Villiers clan as sodomising the nation.[13] Sodomy is both (hetero- and homo-) sexual and political, used to figure the profligate acquisition of rich matches and offices.[14] The final stanza envisages the Villiers family escaping with their booty:

> Harke how the wagons crack
>   With there rich ladinge
> Doll comes vp with her packe,
>   Su's fitt for tradinge.
> Phill: will no longer stay,
>   With her base baby
> What dare the people say
>   When she's a lady.
>   Thes be they, goe so gay
>   In court & citty
>   Would you haue an office pray
>   You must bee thiss witty.

In this politico-economic discourse (the poem is obsessed with both monetary and sexual getting and spending: 'They gett the diuell & all, / That swiue the kindred') sodomy stands as a type of generalised debauchery, explicitly heterosexual, although the sexual rhetoric perhaps glances at the origins of Buckingham's close relationship with James I.[15] The connections between this politico-economic sodomy and crypto-Catholicism is illustrated in another libel, 'As I went to Walsingham', which concludes:

Comme, offer up your daughters and faire wifes,
 No trentall nor no durge
Will open goode Kinge Jeames his eyes,
 But sacrifice to St George.[16]

Sexual debauchery, peculation and Catholicism are interwoven through the image of 'St George' alluding not only to the favourite's Christian name, his Garter badge, as well as the gold coin.[17] The pun almost constitutes Villiers of the gold he has filched, a materialist saint who must be propitiated in popish fashion.

Sodomy as an image of political corruption belongs to 'porno-political rhetoric': the conflation of political and sexual deviance.[18] Here, sexual deviance symbolises a threat to the family/state analogy as Buckingham's family stands as an antitype of the patriarchal model. This perhaps explains the complex interplay between emphasis upon the dominance of the Villiers women (female agency is often registered as either subversive or effeminising), the sexualised appetites which threaten the blood-line of the aristocracy (recycling rumours of the family's low origins) and upon occluded sexual crimes, which suggest a failure to regulate appetite in the favourite. In particular, the libellers often suggest a range of deviancy, from male sodomy to generalised debauchery with women. Thus according to the Scots version of 'Devil take him' 'he could finly dance a galliard / and trims the ladies with his talliard'[19] while 'Upon the Duke' has his ghost lament:

. . . through the Open gate of all Excesse,
In *Luxurie* and *Voluptuousnesse*,
To tread the broad path of a stately dance,
With *Musique*, *Banquetts*, and a Ladies glance,
This did I thinke the *Milkie way* to blisse . . . [20]

The ambivalence of 'a Ladies glance' captures the way in which Buckingham's 'stately dance' along the 'broad' (presumably primrose) path to damnation seemed to undermine not only Buckingham's manliness but the whole of masculine political power. The 'Open gate', of course, recalls the description of women as leaky vessels, while it also echoes the Baconian penetration by libel.[21] Yet even such condemnatory poems have features which complicate responses to the poem. In 'Heaven Bless King James' the heavily ironic tone of the chorus differentiates between criticism of Buckingham's clan and of the monarch embodying, perhaps, a concept of 'loyal opposition',[22] while the humour, although it attacks the Villiers family, paradoxically renders them humorously grotesque rather than dangerous.

Such poems cannot be solely interpreted as 'oppositional' as they generate highly ambivalent audience-responses. The widespread circulation of texts not only demonstrates the operations of political information networks, it also shows varied and sophisticated readerships, particularly amongst the governing elite. Thus, although anti-Buckingham material surfaces amongst the papers of those opposed to the regime, it also appears in collections associated with the court,[23] and libels were often collected by Buckingham's clients, probably for political intelligence purposes and to provide the impetus for counter-propaganda.[24] Indeed, it seems possible that, like modern politicians collecting cartoons about themselves, those involved also found some of them amusing, no matter how savage. These instances suggests a complex response to scurrility, as well as the appropriation of oppositional and even popular forms, by the elite. To understand that complexity we need to consider matters of tone, audience composition, reception and, particularly, performance, more carefully.

'A pillory of ink': transmission and performance in political libel

Archbishop Laud's letter to Wentworth (August 1637), describing three libels recently displayed against him, illustrates the nuances of libel publication and reception. First, a notice on the south door of St Paul's had advertised the church as let by Laud to the devil, the second, a ballad, depicted him and other bishops as captains of a satanic army besieging the saints, foretelling the ruin of the government of the church. Laud describes this as 'the merrier of the two, and is part in verse, and to be sung to the tune of "Here's a health to my Lord of Holland" '. Finally, the third, a board hung on the Standard in Cheap, featured Laud's speech Star Chamber speech against Prynne nailed at one end, singed with fire and its corners cropped with the inscription, 'the man that puts the saints of God into a pillory of wood, stands here in a pillory of ink'.[25]

These three examples epitomise the importance of the public *performance* of libels, especially the impact of public posting in symbolic sites, on meaning. The south door of St Paul's adjacent to Duke Humphrey's walk was associated with news-gathering and transmission, while the Standard in the Cheap was adorned with statues of Fame, and was itself an occasional place of execution.[26] This libel inverts the Star Chamber process against Prynne and his co-defendants, accentuated by the comparison between royal discipline and the oppositional 'pillory of ink', as the libelling process dramatises a trial in the court of public opinion (Fame). The 1628 libel which threatened Buckingham with a 'reformation' was pointedly nailed to a post in Coleman Street, a neighbourhood with strong Puritan associations.[27]

This spatial semiotic carries over into issues of performance and audience. The 1620 proclamation against libels stressed the 'licentious passage of lavish speech' which either originated or transmitted slanders and libels, and enjoined subjects 'not to give attention, or any manner of applause or entertainment to such discourse'.[28] 'Licentious passage' includes both circulation and (sexualised) penetration, while 'applause' implies public performance. Many of the recorded cases combine spoken and written offences, circulation, penetration and performance, as in the case of 'a ballad [on Dr Lamb] being printed, both printer, and seller and singer, are laid in Newgate and some three or four more on suspicion'.[29] In 1623 Buckingham investigated a 'libell . . . sett upp at Court' against him ('worse then the song that went abroad'), offering £1000 reward 'to know the author'.[30] Although Buckingham was obviously concerned with the libel posted at court (another act of symbolic penetration), it is interesting to note that the greater reward is offered for the song that 'went abroad'. These accounts of the oral and performative elements in libelling show how libels impacted far beyond their clandestine circulation amongst the political and regional elites, largely through a strategy of 'popularisation', utilising familiar forms and ballad tunes to increase the audience.[31]

Indeed, many accounts testify to the varieties of dissemination which might be involved, especially where ballad formats were used, as texts moved rapidly from the print milieu into the oral culture (from printer, to stationer, to singer). The case of the scrivener George Willoughby reverses the process as he wrote down a couplet on Dr Lamb which he received from Daniel Watkins who had *heard* it from Lawrence Naylor, a baker's boy, who had himself *heard* the rhyme many times and memorised it.[32] This ability of libels to move across classes and between the print, manuscript and oral cultures of the period illuminates not only a broader political, but a more layered sense of publication and dissemination. Thus, while the privileged, elite, circulation of manuscript libels seems to have concerned the authorities relatively little (although both Mead and Chamberlain were cautious about enclosing libellous verses in their letters), it was the appearance of libels in public spaces, such as the 1628 Coleman Street libel, which provoked official responses. Popular oral forms (songs, ballads, short poems and rhymes) were the major concern precisely because they threatened to dissipate the boundaries of the public sphere and the political nation, encompassing a more heterogeneous audience, comparable to the public theatre.

The number of accusations around seditious speech, especially subversive toasts, which then prompt the investigation and prosecution of written libels, illustrates a social, pub-culture, in which libels might often be heard.[33] Although, it is difficult to ascertain the precise extent and nature of the tavern and alehouse culture of this period within these spaces, libels might be performed amongst other scatological and pornographic ditties belonging to the quasi-licensed forms of communality and festivity. This raises the likelihood of nuanced distinctions which shape libelling performance and reception. For example, an important class-distinction differentiates kinds of pub-cultures, with the taverns less policed than the alehouses which, as lower class institutions, were perceived as more socially and politically dangerous spaces.[34] Importantly, however, both types of venue may have acted as 'neutral spaces' for cross-class, cross-age and even cross-gender mixing, and it may be that the performance of libels within these spaces was less interdicted, possibly as part of a semi-regulated 'subversive' culture, while in more (or, rather, differently) 'public' places, 'in court', 'on a post' in Coleman Street, in a stationer's shop, 'in York House', or other politically sensitive locales, like the Inns of Court, such political scurrility was unacceptable.

Two examples will illustrate the performance potential of these libels. The best known, 'The Clean Contrary Way', provides the clearest example of the interchange between ballads and libelling verse.[35] The title refers to one of the best known refrains and tunes of the period and, like the deployment of 'Lord Holland's Health' for the anti-Laud libel, facilitates recognition and memorisation, effectively popularising the text. The prevalence of memorised short texts, oral transmissions and ballads shows how important communal performance could be and restates the connections of libels with the communal performance cultures of early modern London. In 'The Clean Contrary Way' the well-known song tune is used to underpin a highly ironic mock celebration of Buckingham and James:

> Come heare, Lady Muses, and help mee to sing,
>   Come loue mee whereas I lay
> Of a Duke that deserues to bee made a King
>   The cleane contrary way
>   O the cleane contrary way.
>
> Our Buckingham Duke is the Man that I meane
>   Come loue mee &c
> On his shoulders the weale of the Kingdome doth leane
>   The cleane contrary &c
>   O the cleane &c
>
> O happiest Kingdome that euer was ken'd
>   Come loue mee &c
> And happie the king that hath such a Frend
>   The cleane contrary &c
>   O the cleane &c
>
> Needes must I extoll his worth and his blood
>   Come loue me whereas I lay

> And his sweet disposition soe milde and soe good
> The cleane contrary way
> O the cleane contrary way.

This ballad deploys the commonplace idea of the upside-down or arsy-varsy world to figure the mismanagement of the kingdom and articulate the likelihood that the 'happie . . . king that hath such a Frend' is behaving, literally, 'contrary' to the normal order (preposterously or arse backwards). Yet despite these sexualised puns and the (implicit) accusations of sodomy, the rollicking chorus and the well-known tune both make the words memorable, while also mitigating some of the satirical impact. This is particularly so where the popular tune (as in this case) invites audience participation.

The implications of the musical and performative dimension are clearer still if we turn to 'Listen jolly gentleman' which, although not explicitly about Buckingham himself, concerns most of the members of his coterie. The poem begins with a celebration of the 'old King Harry' and his amorous adventures gradually turning to James's court and its vices:

> Hee liues at Court wheare he hath good sport
>   At Christmas he hath dauncinge,
> In ye Summer tide abroad hee'l ride
>   With his guarde about him prauncinge.
> At Royston and New Marquett
>   Hee'll hunt till he be leane,
> But he hath manie boyes with Masques and toyes
>   Will make him fatt againe.[36]

The poem depicts the court masque as a homosocial if not homoerotic form, contrasting the lords 'yt will daintily doe / But they must haue a wench by yr hand' and the 'durty sport' of the men dancing together.[37] Indeed, even more crucially, these are not men but 'boyes', a term which encompasses a range from roistering gallants to the sexually available pages and servants. In this case the 'braue boyes . . . that make King James so merry', render the king 'fatt againe', leaving him sleek and plump with sexual luxury.

The poem suggests a fascinating awareness of the bedchamber politics of the period 1616–22, yet it also is highly problematic in terms of its tone. Although the attack on the 'dirty sport' and upon court corruption is strongly expressed, the final stanza, with its statement of loyalty, perhaps suggests how the libels sought to construct themselves as a form of loyal criticism. Moreover, any *performance* of the piece might undermine the satiric potency, making it more a jolly, raunchy song about the King, perhaps along the line of modern jokes about the Queen Mother and gin.[38] A sing-along version with rousing chorus suggests an entirely different horizon of reception than that provided by the written text which survives in a collection of oppositional poetry!

These two instances (and the awareness of the authorities about the different routes of transmission) suggest that seventeenth-century audiences could make subtle discriminations based upon the content of the libels, conventions of satire, forms of permitted criticism (such as the petition), and the mode and space of performance. The close interconnections between political libels and the briefer, more transitory oral forms (toasts, healths, short scurrilous rhymes) and the ballad and song culture of alehouses and taverns evidence a much greater fluidity within political culture, as these texts permeate both elite and popular cultures, but also operate within conditions of performance which considerably complicate responses. The ambiguities within the texts and their performance undermines any classification of poems as politically 'pro' or 'anti', suggesting a much more nuanced response to the poems, reaching beyond rather simplistic modern dichotomies about the propagandist or subversive effects of early modern texts. Moreover, these complexities also apply to the sexual narratives of the poems, as texts framed within porno-political rhetoric are translated through music and performance. Although 'Listen Jolly Gentlemen' does not confirm the Baconian invocation of same-sex 'pleasure', it does register a potentially more tolerant or humorous attitude and point towards some texts, where even within the confines of an anti-sodomitical rhetoric other interpretations other readings of sodomy become possible.

'Scandalous behaviour' and the sodomitical counter-narrative

> Nor was his love . . . carried on with discretion sufficient to cover a less scandalous behaviour; for the King's kissing them after so lascivious mode in public, and upon the theater as it were of the world, prompted many to imagine some things done in the tiring-house that exceed my expressions . . . [39]

Although the 'scandal' invoked by both Osborne and D'Ewes echoes the Biblical cry of Sodom which incited God's ire, 'scandal' encompasses more ambiguous ideas, not only of gossip and male (homosocial) networks of information dissemination, but of the power of scandal to define norms of behaviour. Scandals present 'social dramas', provoking affective responses to moral issues which polarise opinions but which, during the 'liminal' period of scandal, actually creates an intense debate and 'cultural indeterminacy'.[40] Thus 'scandal' raises the interesting possibility that Buckingham's modes of self-fashioning and self-representation not only created models of courtly behaviour to be emulated by would-be courtiers but generated a debate that redefined courtly masculinity.[41]

For instance, 'And art thou return'd again' whilst excoriating Buckingham's courtly behaviour as causing military failure also registers some of the favourite's glamour:

> Stay, stay at home then, & at tennis play
> Measure french-Galliardes out of Killigray.
> Venus pauillions doe befitt thee best:
> Periwigges with helmetts are not to be prest:
> To o'rerunne Spaine, winne Cales, & conquere France,
> Requires a souldiers march; noe courtiers dance.[42]

Although the writer deploys the standard collocation of ideas — effeminacy, foreignness, vicious indulgence in sexual sport — which have undermined true English manliness (restrained, practical and above all martial rather than gamesome and courtly), the poem rehearses the very cultural power and courtly behaviour which Buckingham utilised.

Buckingham achieved and maintained power through his adroit manipulation of his extraordinary combination of 'Beauty, Civility, Bounty and . . . Fortitude'.[43] D'Ewes noted how Buckingham was 'full of delicacy and handsome features' commenting on how 'accomplisht' his hand and face were.[44] Others would remark on the grace of his bearing and on the nimbleness of his dancing, designed to show his courtly qualities as well as the length, strength and shapeliness of his legs. 'Accomplishment' suggests that one of the reasons why Villiers attracted such opprobrium, lay in the highly self-conscious power and theatricality of his self-display. Buckingham created an image of himself, shaping a political, 'Buckinghamite' manliness.

The libels responded to Buckingham's personality cult diffused, particularly, through works of art, including his patronage of Rubens:

> Antwerpian Rubens' best skill made him soar,
> Ravish'd by heavenly powers, unto the sky,
> Opening and ready him to deify
> In a bright blissful palace, fairy isle.
> Naught but illusion were . . . [45]

Much of Buckingham's careful patronage policy, especially the distribution of portraits, sought to establish an image for the favourite. Although the transmission of Buckingham's own propaganda and the efforts of his opponents cannot match the penetration of popular consciousness achieved by modern mass media, the wide social, geographical spread of these materials, coupled with the variety of transmissions (printed, manuscript, speech transmission, song transmission, and visual representations) does evidence a widespread, even popular, consciousness of Buckingham's image and manly ideal. Within the rhetoric of rejection and opprobrium which surrounds the sodomite (where the clandestine transmission endows 'secrets' with a spurious glamour), Buckingham's behaviour gains a certain cachet, offering an image of new forms of culture for appropriation in opposition to English philistinism and xenophobia. Buckingham's cultural glamour and eroticised masculinity retains the potential to generate a counter-reading, perhaps associated with youthful rebellion against the moral prescriptions of an older generation.

One of the most interesting possibilities for a sexual counter-narrative concerns 'The War in Heaven' which pictures the gods in revolt over Jove's dalliance with Ganymede:

> Loues Queen stood disaffected
>   To what she had seene
> Or to what suspected
>   As shee in spleene
> To Iuno hath protested
>   Hir seruant Mars
> Should scourge ye Arse
>   Ioue's marrow so had wasted.[46]

The poem combines an attack on Ganymede's 'vpstart' origins with complaints that Jove's unnatural obsession with the 'white-fac't boy' (another term for catamite) has disrupted the order of the universe. Proserpine and the Furies threaten 'To haue him burn'd / That thus hath turn'd / Loue's pleasures Arse Verse', evoking the unhinging of the universe ('The Spheares begin to faulter') caused by Jove's unnatural practices. These images of the arsy-varsy world connect the poem to the porno-political, sodomitical rhetoric of the period, but the explicitness ('Arse') and the allusion to anal sex, clearly distinguishes this text from standard porno-political rhetoric which trades in slurs rather than anatomical detail.

Significantly, the political allusion, unlike in 'Heaven Bless King James His Joy', is not structural to the piece: the political application entirely depends on the title given in the manuscript, the placing of the poem amongst other poems satirising James and Buckingham, or the implication of Buckingham's early office as the King's cupbearer.[47] Perhaps this lack of direct connection may be because the sexual explicitness of the poem ruptures the accepted limits of scurrility and allusiveness but, equally, it is possible that the poem had a dual audience, capable of reading it both as satire *and* as titillatingly pornographic. Indeed, any straightforward condemnation is undermined by the wryly comic vision of the 'disaffected' Venus encouraging Mars to beat Ganymede, an act suffused with erotic implications. Moreover, Jove's final continued dalliance ('Still Ioue with Ganymede lies playinge') allows the possibility of a pleasurable, titillating interpretation.[48]

In such instances the possibility of counter-narratives surfaces, as the ambiguity of such sexual references, even within apparently condemnatory frame, threatens to undo the (apparent) original purpose. In such instances the 'tacit permission' of sodomy as a category facilitates an erotic counter-narrative, perhaps furthered by the glamorised, widely known image of the favourite, in which the libels and satires which sought to detract from his reputation suffered the double-bind of all satire, that to have an effect vices and faults had to be named and described, and in that very act of narrativisation, the potential for the reader to gain pleasure and learn of novel vices, to appropriate the meanings for wholly opposite ends existed.[49] Indeed, although, in general, the image of the sodomite in the seventeenth century mitigates against its subversion and appropriation, there is some evidence for its use to articulate male–male relations in a homosocial context, and expressed through scurrilous verse, 'Tityre-tues or a Mock Song', which illustrates the ways in which images of interdicted relations might be used as part of this anti-culture.[50]

This poem, like much poetic production of the period (especially of scurrile, occasional and political poetry such as 'The Parliament Fart'), derived from homosocial groups, such as the Mermaid and Mitre circles and, even, the Sons of Ben.[51] These all-male circles, associated with tavern culture, in which verse libels were produced and circulated (the 'men' whose gossip D'Ewes records in his diary) were mainly concerned with 'poetry and advocacy of Augustan moderation', exemplified in epistolary and ode forms, in line with their imitation of classical symposia.[52] Some, however, developed more scurrilous verses within a more sexualised culture, particularly the 'Tytre tu' groups of the 1620s, who practised elaborate rituals, deploying their own nomenclature and passwords, their membership signalled with ribbons or bugles.[53] These groups have some affinities with the subversive aristocratic *hetaireia* of classical Athens, although they register generalised discontent rather than political subversion.[54] Their culture was highly sexualised, homosocial (if not homoerotic), and focused upon tobacco-taking, drinking, roistering and, especially, scurrilous poetry. Their name, 'Tytre-tu' derives from Tityros, the genitally well-endowed satyr, while their association in 'taverns and debauched places', courted transgression: the leader was the 'Ottoman' and the members 'giants' ('Giant Asdriasdust', 'Giant Drinkittupall', 'Giant Neuersober', 'Giant Legomitton' and 'Giones: Lady Linauele').[55]

The constellation of possibly subversive religious views, excesses of consumption, sexualised names, associations with foreignness (especially the Turks), and the sense of secrecy, bring the group perilously close to early modern notions of the sodomite. This potential is reinforced by the oaths the group took

> to be true and faithfull to the societie and conceale one anothers secrets, but mixed with a number of other ridiculous toyes to disguise the matter . . .. What mischiefe may lurke under this maske God knowes, but they were very confident and presumed much of themselues to carry yt so openly.[56]

The peculiar mixture of the serious and the ridiculous combined with concealed secrets 'openly' carried encapsulates some of the paradoxes within 'good fellowship', while 'what mischiefe may lurke under this maske' echoes the language of un-named, yet known, sexual crimes, associated with sodomy.

In 1623 two members of the Bugle, Andrew Windsor and George Chambers were arrested at the behest of Archbishop Abbott for papacy and supposed conspiracy:

> Two mad capps were committed late,
>   For treason, as some say;
> It was the wisdom of the State,
>   Admire it all you may.[57]

The poem mocks the authorities' failure to discover any offence even as it implies that their 'fearful sin' exceeds a refusal to drink. The structure parallels the anti-sodomitical rhetoric of the period, the commoners' "cry" for justice echoing the Biblical episode, with ellipsis challenging the reader to complete the possible misdemeanours ('They'd don — we know not what'). Though the poem reiterates the possibly papistry to Windsor and George, it constantly imputes other sins, describing their relations in a highly unorthodox fashion:

> Brave *Andrew Windsor* was the prince
>   George Chambers favourite.
> These two bred this unknowne offence
>   I wo'd they had bine be ——[58]

This striking comparison of the two to 'prince' and 'favourite', alluding to Buckingham and Prince Charles, apparently courts sexual meaning ('bred this unknowne offence').

Yet, despite these inferences, it remains difficult to determine the meaning of these allusions, as the figuring of Windsor as 'Brave' and 'madcaps' may invoke the chivalric narrative with which some pro-Spanish match writers invested the journey to Spain, or, simply establishes the adventurous credentials of the young men, as a gesture of anti-authoritarian bravado. Indeed, the whole point of the poem may be to defend the men against the obvious accusations of sodomy which might follow from an arrest for popish treason, especially in the context of a secret society with subversive oaths of brotherhood. In this sense its aggressive use of the sodomitical rhetoric might be seen as a recuperation of their reputation. The poem also attacks Abbott:

> Let papist frowne what need we care,
>   He lives above their reach,
> And will his silver Mitre weare
>   Though now forgot to preach.
> If hee were but behind me now,
>   And should this ballad heare;
> Sure he'd revenge with bended bow,
>   And I die like a Deere.[59]

Although the passage explicitly retells Abbott's slaughter of one of James I's huntsmen it also strongly implies his interest in sodomising the narrator, as to 'die like a Deere' was a common sexual metaphor which, in the climate of the 1620s, accrued distinctly homoerotic connotations.[60]

On one level 'Tityre-tu' is striking not only in its highly transgressive allusions to Windsor and Chambers relationship, but by figuring these through the prince and the favourite which, given the way their relationship was interpreted and the marginalised near-sodomitical context of the text's production, almost courts disaster.[61] Yet on another level the poem is more remarkable still, in that it carefully distinguishes between its first part, which approves such relations, and the much less permissive description of Abbott as proto-sodomite buggering the narrator with his 'bended bow'. Thus, although the prince/favourite analogy cannot be regarded as straightforwardly approving, it apparently invokes the sodomite as a model of male relations. In its differentiation of two kinds of sodomitical relations, approved (Windsor and Chambers) and calumniated (Abbott and the narrator), the poem distinguishes between inter-male relations which involve equality and mutuality, and those which recall porno-political rhetoric and sodomy accusations where the decorums of power are breached. Is it, therefore, possible that the seventeenth century not only could allow many kinds of homoeroticism and homosociality to operate within the 'tacit permission' of the sodomitical category, but that it could distinguish between kinds of inter-male sodomy, and allow some to exist without opprobrium or prosecution?

Finally, what are we to make of the tune Chevy Chase, to which the poem was sung? This highly popular, jolly ballad tune, sets the poem within a different, almost approving, context, and certainly one which would popularise the text. Was this because the poem repeated a series of mildly scandalous but titillating accusations about dark deeds in high places, or because it satirised clerical authority? Or because, through the forms of popular verse and ballads, a sexual counter-narrative might be insinuated? Certainly, this example suggests how scurrile language and the contexts associated with libellous, pornographic or scatological verse might play a crucial role in allowing the articulation of these counter-narratives and subversive meanings. By placing the poem within the contexts associated with libelling the writer(s) occupy the same liminal social and discursive space, half-allowed, half-interdicted, playing precisely with the edges of public visibility like the 'open secret' of later sexual discourse. In this sense, the political significance of the texts and of their dissemination system for the political culture of early modern England shelters another, very different, ultimately far more subversive, set of ideas and images.

Notes

1   T. Cogswell, 'Underground verse and the transformation of early Stuart culture', in S.D. Amussen and M. Kishlansky (eds), *Political culture and cultural politics in early modern England: Essays presented to David Underdown* (Manchester: Manchester University Press, 1995), 277–300.
2   Cogswell, 'Underground Verse', 287–8. See also p. 79 below and n. 24.
3   J. Goldberg, *Reclaiming Sodom* (London: Routledge, 1994), 4.
4   J. Goldberg, *Sodometries: Renaissance Texts, Modern Sexualities* (Stanford: Stanford University Press, 1992), 3, but also, 3-26; Goldberg, *Reclaiming Sodom*, 4. For a detailed, nuanced discussion of the legal history, see B.R. Smith, *Homosexual Desire in Shakespeare's England: A Cultural Poetics* (Chicago: Chicago University Press, 1991), 41–53.
5   Simonds D'Ewes, 'Life' in BL, MS Harl 646, f. 59r.
6   A. Stewart, *Close Readers: Humanism and Sodomy in Early Modern England* (Princeton: Princeton University Press, 1997), xxi–xx, and M. Warner, 'New English Sodom' in J. Goldberg (ed.), *Queering the Renaissance*, 6 (Durham, N.C.: Duke University Press, 1994), 330–58.
7   A. Bray, 'Homosexuality and the Signs of Male Friendship in Elizabethan England', *History Workshop Journal*, 29 (1990), reprinted in *Queering the Renaissance*, 40–61, 41.
8   BL, MS Harl 646, f. 59v.
9   BL, MS Harl 646, f. 59v.
10 A. Sinfield, *Cultural Politics – Queer Reading* (London : Routledge, 1994), 47.
11 F.W. Fairholt, *Poems and Songs Relating to George Villiers, Duke of Buckingham* (1858) is still the only available anthology of these poems. Fairholt often used poor texts and censored the more explicit passages.

12   In addition to Cogswell's essay (note 1), see also A. Bellany, ' "Rayling Rymes and Vaunting Verse": Libellous Politics in Early Stuart England 1603–1628' in K. Sharpe and P. Lake (eds), *Culture and Politics in Early Stuart England* (Basingstoke: Macmillan, 1994), 285–310 and J. Holstun, '"God Bless Thee, Little David!": John Felton and his Allies', *English Literary History*, 59 (1992), 513–52.

13   Beinecke Library, Yale, Osborn MSS, MS b. 197 (Alston commonplace book), 187–9. The poem is also sometimes known as 'Verses vpon George Villiers Duke of B, & his kindred' (BL, MS Add 61683, f. 74 calls it 'Of the duke of Buckingham & his kindred'). It was partly reprinted by Fairholt from BL MS Add 5832 (Crew MS), a late eighteenth-century copy, with the Ashley stanza omitted. Further copies exist in Bodleian Library, Oxford, MSS Douce 357, Rawl Poet 160, Tanner 306 and Trinity College, Dublin, MS 652.

14   As the stanza on Sir Anthony ('Old Abbott') Ashley's exchange of sodomy for Philippa Sheldon's 'black arse hole' demonstrates.

15   J. Greene, ' "You must eat men": The Sodomitic Economy of Renaissance Patronage', *Gay and Lesbian Quarterly*, 1 (1994), 163–7.

16   Hatfield House, Cecil MSS, 140/125.

17   The half-crown was known as a 'George' (OED 4), thus there may also be a suggestion that Villiers holds half the crown.

18   S. Wiseman, ' "Adam, the Father of all Flesh", Porno-Political Rhetoric and Political Theory in and After the English Civil War', *Prose Studies*, 14 (1991), 134–57, esp. 134 and 144.

19   National Library of Scotland, Advocates MSS, 33.1.7, vol 24, f. 78r (Denmilne MSS).

20   BL MS Sloane 826, f. 172v.

21   'Open gate' may suggest anal penetration; 'Milkie way' = semen?

22   James Howell gives a good instance of this when James was offered a 'very abusive Satire in Verse' which concluded with 'Now God preserve the King, the Queen, the Peers', an ending which provoked the king to laughter and to pardon the 'bitter, but . . . witty knave': cited in P. Finkelpearl, ' "The Comedians' Liberty"; Censorship of the Jacobean Stage Reconsidered' in A. Kinney and D.S. Collins (eds), *Renaissance Historicism* (Amherst: University of Massachusetts Press, 1987), 190–206, 201.

23   'Heaven Bless King James', for example, can be found in the Alston commonplace book (Beinecke Library, Yale, Osborn MSS, MS b. 197), assembled in 1630s Cambridge but linked to the Crofts family who were heavily implicated in royal entertainment culture. Similarly, 'Art thou returned again', an attack on Buckingham's conduct of the Ile de Rhé offensive, appears in the Hippsley MSS a collection assembled by one of Buckingham's naval officers (Somerset Record Office, Hippisley Papers, DD/HI 564).

24   Thus Sir Edward Conway collected material and passed it on the Duke, especially poems on Dr Lamb in 1625: see SP16/523/57 (Conway to Buckingham, March 1625). Conway owned at least six poems on Buckingham (SP14/180/17.2, SP14/153/114, SP16/114/68, SP16/114/70 (two poems), SP16/523/56), along with two masques associated with Buckingham in SP14/122/58 and BL, MS Add 23,229, f. 3r–8r. SP16/114/70 is a copy of 'And art thou dead'.

25   W. Laud, *Works*, ed. P. Bliss, 7 vols (Oxford, 1847–60), vol 7, 371.

26   T. Cogswell, *The Blessed Revolution: English politics and the coming of war, 1621–1624* (Cambridge: Cambridge University Press, 1989), 20–36 discusses the Paul's Walk news culture.

27 T. Birch (ed.), *The Court and Times of Charles I*, 2 vols (1848), 1, 368.
28 J.F. Larkin and P.L. Hughes (eds), *Stuart Royal Proclamations* (Oxford: Clarendon Press, 1973), I, 495–6: 'A Proclamation against excesse of Lavish and Licentious Speech in matters of State' (December 1620).
29 Birch, *Court and Times of Charles I*, vol. 1, 368.
30 January 1623 entry in Sir Simonds D'Ewes, *Diary, 1622–24*, ed. E. Bourcier (Paris, 1974), 112–13.
31 Henry Anett, a washpot at the Middle Temple, was interrogated in 1626 by Sir Robert Heath because he had found a 'scandalous letter' on Buckingham in a pot and showed it to several others (see BL, MS Add 38,855, f. 68).
32 Bellany, 'Raylinge Rymes', 288.
33 For instance, the Scot, Melvin, found himself in trouble for offering a toast to John Felton (see BL, MS Sloane 826, f. 119v) while the initial arrest of Alexander Gill the Younger for the same offence precipitated the search of his papers and the discovery of a packet of anti-Buckingham poems which sparked the full Privy Council investigation.
34 P. Clark, *The English Alehouse: a social history, 1200–1800* (London: Longman, 1983), 5, 147–8 and 157.
35 The text is found (*inter alia*) in BL, MS Sloane 826, f. 164v–166v, the music in C.M. Simpson, *The English Broadside Ballad and Its Music* (1966), 109.
36 Bodleian Library, Oxford, MS Malone 19, fols 87–88.
37 The poem echoes Stubbes' attack on the 'filthie groping and uncleane handling' of mixed dancing in *The Anatomie of Abuses*.
38 Bodleian Library, MS Malone 23, f. 18v–22r, includes a chorus of 'With a hey downe downe goe', allowing for a sing-along version. Significantly, a fragment of this poem survives in BL, MS Add 27879, f. 26 (the Percy ballads).
39 F. Osborne, *Historical Memoires of the Reigne of Queen Elizabeth and King James* (1658), part 2, 127.
40 Cited in E. Cohen, 'Legislating the Norm: From Sodomy to Gross Indecency', in R. Butters, J.M. Clum and M. Moon (eds), *Displacing Homophobia* (Durham, N.C.: Duke University Press, 1989), 169–205, 192.
41 Although the scandals around Buckingham cannot be directly linked to the moment of identity formation which nineteenth-century scholars have located in the Wilde trials, as with Wilde's conviction which could not quite efface the impact of his doctrine of sexual pleasure between men, so the Buckingham scandals may have promoted the very ideas the critics sought to attack.
42 See n. 23 above.
43 J. Hacket, *Scrinia Reserata: A Memorial Offer'd to the Great Deservings of John Williams, D.D.* (1693), sig F4r.
44 BL, MS Harl 646, f. 53v.
45 BL, MS Sloane 826, f. 192r.
46 British Library, MS Add 22603, f. 33r–34r (a Cambridge verse miscellany dating from the 1640s–50s). Other copies of the poem can be found in Bodleian Library, Oxford, MSS, Eng. poet *c.* 50, Rawl poet 160, Tanner 306.
47 The text found several MSS without any direct political allusion, as in BL, MS Add 22, 603. It is intriguing that this text survives in only five copies while 35 copies of the mock blessing 'On the King's Senses' exist.
48 Indeed, similar ambiguities can be found in pseudo-Lucianic satire or the more popular dialogues between Jove and Ganymede such as Heywood's 'Jupiter and

Ganimede' (see S. Coote (ed.), *The Penguin Book of Homosexual Verse* (Harmondsworth: Penguin, 1983), 158–61).

49 Havelock Ellis famously argued Wilde's trial 'brought conviction of their perversion to many inverts who were before only vaguely conscious of their abnormality', cited in Cohen, 'Legislating the Norm', 169.

50 *Wit Restor'd* (1658) reprinted in *Facetiae. Musarum Deliciæ*, 2 vols (1817), vol. 1, 131–2, 131.

51 J. Masten, 'My Two Dads: Collaboration and the Reproduction of Beaumont and Fletcher', in J. Goldberg (ed.), *Queering the Renaissance*, 280–309, esp. 288 argues this period sees a transition from textual production as collaborative and homosocial to patriarchal authorship (282).

52 T. Raylor, *Cavaliers, Clubs and Literary Culture* (Delaware: University of Delaware Press, 1994), 75.

53 The two main groups were known as the 'Order of the Bugle' (a bugle is a decorative bead), and the Order of the Blue (after the coloured ribbons they sported).

54 Raylor, *Cavaliers, Clubs and Literary Culture*, 76.

55 PRO, SP14/155/57.

56 N.E. McClure (ed.), *The Letters of John Chamberlain*, 2 vols (Philadelphia, 1939), 2, 530.

57 'Tityre-tues or a Mock Song' (sung to the tune of Chevy Chase) in *Facetiae*, 1, 131. The poem is attributed to George Chambers.

58 *Facetiae*, 1, 131.

59 *Facetiae*, 1, 132.

60 Raylor, *Cavaliers, Clubs and Literary Culture*, 263–4 (n. 59). In 1619 Queen Anne's Men had performed *Edward II* with its extended Actaeon metaphor and Bacon had at his fall been described as a deer torn by dogs in a Latin libel (see J.D. Knowles, ' "Infinite Riches in a Little Room": Marlowe and the Aesthetics of the Closet', in G. McMullan (ed.), *Renaissance Configurations* (London: Macmillan, 1997), 21), while Buckingham was also often the butt of jokes which used the first part of his name (see 'To hunt the Doe, I haue refus'd' (BL, MS Egerton 2026, f. 12r) and 'Vpon the D. of B.' ('Of British Beasts the buck is King'; BL, MS Sloane 826), f. 184r–185r.

61 It may be that the chronology of events makes this possible: the poem probably post-dates Abbott's death ('He lives above their reach') while the 1658 publication would make an allusion to Charles and Buckingham as sodomites acceptable.

6
Anticlerical slander in the English Civil War: John White's *First Century of Scandalous and Malignant Priests*

James Rigney

Anti-clerical slander is a resilient and long-lived form of expression as two recent British cases illustrate. A court in Edinburgh ruled in June 1996 that Professor Donald McLeod, Professor of Systematic Theology at the Free Church College in Edinburgh was: 'hounded by powerful members of the Free Church of Scotland for more than ten years. They spread rumours and innuendo about his personal life . . . members of the strict religious denomination perjured themselves in court . . . in an effort to ensure Professor McLeod was convicted of five charges [of sexual misconduct] that three Church committees had failed to do.'[1] In the following month David Ward reported for *The Guardian* from Lincoln, where the Dean and Sub-Dean of Lincoln Cathedral seemed likely to resist the Archbishop of Canterbury's attempts to remove them voluntarily from office. Ward canvassed the opinion of the locals: one 'non-attending local businessman' said that he had lived in two cathedral cites [Winchester and Lincoln] 'and there has been the same snobbery, the same feeling of superiority round both Cathedrals. It's all bullshit.' He then recited a rude limerick about a verger.[2] This essay examines the way in which scandalous discourse, like that rude limerick, was put to work during the Civil War as part of the religious policy of the Long Parliament.

An important feature of the Long Parliament's attack on the clergy of the Established Church was harnessing popular anticlericalism to its anti-episcopal proceedings. Among the manifestations of anticlericalism that it exploited was that of exposing clerical immorality. This was a tradition with a long history in England illustrated, for example, by John Heywood's play *John John, the Husband, Tyb his Wife, and Sir John the Priest* (c.1520–22) with its picture of the priest as hypocrite, whoremonger and haunter of stews. The Civil Wars, as the prodigious growth in printed matter during the years 1641–50 shows, were also literary conflicts; their military engagements and political developments were pre-empted, accompanied and reprised by print. In pursuing their aim of purging the ministry of the Church of England the Long Parliament of the 1640s reached into the resources of a pre-literate culture to take one of its major forms of news and exchange, scurrilous gossip, and re-deploy it in print against the clergy.

The text on which this essay focuses is *John White's First Century of Scandalous and Malignant Priests* (1641). This was a record of one hundred Church of England clergymen who had been deprived of their benefices by the Long Parliament because of their unruly lives, their anti-Parliamentary sentiments, or their insufficiency in the performance of their duties. White gathered scurrilous tales about these clerics to produce a prosopography, a collective biography that appropriated orality and exploited the dynamic potential offered by the expanding culture of print during the early years of the 1640s.

White's book

The compiler of *The First Century*, John White (1590–1645) was a lawyer who served in the Long Parliament as MP for Southwark until his death in 1645.[3] He was Chairman of the Grand Committee to Inquire into Clergy Immorality and also chaired its various sub-committees concerned with replacing scandalous and malignant clergy with acceptable Puritan ministers.[4] During the early 1630s he had been involved in a similar project as one of the Feoffees for the Purchase of Impropriations, a group of Puritan activists who had sought to gain control of benefices in order to place Puritan ministers in them. William Laud, Archbishop of Canterbury, had defeated the proposals in the Star Chamber and confiscated the resources of the group in pursuance of his policy of limiting lay influence over parishes and their clergy.[5]

White's status, the origin of the book's information in Parliamentary depositions, and the official order given for its printing, all suggest that *The First Century* can be seen as an official work.[6] In his preface, moreover, White explicitly places the book in the context of Parliament's anti-episcopal project, claiming that by allowing scandalous ministers to remain in their benefices, bishops have acted contrary to their responsibilities:

> They have not onely neglected their Personal Execution of this weighty trust, but also have generally and mostly committed the same to Persons illiterate and insufficient, dumbe Dogges, as the Scripture calls them, that cannot barke, against whom God hath protested for their ignorance, and to men swallowed up with Wine and strong drinke, whose Tables are full of vomit and filthinesse: Whoremongers and Adulterers, who as fed Horses neigh after their Neighbours Wives: Buggerers that change the naturall use into that which is against nature. And to others scandalous of corrupt mindes, and ill affected to the Peace and safety of the Kingdome, men unfit to preach to, or to live among Christians, their wickednesse being so great, as that they are condemned by Heathens: And hereby they have taken the high-way to destroy the souls committed to them, and to drown them in perdition.[7]

In the one hundred cases that follow White sets out to prove the justice of this characterisation.

Furthermore, according to White, the cases revealed in *The First Century* testify to God's goodness in setting up Parliament to extirpate such wickedness; once read they will have the effect of silencing Parliament's critics:

> that the Parliament may appear just in their doings, and the mouth of iniquity may be stopped, this Narrative of the crimes and misdemeanours of these sons of the earth are here published, that all the World may see, that the tongues of the people that speak ill of the Parliament, are set on fire of hell, and lift up against Heaven, and that they hide themselves under falsehood, and make lies their refuge.[8]

Publication therefore stops the mouth of slander with conclusive proof. White's work, however, is itself based upon the searching-out, appropriation and textualising of the transgressive discourse of slander. What happens to slanderous speech here is symptomatic of print's impact on orality generally at this time as gossip, tales, fables and songs are taken from oral circulation, committed to print and then returned, via practices of public reading and report, to the verbal realm. Thus the two spheres were inextricably linked, mutually reinforcing, reciprocally borrowing, repeatedly interchanging. The Long Parliament's use of slander in its campaign against members of the clergy is one of the most striking illustrations of this relationship in action.

Recalling the climate in which his own pamphleteering career began, John Milton, writing in 1654, recollected that at the beginning of the 1640s: 'The vigour of the parliament had begun to humble the pride of the bishops. As soon as liberty of speech was no longer subjected to control, all mouths began to be opened against the bishops; some complained of the vices of the individuals, others of those of the order.'[9]

Milton's imagery of open mouths, crying out against offence had already been used, though to different ends, by the cleric Robert Chestlin in *Persecutio undecima. The churches eleventh persecution* (1648), his pamphlet attacking the Long Parliament's purging of the ministry. Chestlin observed that the phrases: 'O ye scandalous Clergy! and O ye bringing in of Popery! was the belching of every open mouth' during the 1640s.[10] The image used by both Chestlin and Milton partially mediates the reality of the situation which was brought about not so much by the removal of prohibitions on speech as by the removal of prohibitions on writing and publishing. The products of an oral culture are appropriated to a textual form and to a national conflict that becomes progressively more marked by textual exchange and debate.

White begins his work with the eye-catching case of John Wilson, vicar of Arlington in Sussex who was sequestered:

> for that he in most beastly manner, divers times attempted to commit buggery with Nathaniel Browne, Samuel Andrewes and Robert Williams his Parishoners, and by perswasions and violence, laboured to draw them to that abhominable sinne, that (as he shamed not to professe) they might make up his number eighteene; and hath professed that he made choice to commit the act with man-kind rather then with women, to avoide the shame and danger that oft ensueth in begetting Bastards; and hath also attempted to commit buggery with a Mare . . .[11]

After all this, the charges that Wilson, while baptising an illegitimate child, described Christ as a bastard, that he commended images and praying with beads and called the Parliament 'rebels' seem relatively venial.

The eighteenth-century Church historian, and biographer of the ejected clergy, John Walker takes up two columns in *The Sufferings of the Clergy* (1714) to denounce White for the strategy of beginning his book with Wilson. In this decision Walker discerns a policy to make 'a cursory Reader (who just casts an Eye on the Title-Page, and perhaps One or Two more) believe, that all the rest of the Sequestered Ministers were just Equally scandalous with Mr Wilson'.[12] Walker is alert not only to the rhetorical structure of White's book but also the way in which that structure exploits the characteristics of the print market in which the book will be encountered and consumed.

Later cases in White's collection lack the colour of John Wilson but present a seductive catalogue of misdemeanours. Of these drunkenness, frequenting prostitutes, absenteeism, incompetence and litigiousness are the most common and the sexual harassment of parishioners. William Fairfax, rector of St. Peter's, Cornhill, London and vicar of Eastham in Middlesex, it was charged:

seeketh and haunteth the company of women, notoriously suspected of incontinency, and intrudes himself into their company, and into the company of other women, walking alone in the streets in the dark twilight, and tempteth them to uncleannesse, leading them into darke places and into Taverns, fit for such workes of darkness.[13]

Numerous ministers, like John Gruch rector of Walkherne in Hertfordshire, were sequestered for libelling the Parliament or discouraging parishioners from joining the Parliamentary army. Others were deprived for actively upholding the King's cause against Parliament as in the case of John Gordon, rector of Ockley in Sussex, who was sequestered as a negligent drunkard and because, in addition, he was 'reported to have been seene in the Army of Cavaliers, raised against the Parliament'.[14]

Details of the depositions, such as the name and status of the deposers are not recorded in *The First Century* but in a marginal note against the passage in which he speaks of the book silencing the mouths of Parliament's critics, White records that: 'The grossest faults stand proved by many witnesses, seldome less than six.'[15] Despite this assurance it is upon the quality and credibility of his evidence that White's work is most roundly attacked by critics such as Chestlin and Walker.

White's critics

Chestlin claimed that he had written his *Persecutio undecima* because of:

the multitude of scandalous Pamphlets, Parliament Speeches, Centuries, Declarations, published all faced with Authority of Parliament, the Supreme Court of Justice in England, Title enough to charme the world, especially Posterity into a beliefe of such Authentike Records; should no particular counterwake of truth be left to oppose such slanders . . .[16]

His work therefore exposes the complicity of Parliament, 'the Supreme Court of Justice in England,' with slander and untruth and its fourth chapter is solely devoted to what Chestlin terms: 'The Puritan Arts of Framing Accusations in the Parliament against the Clergy, and their Manner of Proving their Charge.'[17] In this he attacks the methods by which the Parliament assembled information against Ministers and the lack of legal recourse for the Ministers against accusations: 'not any one person in that Century,' he complains 'hath had any legall tryall at all; but condemnati quoniam accusati; and the Justice of these times is, satis est accusare'.[18] He also claims that the Committee was prepared to go to inordinate length to find out scandal against a minister: 'If the Parish afforded no evidence [of wrongdoing], or their old acquaintance, downe they sent (in some men's Causes) to the University to hunt out some scandall in the time of their Ministers abode there.'[19]

John Walker likewise attacks the dubious quality of some of White's evidence and those who provide it. In the case of Joseph Draper of St Thomas Southwark and St Thomas's Hospital, Southwark, for example, Walker reports that Draper was ministering to a dying soldier from the parliamentary army that had been brought to St Thomas's after Edgehill and mentioned to him the heinousness of rebellion as a sin for which he ought to seek forgiveness. According to Walker: 'Two Women being by, went and swore blasphemy and treason against him to the Parliament. He was arrested and imprisoned. On Examination, the Witnesses that swore against him, were proved to be persons that came there to be Cured of the P—x.' Walker's marginal comment on this incident is: 'See what Credit is to be given to Whites Calumnies, since he took them from the Depositions of such Profligate Witnesses.'[20]

White's critics allege that his Committees were indifferent to the nature of the evidence provided as long as they had attestations: 'nor scarce durst any parishioner deny, his hand though he knew nothing of the charge for fear of being accounted a malignant, and some parishioners refusing to subscribe because they could prove nothing of the accusations, it hath been replyed, set you your hands, leave us to prove the charge'. The result is that, according to Chestlin, many of blameless lives have surrendered their livings 'to avoid the trouble and charges, and infinite scorne and vexation at Committees, and the shame (as it then was accounted) of being ranked among scandalous Ministers'.[21]

Though he disapproves of this type of gossip Chestlin is not above using it himself in his attack on Parliament. He cites some of John Hampden's neighbours in Buckinghamshire in support of the gossip that Hampden went yearly on subversive visits to Scotland, and records the following servant's gossip about the Puritan leader Lord Saye and his meetings with fellow agitators at Saye's house: 'wherein was a roome and passage, which his servants were prohibited to come neare, where great noises and talkings have been heard to the admiration of some who lived in the house, yet could never discerne their Lord's companions'. Likewise the authority of Parliament, the advancement of which Chestlin sees as lying behind the whole process of investigation and sequestration, allegedly 'so possessed a gentlewoman used to their Lectures, that she durst not in conscience take Physick without an order from Parliament from the House of Commons'. In a marginal note Chestlin locates this woman as living 'in Lime-street in London' thereby ascribing particularity (and thus authority) to such gossip.[22] Finally Chestlin retails the allegation that White, despite his strictures on sexual misconduct among the clergy was himself guilty of frequenting the wives of his neighbours in White Friars.[23]

John White died on 29 January 1644/45; two days later the Royalist newsbook *Mercurius Aulicus* was retailing the story of his alleged infidelities.[24] He was buried in the Temple Church and his memorial inscription included the lines: 'Here lyeth John, a burning, shining light, / His name, life, actions were all White.' The same could not be said for those whose names, lives and actions were catalogued in White's *First Century of Scandalous and Malignant Priests*. There was no second century, though one is forecast in the first book, because, according to Thomas Pierce, White's own party dissuaded him from issuing a second volume because the cases reported in the first were so indecent.[25] Whether indecent or not the *First Century* is a startling appropriation of a rich tradition of anticlerical slander and a successful application of it to the theatre of print in which so much of the conflict of the ensuing twenty years would be played out.

The culture of clerical slander

White's work builds upon, the culture of clerical slander that had developed since the Reformation, especially during the preceding twenty years. In 1632 Francis Stacey of Cole Orton in Leicestershire invented what was said to be a 'rablement of words without rime or reason in derogation of his vicar, Thomas Pestell and further endeavoured to have the same put into verse, further purposing to have had the same put into print'.[26] Many forms of slander, such as shaming ballads, came from a society where status depended on credit within the community: churchwardens had traditionally placed great emphasis on the notions of common voice and common fame when pursuing irregularities at a parish level. White elevated this to a national level and exploited the potential of print, a potential that Francis Stacey had apparently perceived, and which in White's case was supported by the authority of Parliament, to spread and intensify the impact of choric forms such as hearsay, gossip and slander.[27]

The Presbyterian cleric and author Richard Baxter had little doubt about the 'Pride and Impudency' of those who slandered the ministry:

> They are most of them persons of lamentable ignorance; and yet they dare revile at the Teachers, and think themselves wise enough to rebuke and teach them: Many of them are men of wicked lives; and yet they can tell the world how bad the Ministers are. A Railer, a Drunkard, a Covetous Worldling, an Ignorant Sott, is the likest person to fall upon the Minister.[28]

Much anticlerical slander was the consequence of conflicts over local issues such as clergy exemption (or their claims for exemption), from levies.[29] As the vicar of Norborne-cum-Sholden in Kent wrote to Edward Dering, Chairman of the Kent Committee of Religion in January 1640 in response to a petition against him: 'Those that complaine of me doe it not for God's glorie and the good of his Church (for then I could have borne with it), but they violentlie proceed against me out of revenge, envie, hatred, malice, and all uncharytablesness, as I shall make it plainlie to appeare heereafter.'[30] In Chestlin's view the order of the House of Commons inviting all 'active' men to accuse their ministers meant that 'not any Knave or Foole in a Parish whom reproofe for sinnes had made the Ministers Enemy, but now thought himselfe commanded (yes and bound in conscience to obey) to flye in the face of God's Ministers'.[31] As Adam Fox has observed: 'it is difficult to recover either the precise circumstances which surrounded an allegedly seditious outburst, or the hidden sub-texts of animosity and sectional interest which may have underpinned the informing of one neighbour on another'.[32] White's purposes in *The First Century* provide an organic coherence for his collection of gossip from these sources.

The parishioners of Lidsing and Bredhurst in Kent, motivated it seems by Edward Alchorne, a Gentleman of the Parish, complained in February 1641 against the performance, contentiousness and (in the case of one parishioner) violence of their minister, Richard Tray. There were four signatures and three marks on the petition. In April of the same year Tray wrote to the Kent Committee on Religion in his defence. He included a statement by two arbitrators in a dispute between him and one of his parishioners and various recantations by some of his accusers:

> I, William Kemsley, of Bredherst, yeoman, doe by these presents testify, that Mr Ed. Alchorne did oftentimes solicit me, at Hartlipp alehouse, to set my hand to his petition to be preferred against Mr Tray, our minister, to the high Court of Parliament; but I twice or thrice denying, at length, with much importunity he got my hand thereunto, beeing much, I confesse, overtaken with drink; but I never heard above 2 or 3 lines thereof; and for the rest, I doe not know what was therein; I would faine have put him off; but still solicits me thereto, perceiving me to be much in drink. I am very sorry for soe dooing; for I never knew nor heard but very well of Mr Tray . . .[33]

Similar claims of importunity by Alchorne and ignorance on the part of the petitioners were put forward by Moses Long and John Drew and John Paine (the latter two of whom were unable to sign their name), and both Long and Paine claimed that Alchorne got them drunk to get their signatures.[34]

In a similar case the parishioners of Snargate in Kent wrote to Sir Edward

Derring, Chairman of the Kent Committee in April 1641 to recall their petition against their vicar E. Nicholls and the curate Mr Jo. Freeman:

> our intent was not, by any meanes, to disgrace him, or, in any wayes, to disparge his sufficiency in not being able to discharge the Cure of soules committed to his charge; and we confesse him to be both very able, sufficient, and painefull, in dispensing the word of God; but onely he seemed to carry himselfe something too lofty, and to be hasty towards us, which thing we perswade ourselves will be much amended.[35]

'Active' men within a parish, anxious to proceed against a cleric, needed to be certain that their evidence would not defect in this way. In January 1640, William Finch of Woodchurch in Kent complained to the Kent Committee about the Popish practices of the minister of Woodchurch, Edward Boughen:

> I verily beleeve he will not deny any of theise his actions, words, or gestures: If he should, there are sufficient witnesses to prove every perticular, whose names I shall readily give you, if parishioners doe not shortly joine in an information concerning the premisses; theise I have privately certifyed, fearing lest that the parishioners may too long delay.[36]

Conclusion

By 1644 Parliament was once more in pursuit of scandalous ministers prompted by legislation such as An Order for Regulating the University of Cambridge, and for removing Scandalous Ministers in the Seven Associated Counties which established Committees under the chairmanship of the Earl of Manchester with power to collect evidence and remove clergy from their livings on its strength. The surviving records of these committees (giving far more detail than White makes available in *The First Century*) provide rich material for further study of White's influence: in areas such as the weight attached to approximations and phrases such as 'words to that effect', and perhaps most interestingly, the regularity with which charges of sexual misconduct are levelled by women parishioners. While Thomas Metcalf attested to the anti-Parliamentary remarks of the Minister of Bartlow in Cambridgeshire, it is his wife Anne who, along with Lucy Goodwin, deposes that 'Hee hath had a Bastard laid unto him by the woeman in travaile & the Father of the woman reports he gave 15s to keepe it.' And it is Frances Smith, wife of William Smith, Tanner of the same Parish, who alleges that the Minister, John Baker, took his wife's 22-year-old sister, Susan Tirrel and '. . .

laid her over his knee and there did slap her bare buttocks and then tried to do the same to another woman'.[37] Clare Brant has recently written that the violence of scandal is most often said to arise from feminine envy and its attendant malice. The deployment of female voices in these collections of slander raises interesting possibilities about the ways in which women's perceptions are used in local regulation and its larger representation.[38]

As religious prosopography, White's work has clear parallels with, if different purposes from, for example, Foxe's *Book of Martyrs*. Its great influence lies on the works that follow it, most notably Calamy and Walker's martyrology of clergy from the respective parties of the Civil War Church of England.[39] But most immediately its impact can be seen in the newsbooks and pamphlets of the English revolution which tapped and circulated rich mines of gossip, slander and sedition as part of the polemical chorus that accompanied the Civil War. As Walker commented on the case of Daniel Featley after these proceedings of the Parliament, 'tis not to be wonder'd at that he was abused and vilified in the diurnals and weekly papers'.[40] White's importance seems to me to lie in the way he perceived and exploited the potential relation of orality and print in maximising the impact of slander.

White's most direct heir is perhaps Thomas Edwards in *Gangraenea*, a catalogue of current heresies published in 1645. Though using published sources to explicate and classify heresies, Edwards relies on oral testimony to illustrate and warn of the dangers they pose. Lucasta Miller has recently shown how John Milton's *Doctrine and Discipline of Divorce* (1643) made its way into the heresiologies of Edwards, Robert Baillie and Ephraim Paggitt.[41] In the second part of *Gangraenea* (published in 1646), the *Doctrine and Discipline of Divorce* is defined as a sectarian text not by any reference to its author's intentions but by reference to its readership: especially to its alleged influence on the radical Mrs Allaway.

In his life of White, Anthony Wood recounts a story told by Thomas Pierce, an ejected Fellow of Magdalen College, Oxford (and also by Thomas Fuller in his *Church History*) that Charles I was shown White's book when it was published and that the King 'would not give his consent that such a book should be written of the vicious lives of some parliament Ministers, when such a thing was presented him. 'Whereby', concludes Pierce, 'you see that vast difference between the spirit of Majesty and the impotent spleen of their author.'[42] What we also see is a member of the Royalist party anxious to emulate White and perhaps have the same or greater impact. Although on this occasion, if Pierce is to be believed, the strategy was rejected, by the time the Royalist newsbook *Mercurius Aulicus* began to be published, White's lesson about the potency of slander and gossip had been thoroughly learned and adopted.

Notes

1   *The Times*, 26 June 1996, 2.
2   *The Guardian*, 8 July 1996, 8.
3   For further references to White see DNB and Peter Smith, *A Sermon Preached Before the Honourable House of Commons at their Monthly Fast*, May 29, 1644, (1644), 32.
4   White's contemporary critic, Robert Chestlin, claimed that 'anticlerical speeches, and publishing those Speeches in print on purpose to infect the people, and fire their mindes . . . and this railing against the Clergy, was the only way to be made a Chairman of a Committee,' *Persecutio Undecima* (1648), 17.
5   See Gary Gorman, 'A Laudian Attempt to Tune the Pulpit: Peter Heylin's Sermon Against the Feoffees for the Purchase of Impropriations,' *Journal of Religious History*, 7 (1975), 333–49. Anthony Wood later attributed White's persecution of the clergy to his resentment over this episode in his *Athenae Oxonienses. An Exact History of all the Writers and Bishops who have had their education in the University of Oxford. To which are added the Fasti, or Annals of the said University*, 4 vols, ed. Phillip Bliss (1813–20), III, 144.
6   See, *An Order Made to a Select Committee Chosen by the Whole House of Commons to Receive Petitions Touching Ministers* (1640). C.T. Hansard provides a sense of the parliamentary climate that led to the establishment of the Committee in his *The Parliamentary History of England, from the Earliest Period to the Year 1803*, 36 vols, (1807), II, 670.
7   John White, *First Century of Scandalous and Malignant Priests* (1641), sig. A2v.
8   Ibid., sig. A4.
9   John Milton, *The second defense of the English people* (1654), trans. Robert Fellowes, in John Milton, *Prose Writings*, ed. K.M. Burton (1958), 344.
10 Chestlin, *Persecutio undecima*, 8–9.
11 White, *First Century*, 1.
12 John Walker, *An Attempt towards Recovering and Account of the Numbers and Suffering of the Clergy of the Church of England, Heads of Colleges, Fellows, Scholars &c, who were Sequester'd, Harass'd &c in the late times of the Grand Rebellion* (1714), 406.
13 White, *First Century*, 7.
14 Ibid., 4.
15 Ibid. sig. A4.
16 Chestlin, *Persecutio undecima*, 4.
17 Chestlin was imprisoned for preaching against the Parliament (see the list of dangerous points in his sermon in Bodl. MS Tanner 64.76). In *Persecutio undecima*, 34, Chestlin cites one case of an anonymous minister being interrogated by an ignorant committee, and in the margin identifies this cleric as 'Mr Chestlin'.
18 Chestlin, *Persecutio undecima*, 27.
19 Ibid., 28.
20 Walker, *The Sufferings of the Clergy*, 167.
21 Chestlin, *Persecutio undecima*, 28, 24; 17, 23.
22 Ibid., 55, 55.6. This device is used to great effect by Thomas Edwards in his exposure of prevailing heresies, *Gangraenea*, published in two parts in 1645 and 1646.

23   Chestlin's allegation is picked up and reproduced by Anthony Wood in his life of White in *Athenae Oxoniensis*, III, 145.

24   *Mercurius Aulicus*, 31 January 1644/5, 1362.

25   White's work was reissued in 1712 under the title *A New Year's Gift for the High Church Clergy: being an Account of the Sufferings of a Great Number of the Church of England*. For a sense of the context of this re-publication see also *The Merciful Judgement of the High Church Triumphant on Offending Clergymen and others in the Reign of Charles I* (1710).

26   Huntington Library, Hastings mss, legal box 5 (9), f. 86r, cited in Adam Fox, *Aspects of Oral Culture and its Development in Early Modern England* (PhD thesis, University of Cambridge, 1992), 232-3.

27   The printing of slander was a well established polemical practice. That print offered a more effective and telling means of spreading slander is shown by the case of Dr William Stoughton. The seventeenth-century diarist John Rous records that a carrier coming from Stoughton's living in the West Country, 'bringing some monyes for his wives childrens portions, he was traduced (as it seemeth) to be a favourer of New England, and a collector of contributions for those ministers there&c.: so that a pursevant was sent to the carrier, and many halbard-men for him, and his study was sealed up &c.: but within 2 or 3 dayes, re cognita, he returned with credite in the Earl of Holland's coach.' See, Mary Ann Everett Green (ed.), *The Diary of John Rous*, vol. 856 (London: Camden Society, 1855), 80.

28   Richard Baxter, *One Sheet for the Ministry Against the Malignants of all Sorts* (London and Kidderminster, 1657), 6. Baxter had also criticised Sir Henry Vane, a Parliamentarian who held religious views of an intensely personal nature, for his responsibility for the break-up of the godly party since he not only argued for liberty of conscience, but also taught his clients: 'to revile the Ministry, calling them ordinarily Blackcoats, Priests, and other names which then sounded of Reproach'. See his, *Reliquae Baxterianae* (1697), ed. Matthew Sylvester, 75.

29   See, for example, the cases in J.S. Cockburn (ed.), *Western Circuit Assize Orders, 1629-1648*, 4th series, 17 (London: Camden Society, 1976), 137 and 158, and B.C. Redwood (ed.), *Quarter Sessions Order Book, 1642-49*, LIV (Sussex Record Society, 1954), 8.

30   Lambert B. Larking (ed.), *Proceedings Principally in the County of Kent, in Connection with the Parliament called in 164? and especially with the Committee of Religion appointed in that Year* (London: Camden Society, 1862), 110.

31   Chestlin, *Persecutio undecima*, 17. In *The Sufferings of the Clergy*, 169, Walker records that the charges against Daniel Featley were laid by three mechanics in his parish who had previously been indicted for Brownists at the County Sessions.

32   Fox, *Aspects of Oral Culture*, 262-3.

33   Larking, *Proceedings Principally in the County of Kent*, 171.

34   Ibid., 172-3.

35   Ibid., 199. Sometimes the written record of a petition contains a purely oral survival; so William Day of the parish of Rolvenden in Kent, affirming that the vicar Thomas Higginson allowed him to steal fire wood from another man's property was recorded as follows: 'Witness to this, William Day, who is since dead.; Witnesse that he said it, Robert Gibbon and James [His mark] Chittenden.' (237).

36   Ibid., 122.

37 BL. Add. MS 15672, f. 12–13.
38 Clare Brant, 'Speaking of Women: Scandal and the Law in the mid-Eighteenth Century', in Clare Brant and Dianne Purkis (eds), *Women, Texts and Histories, 1575–1760* (London and New York: Routledge, 1992), 242–70.
39 According to the DNB entry on Walker, his friend John Lewis disparaged The Sufferings of the Clergy as a 'farrago of false and senseless legends' (73). Edmund Calamy, *An Account of the Ministers, Lecturers, Masters and fellows of Colleges and Schoolmasters, who were Ejected or Silenced, after the Restoration of 1660* (1713) (first published as part of *Edmund Calamy, An Abridgement of Mr Baxter's History of his Life and Time*, 1710).
40 Walker, *The Sufferings of the Clergy*, 169.
41 Lucasta Miller, 'The Shattered Violl: Print and Textuality in the 1640s', *Essays and Studies*, new series, 1993 (46), 25–38, 27.
42 Thomas Pierce, *The New Discoverer Discover'd by Way of Answer to Mr. Baxter his Pretended Discovery of the Grotian Religion* (1659), 141, cited in Wood, *Athenae Oxoniensis*, III, 146.

7

His Praeludiary Weapons: mocking Colonel Hewson before and after the Restoration

Neil Durkin

On 5 December 1659 there was a serious riot in the City of London. It left perhaps six apprentices dead and many more injured. 'Yesterday's fray in London will most likely make a great noise in the country,' said Pepys, the following day, writing to his patron Edward Mountague. It was, Pepys reported:

> the hottest in the pursuit and the quietest in the Close of any wee have hitherto known. In the morning a Common councell being mett, some young men in the name of the Citty apprentices presented theyr peticion . . . to the Lord Mayor and Common Councell. This meeting of the Youth was interpreted as a forerunner of an insurreccion, and to prevent that, the Souldiers were all (horse and foot), drawne into the Citty . . . the souldiers as they marcht were hooted at all along the streets, and where any stragled from the whole body, the boys flung stones, tiles, turnups &c. at [them] with all the affronts they could give them, some they disarmed and kickt, others abused the horses with stones and rubbish they flung at them; and when Collonel Huson came in the head of his Regiment they shouted all along a Cobler a Cobler; in some places the apprentices would gett a football (it being a hard frost) and drive it among the souldiers on purpose, and they either darst not (or prudently would not) interrupt them; in fine, many souldiers were hurt with stones, and one I see was very neere having his braines knockt out with a brick batt flung from the top of an house at him. On the other side, the souldiers proclaimed the proclamacion against any subscripcions which the boys shouted at in contempt, which some could not beare butt lett fly theyr musquets and killed in several places (where I see one in Cornhill shott through the head) 6 or 7. and severall wounded.[1]

Apprentices had been at the centre of many of the disturbances of mid-seventeenth-century London and Colonel Hewson's regiment, following the orders of the Committee of Safety, of which he was one, acted to quell a

London uprising that was itself a common occurrence in Interregnum Britain.[2] When groups of boys and young men began assembling on the streets of the city on the morning of 5 December 1659, onlookers could justifiably have seen their gathering as typically mixed-motive, anti-authority discontent, a defence of trade as much as an assault on an unpopular soldiery. In fact, at the start of the month, armed with news that a petition calling for free elections was being drawn up by City apprentices, the Committee of Safety had hastily issued a catch-all proclamation forbidding the petitions of 'ill-disposed persons'.[3] Ostensibly it was this that Hewson's troops were in the city to read and enforce, though their numbers indicate that they also anticipated serious opposition. The fighting witnessed by Pepys was also seen by Thomas Rugge, the London barber:

> Theire was many affronts offred and a great many of uncivill actions
> . . . especialy to Colonelle Hewson Regiment of ffoote, they ware more
> abused then any other. Hee was a Cobler by his trade, but a very stout
> man and a very good Commander of foote, but in regard of his former
> employment, and the aprentises once got into theire mouths [they very
> well employed their mouthes]: hee had but on eye, but they calld him
> blind Cobler blind hewson and did throw ould shewes and old slipers
> and turnapes topes battes and stones and tiles, att him and his soulders
> . . .

Six months later, of course, the king and his exiled court would be back in the country and the Restoration a confirmed fact. In the apprentice opposition to army-based government in the 1659–60 winter, however, proto-Restoration writing reveals itself as a scurrilous precursor to a sophisticated satire to come. Specific, aggrieved polemics found a taunting voice. At once the language of the heckler, it was a strain of political barracking, cackling laughter edged around with the threat of revenge to come. 'Blind Cobler blind hewson': the apprentices vilified the soldiers – 'with many affronts' – as much as they bombarded them with ready-made missiles and used football as a cover for affray. Rugge reported that the apprentices had guns ('amonge the Rude multetude their ware som did fier a pistoll att the souldiers'), and according to the *Monthly Intelligencer* newspaper one of Hewson's lieutenants was shot in the knee. But insults themselves were well-aimed and damaging: 'They very well employed their mouthes.' Heckling the Committee of Safety's hard-pressed soldiers was always more than youthful agitation or the hurly-burly of early football rampaging. In defence of a petition calling for free elections or the return of excluded members, and in defiance of an army whose back pay it nevertheless wanted paid (and therefore disbanded), the apprentices fed into a discourse that would come out the other side of the Restoration as mock-heroic.[4]

The apprentices' petition had been addressed to the Corporation of London, the 'right worthy and grave Senatours, the Lord Mayor, Aldermen, and Commonality of the City of London in Common Council'. Caught in the middle the Common Council had somewhat lamely instructed citizens to keep apprentices indoors for fear of 'raising of any tumults'. This barely worked. Journeying to the capital on the 12th, Ralph Josselin noted the icy streets and the 'city very full of tumults'. The riot's political significance was apparent to all. It had caused a 'greate heart burneing in the Citty' wrote one correspondent to Monck's secretary William Clarke, and declarations for a free parliament from the garrison at Portsmouth and elsewhere were enough to occasion a flurry of excited correspondence amongst Clarendon's party, monitoring the situation on the Continent with the aid of agents' letters. After their dispersal on 5 December the apprentices kept up their campaign. Addressing a 'further humble Petition and Remonstrance' to the Lord Mayor and Common Council aldermen on the 13th, the apprentices complained bitterly of the 'Mercenary Souldiers' and their 'barbarous Usage of Us'. Their petition called for the raising of a City Militia to defend against the 'Granadoes' of the army coupled with the familiar urging of a free parliament. On 2 January the apprentices issued a satirical poem mixing the usual scatological abuse against the Rump with bloated threats that 'If [the petition] be frighted by the Proclamation / Our Sword Establish shall a Reformation', and by early February addresses were being made directly to General Monck himself, by then the nation's most significant political player.[5]

One lasting residue of the December suppression was a personalised campaign against Hewson himself. In January 1660 apprentices from Fleet Street and St Paul's 'made in snowe the Effigies of Colonell Hewson wth one Eye in heade and wth an old face, and a haulter or Rope a bout his neck', and on the 25th a gibbet was set up in the road in Cheapside with Hewson's picture placed upon it. Sinister and comic – the Hewson snowman had 'ould shewes lying by him', and Rugge himself could not forbear the mordant remark that the apprentices 'did remember his box after christmass' – the apprentices' tactics displayed a scurrilous mode typical of the eve-of-Restoration period. Judging from tracts issued throughout 1660, it is clear in fact that the apprentices did remember Hewson's actions against their number. By October 1660, when, as Jonathan Sawday has shown, the very notion of memory had become politicised, Hewson would be awarded his place in Thomas Riders's *Black Remembrancer*, and he was 'Nasty John Cobler Hewson' in the instructively titled *Schedule, List, Scrowle or Catalogue* of royalist targets named on the very eve of the Restoration.[6]

While several of the period's royalist broadsides against Rump and army hate-figures did little more than round up the usual suspects some gave

Hewson particularised treatment. In *The Out-Cry of the London Prentices For Justice to be Executed upon John Lord Hewson*, a pamphlet published around the middle of January 1660, Hewson became a 'one-eyed Varlet', 'this Polyphemus'. '*Sound Drums and trumpets! will you buy Brooms, have you any Shoes to felt?*', mocked the pamphlet writer, attributing the street-seller's cry to the ironically-titled 'noble Lord Hewson, Baron of Bungle Hall'. Mixing grievance for the 'Outrages and affronts' committed against the London apprentices with crowing satire, the *Out-Cry* exploited the reversal in Hewson's fortunes in early 1660. For, part of what historians have identified as General Lambert's Wallingford House group, Hewson's fall from power in January 1660 paralleled Lambert's, as the general's troops melted away in the days spent anticipating Monck's next move in that winter's phoney war. Throughout January, and indeed right through to the Restoration in May, radicals were being expelled from regiment officer groups, from provincial garrisons, from the City Militia, and from the government's newspapers. By 11 February, with his troops in control of London, Monck and his chief officers had instructed Parliament to make the necessary preparations for dissolution and fresh elections, and the 'Roasting of the Rump' was underway. Events were moving swiftly. By 10 April Lambert would be escaping from custody in the Tower to muster support for a last-ditch rendezvous of what remained of the army's republican die-hards, and satirists ingeniously kept up with the times by issuing mock Hue-and-Cries that often anticipated genuine proclamations for the apprehension of renegades. The January *Out-Cry*, for example, had contained a mock 'HUE-AND-CRY or *Proclamation*, after Coll. *Hewson*', informing loyal citizens of the outlaw's tell-tale signs, 'That you may know him when you meet him'; wearing a 'Last' rather than a knight's 'Sword', no longer the titled upstart but just simple 'Blind Hewson'. The apprentices' scourge 'you may better . . . descry / By's aged Person', sniped the *Out-Cry*, a jibe at what Rugge and others considered to be Hewson's unusually 'old face'.[7]

The spring of 1660 saw a steady flow of anti-Hewson portraits appearing on the streets of London. On 15 March Thomason bought a broadsheet called *The Black Book Opened*, a mockplaylet in which Hewson appeared as a stooge of the 'Diabolicall Saints'. Only the most ridiculous of a self-confessed entourage of 'King-Killers', he was discursively rounded up with Thomas Scot, Thomas Harrison, Miles Corbet, John Barkstead, William, Lord Munson, Robert Tichborne and Edmund Ludlow. Hewson had an ignominious starring role: 'Enter Cavalier and Hewson the Cobler. / Well meet blind Harper, whether away so fast?' With polemic overpowering its barest pretence at dramaturgy (the title-page facetiously announced that it was to be acted 'by a Company of Blind *Bloomsbury* fidlers'), the *Black Book*

Opened had Hewson's imagined response to the return of the king as a trite but keenly topical exclamation – 'Heaven forbid! I'de rather all the Apprentices in *London* should rise, had I but my Regiment again.' A pattern was being established. From January 1660 onwards Hewson would come to feature in royalist tracts as a buffoonish, self-incriminating tradesman responsible for a heinous crime. Guilty, with 'a shaking Ague through fear of a King'; haunted, brooding over actions committed against one-time brethren, the apprentice cobblers; yet unrepentant, a cowardly social climber pathetically lamenting his lost 'Colonels place', the caricature Hewson would live a curious spectral life on the pages of the royalist press. By September, *A Charge Of High-Treason Prepared by the London-Apprentices against Col. Hewson* had this finely worked out. Charged with the murder of Charles I and the banishment of the Stuarts, of the unlawful sale of sequestered lands and the destruction of seal and arms ('when the Devil was in him'), this Hewson is a cringing wretch. Announced (quite fictitiously) as having been 'taken near Plymouth', an abject Hewson issues a 'Lamentation' based on a vision of a seemingly wounded figure with 'a pale Ghostly face'. Clearly the product of Hewson's fevered conscience, the admonitory ghost harasses Hewson with the accusation 'was it not enough for thee to be mock-honorouble, but thou must commit wilfull murther upon thy Brother Cobler?' His urine tested by an attendant doctor, the *Charge*'s Hewson is miserably reduced, left with '*Nothing but Death, Nothing but Death*'.[8]

Under the guise of supposed legal sanction the apprentices played out a theatre of revenge in these texts. It was, as the Cavalier in the *Black Book Opened* remarked, 'wonderful when Devils tell the Truth', and yet more wonderful when one's implacable enemies conveniently acted out their own fall and damnation. As early as mid-January, with Lambert on the run and Hewson in hiding, the single-sheet press anticipated a reckoning for 'Nine worthies' deserving of the hangman's noose. Last named after Cromwell, Vane, Lambert, Lilburne, John Desborough, Robert Duckenfield, Packer and Creed, Hewson here eluded his fate, much to the speaker's chagrin: 'Tis vain to look for dead mens shoos, / Else I had had Hewson in a noose'. Each of twenty-one bawdy stanzas in *The Hang-Mans Last Will and Testament* concludes with the tavern cry of '*I and my gallows groane*', simultaneously a macabre desire for revenge and a register of frustration at enemies thought to be escaping the gallows.[9]

With both the country and Hewson's future darkly uncertain in the winter and spring of 1660, it was to the firmer ground of Hewson's past that his opponents turned. This past was, it seems, only murkily known to his contemporaries, but its very obscurity granted licence to the scurrilous. For the 'honest shoemaker in Westminster', a man who had once supplied the

Massachusetts Bay Colony with eight pairs of 'welt neat's leather shoes', never escaped the stigma of his origins. 'Why not a Cobler a witness', asked *'Seely, Of London Cobler'* in the *Black Book*, before introducing a retinue of tradesmen types (*'Evans* the Welch Smith' and so on) all likewise in search of their dues. More than any comparable figure the alluring subject of Hewson's social origins was in the mouths of his detractors in the months before and after the Restoration. 'For Nobilities sake we may not forget . . . / That Valiant *Mars* his true Son', mocked *The Gang* (mid-January 1660), for 'His Cobling Feat / Lack't a Parliament Seat / That marks-man one eyed *Hewson'*. A bawdy song claiming to be to the tune of 'Robin Hood', *The Gang* rehearsed familiar attacks on upstartery – from Lambert the 'dapper Squire' to Packer the 'toyling ditcher' – but it was Hewson who came in for exemplary treatment, his assets discursively seized back in a new twist on the Robin Hood myth. The hunted Hewson of the September 'Plymouth' tract bitterly regrets that he had ever 'climbed to dignity': as if a spirit from a former life and sphere, the ghost of Hewson's 'Lament' approaches him 'Crying, *Cobler, Cobler, Cobler'.*[10]

Not only h(a)unted by past crimes but a past life, the Hewsonian royalist construct of the 1660 pamphlets was a powerful embodiment of social anarchy revisiting itself; a convenient, satisfying morality lesson on the dire consequences of craftsmen scrambling out of their allotted place in life. Likewise *The Lamentation of a Bad Market* (dated by Thomason 21 March), for instance, presented readers with a quarto's worth of mockery at the expense of Lambert, Fleetwood, Hesilrige and *'Hewson* the Cobler', purporting to reveal a scared band of opportunists trapped by their own rise to power:

> Oh! that as first we did begin
> With a Coblers Awl, and a Taylors Pin;
> With Carpenters Rule, Brewers Sling,
> Weavers Trade, Pedlers Pack,
> Tinkers Budget, Millers Sack:
> We could but now to work again,
> All in our pristine Trades amain:

Ironically cornered through attainment of 'position', these erstwhile tradesmen yearn for the lost security of calling or station. Lower even than animals (unable like 'the Dog' to 'return to his own vomit'), they cringingly bemoan their loss of primal innocence. Theirs is a lament at reversal, a longing for their earlier condition. 'Our chiefest cover and business then', they conclude, 'were to get bread to feed our selves, and Clothes to cover our nakedness, and to become the best Workmen in the several Trades and

Occupations our Fathers gave us education in, as Thimble-makers, Razor-makers, Taylors, Coblers, Carpenters, Weavers, Brewers, Pedlers, and such like Vocations'.[11]

If the allusion to Genesis here – possibly a confused one, as Adam and Eve cover their nakedness only after their Fall (Genesis 3:10–21) – suggested nothing less than a supposed commonality of Christian piety in the face of inscrutable socialised relations, it also rehearsed an urgent imperative concerning the dangers of overreaching at a time of political uncertainty. Just as Eve had unwisely neglected rightful labours, so the *bêtes noires* of the royalist press were depicted as falling into danger precisely because they had presumed to desert their allotted occupations. During 1659–60 this ideology was nothing if not commonplace. For example the goldsmith Barkstead ('a Lord of the new stamp') came in for repeated attack, and Robert Tichborn and John Ireton were singled out in a pair of tracts scorning them for their disreputable ascent to eminence – all grubby covetousness and ruthless familial Machiavellianism. Above all though it was Hewson who received exemplary attention. The second of the Tichborn-Ireton pamphlets – the so-called *Apology* – was, according to its title-page, 'Printed for everybody but the light-heel'd Apprentices and Head-strong Masters of the wincing City of London', an ironic swipe, perhaps, at City leaders and compliant masters seen as hostile to the apprentices. It was in this specific context that Hewson's name became synonymous with the army's contempt for the City, and here that royalist-apprentice hatred rebounded back as one most contemptuously class-based.[12]

In many ways Hewson was a godsend to the underground royalist press. Denouncing him as a cobbler drew special force from it being a common labouring trade and the shoe fitted in the case of John Hewson, for, asked the *Out-Cry*, drawing on proverbial wisdom, 'What can be Registered of's former fame, / But that he was *Sutur ultra Crepidam*'. Hewson's behaviour (and fall) appeared to bear out the worth of the ancient injunction 'cobbler, stick to your last' (*ne supra crepidam sutor judicaret*). 'Let the kobler medle wyth clowting his neyghbours shoes, and not be a captaine in felde, or meddle wyth maters concernynge a common wealth', Erasmus had elaborated. From a commander of foot in the several Civil War campaigns, Hewson had progressed to staunch Council of State committee man, an ascent that included an honorary Oxford MA in 1649, the governorship of Dublin, significant monetary rewards, the office of MP for Guildford and a Cromwellian knighthood in 1657. Translated as the well-rewarded man of 'quality', a colonel entrusted with key strategy in the Irish campaign, Hewson's was the classic career soldier's rise: steep yet unstable. By 1659, with the publication of James Howell's *Proverbs*, we can see that the anti-Hewson campaign chimed in with the consolidation of proverbial lore: outside of their booths, meddlesome cobblers represented a threat to the state. While the proverb's simplistic logic seemed generally applicable to all trades, it was nevertheless shoe repairers that repeatedly illustrated its sense when proverbs were compiled, thereby reinstituting its 'ancient' pedigree and marking out cobbling as the trade *par excellence*.[13]

Hewson had precisely turned military careerist and meddled with matters concerning a commonwealth, and the winter barrage against authority's newest hate-figure also had an entirely predictable pre-history. News of Hewson's elevation to the lords was too much for Sir Richard Browne, for example. The royalist correspondent heaped heavy sarcasm on Cromwell's 'doughty knights', particularly 'Huson, the shoemaker', whose armorial device, 'his praeludiary weapons', would best be 'Sir Hugh's bones, and an awl'. When Hewson later took his place in the upper house Robert Rich, Earl of Warwick, refused to take his own seat. He 'would not be perswaded to sit with Col. Hewson and Col. Pride, whereof the one had been a shoomaker, and the other a drayman'. The pairing of Hewson and Pride also occurred in the Earl of Berkshire, Thomas Howard's denunciation of Cromwell's low-born lords as 'base mechanick fellowes'.[14] And a pamphlet from January 1660 reproduced this aristocratic disdain for social inferiority almost exactly:

> Who can but laugh to see the Cobling Clown
> (And dirty Drayman) in a Scarlet-Gown
> Lord it along? Sure 'tis a wondrous Fate
> To see such Monsters in a Robe of State.
>
> I laugh to see so many swaying swords
> Swear for zeal they hate a House of Lords:
> When Quaking Coblers but with half they eies,
> They hope thereby to rule and revelize.

Quaking (in 'Quaking Coblers'), the standard put-down of sectarian puritanism for the period, associated cobblers here with generalised religious sectarianism. But 'with half their eies' was an unmistakable reference to the unnamed Hewson and *Englands Murthering Monsters* was one of a multitude of similar denunciations, just as the same month's *Out-Cry* claimed that 'his head's of greatest note, / For it appears to each man's Eye to flote / In the Ayre: I guesse by's shaking's meant, / His threatning of the famous Parliament'.[15]

By August of 1660 a fourteen-page pamphlet calling itself *The Lamentation of the Safe Committee* could mesh together a number of the motifs of the shorter winter tracts in a relatively elaborate playlet form. Here, though the agonisingly static 'drama' provided for no more than the stylised walk-ons enacted by the familiarly contrite cardboard cut-outs of Fleetwood, Hewson and Desborough, the supposed meeting at '*Hangmans-Fayre*' deftly rehearsed themes played out in the earlier broadsheets. In similar vein to the *Bad Market* lamentation, Hewson once again wishes that he 'had took a Coblers stalle' during the turbulent winter of 1659–60; and if the killing of the 'prentice boy' had enabled Hewson to acquire what Fleetwood ironically terms his 'honour', then Hewson himself is quick to recognise that Fleetwood's own 'terrible shaking' is the 'affright' engendered by the king's return.[16] Absurdly heightened regret, bitter infighting, haunted consciences, shaking bodies, a gallows humour made literal with a focus on the scene of execution, a longing for a return to pre-revolutionary occupations, and a fleeting promise of escape to foreign lands. These had become the trademarks of the anti-Hewson literature.

With the Restoration backlash a confirmed fact later in the year, Roger L'Estrange declaimed against the fact that 'The meanest Redcott' in the army had tried to catch at 'the reynes of Government'. More pointedly the pamphlet writer 'W.C.' took the opportunity to denounce the 'cobblers' and others of low status who had risen to unprecedented heights before 1660.[17] Literally operating at street level, the broadsides and pamphlet tracts of the pre-Restoration winter anticipated the full bloom of royalist propaganda under professionals like L'Estrange. The single-sheet tracts were curiously powerful. Anonymous, pseudonymous, appearing under the unlikely imprimaturs of 'Charles Gustavus', 'Gustavus Adolphus' (earlier Swedish kings) and 'Theodurus Microcosmus', they projected a gleeful irreverence. Simultaneously aping and mocking the form of official proclamations with their HUE-AND-CRY titles, while sending up the meeting-house propriety of puritan ministers, they delighted in the manufacture of prison confessions, repentances, hysterical lamentations, dialogues and minimally-dramatic sketches. Broken and irregular typographies huddled under huge titles, crammed onto heavily-inked sheets. The broadsides subverted the norms of the publishing shops, with their lists of titles, bindings, book sizes and prices; broadsides were commonplace. They were the library of the street, appearing in taverns, in the satchels of ballad sellers and hawkers of chap books and in the print-stained hands of apprentices to the printing trade.

Their radically unregulated state made them irresistibly potent in their licence. In all senses *unbound*: unlicensed and beneath the scope of the Stationer's Register; and, as it were, *amorphous*: shabby shapeless single sheets, literally spineless, and to some metaphorically so in their anonymity – the broadsheets implicitly mocked the pseudo-'balance' of even partisan tracts, those tracts that retained a traditional disputation form of point-by-point proposition and rebuttal. The approach of the broadsheets was in all senses more irreverent. Theirs was the unashamed stance of the *monoculus*, single sheets with a one-eyed view out into the world. Hounding a figure like

Hewson was tailor-made to their form; the short eight-page pamphlets doing little more than repeat this exercise, matching their octavo form to a broadsheet content, folding, as it were, their theme three times to produce a neat but scurrilous booklet.

If broadsheets and short tracts suggested a discursive formation elusively beyond the full control of the printing industry, they also denoted urgency, literature quickly responsive to rapidly changing political situations. After the Restoration the abusive pamphlets aimed at Hewson and his party did, largely, fall away, their *raison d'être* having vanished with the final collapse of the republic. But of course Hewson, like Ludlow, had actually eluded the Restoration's reckoning, with what, for him, would have been its inevitable punishment and near-certain death. This can explain the vivid and macabre exaggeration of the Plymouth 'capture' pamphlet, published in September 1660, with its highly lurid picture of vengeful wish-fulfilment. Spinning its story out over several loosely dramatised pages, the capture publication moved much further and more centrally into the realm of fictive creativity than its normally abbreviated predecessors.

In John Tatham's early Restoration comedy *The Rump*, Hewson ('Huson') appeared in what was a farcical account of social-climbing centred on John Lambert's household. The plays ends with the predictable rout of its main characters, and the Committee of Safety interlopers utter their standard regrets over their disastrous departures from trade and profession. Hewson's character functions chiefly as a stooge to the other characters. His nonsensical parroting of the speeches of others causes even Cobbet to comment that 'Your Language cannot be Translated, Brother'. Unsurprisingly his most important scenes come during the play's dramatisation of the December City riot. '*Whoop Cobler, Whoop Cobler*' is the apprentices' harangue when Hewson and his 'Mirmydons' attempt to subdue the rioters. And the rioters themselves are interestingly portrayed. Brandishing clubs and in one case a pistol (or 'small Engine'), their street violence is part comedy and part vivid social threat. 'Come boyes, come, as long as this Club lasts fear nothing, it shall beat out Husons tother Eye', says Apprentice number one, whose role as foolish braggard ringleader mirrors Hewson's ragged command of his soldiers, soldiers as busy debating their future in the disintegrating political scene as they are in policing the disturbances.[18]

While *The Rump* worked with a comedy of political and domestic intriguing set in the recent past, it differed from the contemporary tracts in being an extensive retrospective reworking. At the other chronological remove in the Hewson literature is *Walk Knaves, walk*, a mock-sermon published as early as July 1659. This demonstrates that Hewson was more than a simple butt of jokes well before his troops had opened fire on teenagers in the City. Here the writer purported to take for his sermon's text 'Hewson [chapter] 1. [verse] 2'. In what it called 'Good Counsel against Cold Weather', this pamphlet lengthily lampooned Hewson through the conceit of drawing on Hewsonian expertise to advise on the purchase of good footwear. 'Now because the times are bad', it says, 'and the Winter draws near . . . therefore buy ye wax Boots'. 'Buy ye wax boots', it repeats over and over again, 'Bad times require good boots'. And if the 'Cavaliers prevail', then with the right footwear 'it may be possible for us, to passe over the Sea [to Amsterdam] in waxed boots'.

What scant biographical information exists on Hewson's fate during 1660 confirms the unwitting prescience of *Walk Knaves, walk*. Exempted from the Act of Indemnity, obscure exile in the Low Countries did indeed lie in store for the former colonel. Yet serendipity aside, *Walk Knaves, walk*'s blend of nicely-laced humour, garbled learning and tall-story exaggeration marks the beginning of the transformation of Hewson the colonel into Hewson the mock-heroic Cobbler-Warrior. Contemporaneously a cobbler was considered an artisanal translator, one whose labour transforms, changes, alters. *Walk Knaves, walk* performs its own translation, into skeletal mock-heroic. In its account of Alexander the Great's death ('without his Winter Boots, he took such an extreme Cold in his Feet . . . and within four days after dyed at Babylon'), and Achille's demise ('which accident had never happened to him . . . had he not two days before, pawned his boots to Ulisses'), the attack on Hewson embarked on mock-heroic comparisons deflating Hewson's then considerable status for the delight of any classically-educated royalist readership.[19] By the winter of 1659–60 the city apprentices – thought by Edmund Ludlow to be a hotbed for 'men of the King's party, and of desperate fortunes'[20] – would have found *Walk Knaves, walk* the more pertinent; and by the following winter the sketchy mock-heroic of this pamphlet had been succeeded by the full-scale treatment of *Don Juan Lamberto; or, a Comical History of the Late Times*, the most extraordinary of the Hewson texts.

Published, it seems, in the last months of 1660 under the supposed authorship of 'Montelion, Knight of the Oracle', and 'vending very fast' and prompting a Second Part in subsequent editions,[21] *Don Juan Lamberto* comprehensively recast royalist *bêtes noires*, creating a teeming political world of giants, dwarves, sorcerers, fair damsels, enchanted forests, and fierce dragons – a blatantly farcical faux-medieval romance. Embellishing its vivid characterisations with rough illustrations ('curious plates' in Anthony à Wood's view), Lambert became 'Lamberto' – the 'Golden Tulep', Vane 'the Knight of the mysterious Allegories', Fleetwood 'the contemptible Knight', Richard Cromwell 'the Meek Knight', Hesilrige 'Don Hazlerigo', Scot 'Scoto the Negromancer', Ludlow 'Knight of the Powdring-Tub', Peters the 'Arch-

Priest *Hugo* Petros', and Martin 'Sr. Harry *Martino*, the Knight of the *Turpentine Pill*'. Hewson was prominent amongst a group of giants: the 'Gyant Creed' or 'Credo', the 'Gyant Okey', 'Cobbetto', 'Hackero', 'Rodesbo', and 'the grim Gyant Desborough'. He was transposed as Husonio, or 'the Gyant *Husonius*, called also Polyphem', and it is clear that giants are this world's lower-status upstarts, overgrown and horribly inflated. Husonio is shown doing the dirty work on behalf of power-hungry ogres. He assists in Vane and Lambert's plan to replace Christian worship with the idolatry of eight deities (four female, four neuter, we are told) and to overrun the authority of the Committee of Safety, or here simply the 'forty tyrants'.[22] Historical events are frequently recognisable within the overblown paraphernalia of romance, and the riot of 5 December 1659 is recreated as a mock-heroic misadventure:

> . . . it hapn'd one morning that the weather being cold, the young men of the City of London went to play at Football in the streets; Which being related to the Councel of Safety, they were sore afraid, fearing lest the Christians having such a pretence to assemble together might rise against them; wherefore they sent command immediately to the Gyant *Husonius* to go into the City, for fear of the worst . . . The Christians hearing of his coming, shut the Gates of the City, thinking to keep him out; but the Gyant pusht them open, with as much ease, as if they had been made of Pastboard; and finding his own Shield defective, he made use of one of the Gates for his Buckler all that day . . . The Gyant who had but one Eye, and being jealous that the Christians intended to put out that too, was sorely enraged; wherefore in great fury he laid about him with his huge Elm among the multitude, killing six of the Christians at one blow; which the Christians beholding they incontinently fled away: That, when the Gyant *Husonius* saw, he thought it good time to satisfie his hunger, as well as his revenge. Thereupon he streightway went and took up one of the dead Christians, and so sitting down upon the ridge of a house in a moment, devoured him raw without either bread or salt . . .[23]

After the indignation of the early apprentices pamphlets, *Don Juan Lamberto*'s account of the Gyant Husonio eating dead apprentices raw without either bread or salt, was both revisionism and burlesque (simultaneously 'high' and 'low'), a relatively genial satire without the cutting urgency of the politically dispossessed.[24]

Rather, it exuded a confidence based on hindsight, countering, as it were, Hewson's historically committed one-eyedness with the double vision of victorious retrospection. Personal and national histories were rewritten as a bastardised medieval knock-about. For instance, John Lisle (the 'Seer *Lisle*')'s accession to power involves a devil's pact with 'a thing out of the

Earth like a great Seahorse, with long hair as black as Charcoal', a 'spirit', which 'walked and walked over him, and at length piss'd in his face'. After various abominations committed against the Christians on behalf of the 'Soldan', Lisle receives help from the 'Sable-browd Inchantress' called Mariana. Procuring a camel's hair wig and beard as a disguise, and sleeping with a damsel ('the fair Philotheta', 'the Soul of a Poulterers Wife'), Lisle finally effects his Restoration escape to Egypt.[25] In a chapter which shadows Lambert's winter-long military stand-off with Monck in the north of England, *Don Juan Lamberto* is at its most fantastical. Lambert's intention is to build a huge defensive wall in Northumbria to keep Monck from invading from the north, to keep his disgruntled soldiers occupied and possibly to discover riches in the soil. The wall is to be fifty coaches wide, to have an enormous brass gate fastened with bolts the size of church steeples and to be 'guarded by never-sleeping Dragons, which were to be sent for from *Lydia*, as also by Mastiff Dogs, which were to be kept hungry for that purpose'. Meanwhile, now facing defeat, Husonio, along with the other soldier-giants, fumes against the gods and resolves to pile together hills and mountains from which to mount an assault on the heavens. He is sent to the African Atlas range, walking on stilts with strides ten miles long. After the narrative calmly reports Husonio's slaughter of three million knights, he and Hackero decline conflict with 'Atlas' himself before succumbing to early morning humiliation at the hands of 'five Milkmaids' who turn out to be fierce 'Amazon Virgins'.[26]

This is Husonio's fate at the end of Part One, yet like Lisle he returns in Part Two, there to partake of increasingly bizarre post-Restoration adventures. In fact Hewson's historical escape overseas in 1660 explains Husonio's prominence: attempting to find a 'Den', enlisting 'an Astrologer and a Book of Mapps', packing his 'Club' and a 'Cloakbag', following the guidance of a 'certain great and puissant Flea . . . the *Spirit Pipantabor*' (conveniently secreted in his ear), engaging in epic contest with Neptune (and his wife), and, after many occurrences – which revolve increasingly around his Pantagruelian appetite and propensity for Gargantuan farting – building his castle in the air and eventually falling into 'the bottomless Pit'. By the end of Part Two Husonio has become a heavily worked burlesque figure. Yet for all of its apparent crudity *Don Juan Lamberto* operated on many levels. Employing the broad scatological humour of the broadsides and Rump ballads, investing its narrative with authorial irony ('it may seem incredible', it says of the giant stilts episode, 'but . . . we do not find it set down in the Apocrypha'), and scattering its self-consciously implausible events with piquant jests, it nevertheless reveals a startling political vision:

> they [Lambert and Vane's party] intended to have destroy'd all the old inhabitants of *Brittaine*, both Nobles, Gentry and Yeomen, by making

their own party Lords over them, who were all of a new race . . . and
such therefore whom no tyes of consanguinity had interest to make
them in the least mercifull.[27]

As pre-Swiftian satire *Don Juan Lamberto* clearly sought to undermine
whatever vestiges of honour still attached to the Cromwellian cause after the
Restoration. *Don Juan Lamberto* occurs in Paul Salzman's survey of English
prose, where he lists this 'anti-Romance', a precursor to *Hubidras*, as one of
only five surviving political allegorical romances of the period. Samuel
Butler's own description of satire – as 'a kinde of Knight errant that goe's
upon Adventures, to Relieve the Distressed Damsel Virtue, and Redeeme
Honor out of Inchanted Castles, And opprest Truth, and Reason out of the
Captivity of Gyants Magitions' – is entirely appropriate in this context,
realising something of *Don Juan Lamberto*'s redaction of chivalric romance
in the definition itself. Contemporary readers evidently saw the text as
nothing less than a 'Satire upon the Republicans', with Wood adjudging both
parts 'very witty and satyrical'. As Butler testified, satire's seventeenth-
century deployment of medieval romance was a serious matter, in *Don Juan
Lamberto*'s case exemplifying what Claude Rawson refers to as the 'demonic
gigantifications of English mock-heroic tradition'.[28] Pictured on the
frontispiece to later editions as a bearded, long-haired giant, wearing armour
but brandishing a huge cudgel and a shield adorned with the trefoil leaf
playing card (the ace of clubs), *Don Juan Lamberto*'s Husonio was a
throwback to the carnival giants of medieval guild processions and still
further to the folk-loric tradition of forest-inhabiting Wild Men, *homo
sylvarum*. Already irrevocably damned by his shoe-repairer origins, Hewson's
passage back to the creatures of guild processions and primitive myths flowed
through such linguistic circuits as 'Prentices and clubs', the traditional
rallying cry of the London apprentices.[29]

Hewson's reputation was not just sullied in *Don Juan Lamberto*. It was
flipped giddily upside down, coming to land, as it were, in a place where the
original sins of social transgression and of bearing arms against a king coded
the text's mock-heroic. From receiving ship-loads of ordnance to do the
inglorious work of the Commonwealth through the 'praeludiary weapons' of
career advancement, Hewson's swift fall from power in 1660 is taken further
by Don Juan Lamberto, a reduction itself condensed still further into the
primitive weaponry of the wild man club. Catapulted into a dimension of
mythic-scaled ineptitude, Hewson as Husonio is condemned to roam the
benighted forests of *Don Juan Lamberto*'s text precisely because his historical
escape had cheated his enemies of the revenge that had been due to them.

Pondering the proximity of the book's appearance and Charles's
'wonderful' restitution in 1660, Scott was moved to read mid-seventeenth-

century history as medieval romance. For with the king's return, he wrote, 'the whole fabric of government and all who protected and guarded it, seemed to dissolve at the very appearance of the king, as the walls of an enchanted castle with its fosses, drawbridges, turrets, and barbacan, vanish into air as soon as the destined knight blows his horn before its gates'.[30] The opposite of Scott's fanciful apprehension was true, of course, because Montelion's looking-glass world of romance was precisely one where regicides like Hewson were hunted down afresh. For those who really did slip the net *Don Juan Lamberto* was relentless, discursively scouring the world in a displaced hunt throughout a series of early 1660s reprints. In the riot scene the 'bassness of his proportion' identified the demonic giant Husonio with the monstrous Revolution itself, deformed and out of all proportion or degree, the seventeenth-century term for social status. 'What became of his family is unknown', wrote Noble, and for royalist propagandists of this stamp it was indeed fitting that Hewson's obscure origins should be matched by the murkiness of his demise. The last rumour of Hewson's whereabouts came with the arrest of a wandering tobacco seller in 1666 under suspicion of being Hewson, thus neatly reinforcing a sense of Hewson's lowly place.[31] After the king's entry in 1660, with the boot firmly on the other foot and many of those apprentices of the king's party acceding to positions of security and power, the frantic character polemics of the republic's final winter gave way at the Restoration to a more elaborate hybrid of satirical historical romance.

Notes

1   Samuel Pepys, [6 December 1659], letter to Edward Mountague, in R.G. Howarth (ed.), *Letters and the Second Diary of Samuel Pepys* (J.M. Dent & Sons, 1932), 14–15.

2   Steven R. Smith, 'Almost Revolutionaries: the London Apprentices during the Civil Wars', *Huntingdon Library Quarterly*, 42 (1978–9), 316–22. For contemporary examples, see [Anon.], *The Thankfull Acknowledgment and Congratulation of Divers well-affected Apprentices within the ward of Cripplegate without* (n.p., 6 May 1649), n.p. [Thomason Tracts (hereafter TT): 669.f.14.(30.)]; [Anon.], *The Resolved Apprentices, or A Reply of the well-affected Apprentices of the City of London, Inhabiting in the Ward of Bridge within* (n.p., 17 May 1649), n.p. [TT: 669.f.14.(32.)]. See also K.J. Lindley, 'Riot Prevention and Control in Early Stuart London', *Transactions of the Royal Historical Society*, 5th series, 33 (1983), 109–26.

3   [Anon.], *A Proclamation by the Committee of Safety* (Henry Hills and John Fields, 1 December 1659), n.p. [TT: 669.f.22.(13.)]. And see John Nicoll, *A Diary of Public Transactions And other Occurrences Chiefly in Scotland, From January 1650 to June 1667*, ed. D. Laing (Edinburgh: Bannatyne Club, 1836), 259; Sir Richard Baker, *A Chronicle of the Kings of England From the Time of the*

Roman's Government unto the Death of King James (G. Sawbridge & T. William, 1670), 697.

4 Thomas Rugge, 'Mercurius Politicus Redivivus Or A Collection of the most materiall Occurrences and Transactions in Publick Affaires Since Anno Dm:1659', 2 vols (n.d.), British Library Add MSS 10, 116–17, f. 36r–v; [Anon.], *The Monethly intelligencer*, (Thomas Johnson, January 1660), n.p. See Noel Malcolm, *The Origins of English Nonsense* (HarperCollins, 1997), 3–124, for the history of mock-heroic and related discourses.

5 [Anon.], *The most humble Petition and Address of divers young men, on the behalf of themselves and the Apprentices in and about this honourable City* (n.p., 5 December 1659), n.p. [TT: 669.f.22.(15.)]; Common Council Journal 41x, f.212r; Ralph Josselin [12 December 1659], in Alan Macfarlane (ed.), *The Diary of Ralph Josselin 1616–1683* (Oxford: Oxford University Press for the British Academy, 1976), 455; William Clarke [6 December 1659]), letter and newsletter in C.H. Firth (ed.), *The Clarke Papers: Selections from the Papers of William Clarke*, 4 vols (Camden Society, 1899–1901), new series, XLIX., LIV, IV, 1668; see letters (1657–60), calendared in F.J. Routledge (ed.), *Calendar of the Clarendon State Papers: Preserved in the Bodleian Library*, 5 vols (Oxford: Clarendon Press, 1872–82), IV, 477–84; [Anon.], *To the Right Honourable our Worthy and Grave Senetors the Lord Mayor, and Aldermen* (n.p., 13 December 1659), n.p. [TT: 669.f.22.(19.)]; [Anon], *The Apprentices Hue-and-Cry after their Petition* (n.p., 2 January 1660), n.p. [TT: 669.f.22.(49.)]; [Anon], *To His Excellency the Lord General Monck. The Unanimous Representation of the Apprentices and young men Inhabiting the City of London* (Thomas Ratcliffe, 2 February 1660), [TT: 669.f.23.(33.)].

6 Rugge, 'Mercurius Politicus Redivivus', f. 48v; Samuel Pepys (25 January 1660), in Robert Latham and William Matthews (eds), *The Diary of Samuel Pepys*, 11 vols (London: Bell & Hyman, 1970–83), I, 28; Thomas Riders, *The Black Remembrancer for the Year of our Lord God, 1660* (Tho. Johnson, 8 October 1660), [TT: 669.f.26.(18.)]; [Anon.] *Lucifers Life-Guard* (n.p., 28 May 1660), n.p. [TT: 669.f.25.(34.)]. See Jonathan Sawday, 'Rewriting a Revolution: History, Symbol and Text in the Restoration', *Seventeenth Century*, 7 (1992), 171–99.

7 [Anon.], *The Out-Cry of the London Prentices for Justice to be Executed upon John Lord Hewson* ('Gustavus Adolphus', 16 January 1660), [TT: E.1013.(12.)], 3, 6, 3, 4, 78; Rugge, 'Mercurius Politicus Redivivus', f.48v. For the purges of January onwards, see Ronald Hutton, *The Restoration: A Political and Religious History of England and Wales 1658–1667* (Oxford: Clarendon Press, 1985), 85–118; *Dictionary of National Biography* [hereafter *DNB*], s.v., John Lambert.

8 [Anon.], *The Black Book Opened, or Traytors Arraigned and Condemned by their own Confession* ('Theodorus Microcosmus', 15 March 1660), [TT: 669.f.24.(12.)]; [Anon.], *A Charge of High-Treason Prepared by the London-Apprentices, against Col. Hewson; And the strange Apparitions that appeared unto him, immediately after his being taken near Plymouth in Cornwal; With his Speech and Confession to the Vision* ('C. Gustavus', 24 September 1660), [TT: E.1045.(9.)], t.p., pp. 2–4.

9 *Black Book Opened*; [Anon.], *The Hang-Mans Last Will and Testament* ('Charls Gustavus', 17 January 1660), [TT: 669.f.22.(72.)]. Anthony à Wood, quoted in *DNB*, s.v. John Hewson; Alexander Young, *Chronicles of the First Planters of the First Colony of Massachusetts Bay* (Boston: Charles C. Little and James Brown,

1846), 26 February 1628. And see Richard L. Greaves and Robert Zaller (eds), *Biographical Dictionary of British Radicals in the Seventeenth Century*, 3 vols (Brighton: Harvester, 1982–84), II, 82–2.

10   *Black Book Opened*; [Anon.], *The Gang or the Nine Worthies Gang or the Nine Worthies and Champions, Lambert, &c.* ('Charls Gustavus', 17 January 1660), [TT: 669.f.22.(71.)]; *A Charge Of High-Treason*, 3.

11   [Anon.], *The Lamentation of a Bad Market: or, Knaves and Fools foully foyled, and fallen into a pit of their own digging* ('Printed for the Charge of John Lambert, Charles Fleetwood, Arthur Hesilrig and — Hewson the Cobler, and are to be distributed to the fainting Brethren', 21 March 1660), [TT: E.1017.(26.)], 8, 6, 4–5.

12   [Anon.], *The Apology of Robert Tichborn and John Ireton* ('Printed for every body but the light-heel'd Apprentices and headstrong Masters of this wincing City of London', 2 March 1660), n.p. [TT: E.1017.(3.)], t.p.; [Anon.], *Bretheren in Iniquity: or a Beardless Pair: Held forth in a Dialogue Betwixt Titchburn and Ireton, Prisoners of the Tower of London* (Daniel Webb, 30 April 1660), n.p. [TT: E.1021.(16.)].

13   *The Out-Cry*, 8 (misprinted as 7). On the history of the proverb, see M.P. Tilley, *A Dictionary of the Proverbs in England in the Sixteenth and Seventeenth Centuries* (Ann Arbor: University of Michigan Press, 1966), 107: C479; *The Oxford Dictionary of English Proverbs*, 3rd edn (Oxford: Clarendon Press, 1970), 130; Ivor H. Evans, *Brewer's Dictionary of Phrase and Fable*, rev. edn (Cassell, 1981), 250; James Howell, *Proverbs, or, Old Sayed Sawes & Adages, in English (or the Saxon Toung) Italian, French, and Spanish whereunto the British, for their great Antiquity, and weight are added* (1659 [1660]), 12, in Howell's, *Lexicon Tetraglotton, an English-French-Italian-Spanish Dictionary*, 3 vols. (J.G., 1660). See also [Anon.], *The Entertaining History of the King and Cobler* (Nottingham: 'Printed for the Walking Stationers', 1796). For the shoemaker's trade, from prosperous shoemaster to near-destitute out-working journeyman, see Peter Linebaugh, *The London Hanged: Crime and Civil Society in the Eighteenth Century* (Harmondsworth: Penguin; 1993), 230–5. On Hewson's career, see Ian Gentles, *The New Model Army: In England, Ireland and Scotland, 1645–1653* (Oxford: Blackwell, 1994), especially, 70, 219, 249, 299, 310, 348; A.S.P. Woodhouse (ed.), *Puritanism and Liberty: Being the Army debates (1647–49) from the Clarke Manuscripts* (London: J.M. Dent & Sons, 1986), 455, 467; Samuel R. Gardiner, *History of the Great Civil War 1642–1649*, 4 vols (New York: AMS Press, 1965), IV, 24; *Calendar of State Papers, Domestic*, 1650; 131, 575 [hereafter *CSPD*]; *CSPD*, 1653–54, passim; *CSPD*, 1654, 445, 504; *CSPD*, 1656–57, 128–9; *CSPD*, 1659–60, 13.

14   Sir Richard Browne's letter (25 December 1657), extracted in *CSPD*, 1657–58, 232; Edmund Ludlow, (1659) in C.H. Firth (ed.), *The Memoirs of Edmund Ludlow Lieutenant-General of the Horse in the Army of the Commonwealth of England 1625–1672*, 2 vols. (Oxford: Clarendon Press, 1894), II, 32; Bulstrode Whitelock (7 June 1660), in Ruth Spalding (ed.), *The Diary of Bulstrode Whitelocke 1605–1675* (Oxford: Oxford University Press, 1990).

15   [Anon.], *Englands Murthering Monsters set out in their Colours, in a Dialogue between Democritus and Heraclitus* (n.p., 5 January 1660), n.p. [TT: 669.f.22.(54.)], stanzas 8, 18: pamphlet signed 'G.P.'; *The Out-Cry*, 78.

16   [Anon.], *The Lamentation of the Safe Committee. Or, Fleetwood's Teares, Hewson's Last, Desborough's cart, Met together at Hangmans-Fayre* (William Gilbertson, 28 August 1660), [TT: E.1844.(2.)], t.p., 2, 8.

17   Quoted in Carolyn A. Edie, 'The Popular Idea of Monarchy on the Eve of the Stuart Revolution', *Huntingdon Library Quarterly*, 39 (1975–6), 358, 362 n. 55.

18   John Tatham, *The Rump: or the Mirrour of The late Times. A New Comedy* (W. Godbid, 1661), 2nd edn; quotes: 11 (I, i), 40–1 and passim (III, i), 57 (V, i). In another work Hewson himself will also be depicted flourishing a club: see below.

19   [Anon.], *Walk Knaves, Walk, a Discourse Intended to have been spoken at Court And now publish'd for the satisfaction of all those that have participated of the sweetness of publike Employments* (n.p., 1 August 1659), [TT: E.993.(14.)], t.p., 1, 9, 11, 16–17. It purports to be by 'Hodge Turbervil', 'Chaplain to the late LORD HEWSON'. Neither C.H. Firth's *DNB* article or T. Lui's in *Greaves and Zaller's Biographical Dictionary* (1982–84) are able to establish the circumstances of Hewson's exile or death (evidently rumoured to have been in 1662).

20   Ludlow, *Memoirs*, 177.

21   Anthony à Wood, quoted in Walter Scott (ed.), *A Collection of Scarce and Valuable Tracts*, 13 vols (Edinburgh: T. Cadell and W. Davies, 1809–15), 2nd edn, VII, 104–57, footnote on p. 105 [hereafter *Somers Tracts*]. 'Montelion, Knight of the Oracle', *Don Juan Lamberto; Or, a Comical History of the Late Times* appears in the Stationer's Register for 8 September 1660, but the Transcript questions whether this should be a December entry: [G.E. Briscoe Eyre,] *A Transcript of the Registers of the Worshipful Company of Stationers: From 1640–1708 AD.*, 3 vols (printed privately, 1913), III, 284. The earlier date is the likelier, however, as Thomason's copy is dated 15 November 1660.

22   *Don Juan Lamberto*, Pt. 1, A1r, and ch. I (Lambert); A3v and ch. III (Vane); ch. IX (Fleetwood, Cromwell); ch. XIII (Hesilrige, Scot); Pt. 2, L3r (Ludlow); Pt. 2, M4r (Peter); Pt. 2, O4v (Martin); Pt. 1, ch. XIV [wrongly given as IX] (Creed); Pt. 1, ch. IX (Desborough); Pt. 1, D4r (Hewson). Woodcuts did not appear until the second and subsequent editions; see *Catalogue of Prints and Drawings in the British Museum: Political and Personal Satires*, I (Chiswick Press, 1870), 511–14 (no. 920). Wood despaired of the fact that their popularity caused booksellers to tear the illustrations out of many editions of the book: as quoted in Scott's *Somers Tracts*, 105.

23   *Don Juan Lamberto*, Pt. 1, F1vF2r [last wrongly numbered H2].

24   *The Out-Cry*, 4. For a good example of a Republican satire sensing political reversal, see: [Marchamont Nedham], *Newes from Brussells in a Letter from a Neer Attendant on his Majesties Person. To a Person of Honour here* (n.p., 10 March 1660), n.p. [TT: E.1017.(38.)].

25   *Don Juan Lamberto*, Pt. 2, chs. III; *Prints and Drawings*, 520–21.

26   Hutton, *The Restoration: A Political and Religious History of England and Wales 1658–1667*, 73–84; *Don Juan Lamberto*, Pt. 1, F3vF4r; Pt. 1, G1vG2v.

27   *Don Juan Lamberto*, Pt. 2, ch. III, XI; Pt. 1, G1v; Pt. 1, E2v.

28   Paul Salzman, *English Prose Fiction 1558–1700: A Critical History* (Oxford: Clarendon, 1985), 155–6, 270–82; Butler quoted in Earl Miner, 'The Restoration: age of faith, age of satire', in *Poetry and Drama 1570–1700: Essays in Honour of Harold F. Brooks*, ed. Antony Coleman and Antony Hammond (Methuen, 1981), 92. A manuscript insert (a bookseller's?) in the British Library's Grenville Collection copy (Grenville 4132: a 1661 second edition) reads: 'Don Juan

124   Subversion and Scurrility

Lamberto. 2 parts. 4o. 1661. the second part of this Satire upon the Republicans is seldom to be found added to the first. This Copy has both Parts.' Wood, *Athenae Oxonienses*, II, 826; Claude Rawson, *Satire and Sentiment 1660–1830* (Cambridge: Cambridge University Press, 1994), 15.

29   *Prints and Drawings*, 519 (no. 931); cf. nos 933–5, 521–2, and woodcuts in *Don Juan Lamberto*, Pt. 2, K2v and K3v. On wild men, see for instance, Francois Laroque, *Shakespeare's festive world: Elizabethan seasonal entertainment and the professional stage*, trans. Janet Lloyd (Cambridge: Cambridge University Press, 1991), 10–11, 29–45 and illustration 10.2. A 'carnival-type giant, with illuminated eyes' was typical of the provincial and London corporations' entertainments (ibid., n. 242, 3462); see the references to guilds paying for giants in Chester, for example: Lawrence M. Clopper (ed.), *Records of Early English Drama: Chester* (Manchester: Manchester University Press, 1979). For 'Prentices and clubs', see *Oxford English Dictionary*, s.v. Club.

30   Scott, *Somers Tracts*, VII, 104, editorial commentary. An examination of the John Rylands Library copy (22301) of *Don Juan Lamberto* will readily reveal the eager, annotating approach of Scott. Plentiful annotations are pasted in on torn pieces of paper. These clearly form the basis to his editorial remarks in *Somers Tracts*.

31   Mark Noble, Rector of Barming, *The Lives of the English Regicides*, 2 vols (London: J. Stockdale, 1798), 354; 354; DNB; CSPD, 1665–6, 321.

8
Innuendo and inheritance: strategies of scurrility in medieval and Renaissance Venice

Alexander Cowan

Honour and shame lie at the heart of Mediterranean value systems.[1] The individual's position in society depends upon reputation, which in turn depends upon the extent to which they are perceived by those around them to conform to a complex of social ideals. This essay considers the criteria according to which honour could be established or undermined in early modern Venice by investigating the use of calumny, the deliberate attempt through the use of language to blacken someone's reputation in order to gain personal advantage. Venice would appear to have been an ideal setting for such behaviour. Special letter boxes in the form of a lion's mouth were placed at key points in the city as repositories for anonymous letters identifying people as heretics, blasphemers or enemies of the state. We know from the records of the Venetian Council of Ten that these denunciations were followed up with great care, even if most of them were proved to be exaggerations of unusual behaviour, or to be the product of local disputes and enmities.[2] Early modern Venice was an authoritarian state, but it proved to have been far more flexible and understanding than Romantic novelists of the nineteenth century or even English dramatists of the seventeenth century would have us believe.[3]

This essay is less concerned with the general atmosphere of suspicion and anonymity than with calumnies of a more open kind. The context is reasonably straightforward, although the ramifications are less so. Early modern Venetian society was divided into three groups, the *nobili*, *cittadini* and *popolani*. This had been the case since at least the thirteenth century, and it was enshrined in a long series of laws which ensured that political power and high social status remained the prerogative of the *nobili* – patrician families, whose legitimate male members had the sole right to sit on the city's

Great Council (the *Maggior Consiglio*), from whom all magistrates were elected.[4] The *cittadini*, representing a further 2 per cent of Venetian society, were honoured with a range of privileges, which, once acquired opened up the possibilities of international trade, membership of the professions, and, for a select few, the opportunity to serve in the Venetian civil service.[5] The *popolani*, as their name suggests, were the 96 per cent of the population who had no privileges and were excluded from the worlds of government, administration, the professions, and international trade. They were the craftsmen, the print-workers, the arsenal workers, sailors and shopkeepers, their wives and daughters.[6]

These discussions of attempts to damage reputations in early modern Venice are based on a study of the records known as the *Prove di Nobiltà*, official investigations into claims by Venetians that they had the right to patrician status, either by birth, or, in the case of women, by marriage.[7] Since every legitimate son of a Venetian patrician was entitled to take his place as a member of the *Maggior Consiglio*, it was essential to ensure that no mistakes were made which might allow in men of base birth.

One might ask why it should have been necessary to make sure that the credentials of young patricians entering the *Maggior Consiglio* were entirely sound. The answer lies only partly in the Venetian patriciate's insistence on its own purity as a hereditary elite. By the fifteenth century at least, the patriciate was now too large for men asking to join the *Maggior Consiglio* when they came of age to be accepted on the grounds that they were known to most other patricians. In the early sixteenth century there were as many as 2,500 male patricians over the age of twenty-five sharing relatively few family names and relatively few first names and patronymics.[8] To make matters worse, dynasties of patrician families long resident on the Venetian islands of Crete or Cyprus had developed. Any one of their legitimate male descendants could come to Venice, a city where he was unknown to all but a few, and claim a seat on the *Maggior Consiglio*.[9]

Even the possession of a family name identical to those borne with such pride by members of the patriciate might not be all that it implied. Some patricians bore illegitimate children but recognised them as their own sons. Others married below them, but once again passed on their family names to sons who did not meet the criteria of patrician status. The risk of confusion in circumstances such as these magnified fears of social contamination among the elite, fears which became ever stronger during the sixteenth and seventeenth centuries as patricians conformed more and more closely to an aristocratic lifestyle.[10] Disdain for men who soiled their hands while earning a living indeed became a mark of most European aristocracies at the time.[11]

The responsibilities of the Venetian *Avogaria di Comun*, the magistracy entrusted with safeguarding the purity of the patriciate consequently expanded in proportion to the social anxieties of the elite. What began as a fairly straightforward solution to the problem of identification among aspirant members of the *Maggior Consiglio*, the recording of all baptisms, marriages and deaths of the legitimate male sons of patricians in the Golden Book, became an enormous edifice of reports and investigations. Marriages and births outside the city of Venice had to be reported to the *Avogaria* as soon as possible, accompanied by supporting evidence. A copy of every patrician marriage contract drawn up by a notary in Venice had to be deposited with the *Avogaria di Comun* as soon as it had been signed. This fulfilled the double function of providing a legal record of a betrothal involving two patrician families and of ensuring that sumptuary legislation – introduced to limit the size of dowries – was adhered to.

The *Avogaria di Comun* was particularly concerned with the possibility that aspirant male patricians might have been born of a marriage in which the partners were of unequal social status. A base-born woman could not be allowed to take on patrician status simply because she had married a patrician. If she did so, it was believed that she would introduce her baseness into the patriciate through her sons. A whole series of laws was passed regulating marriages between male patricians and non-patrician women. The frequency with which the subject arose for consideration clearly reflects the growth of out-marriages among the patriciate.[12] Laws were passed in 1422, 1526, 1533 and 1550, but the most detailed legislation of all was brought before the Venetian Senate in June, 1589. Following wilful deception on the part of patricians and their partners, this new act now stated that

> all . . . marriages with women who are not of legitimate marriage, born of Nobles as above or of another status, can not be accepted in future by the simple office of the Avogaria, but when such a case arises, the *Avogadori di Comun*, under oath of the Sacrament, apart from evidence to be brought by the interested parties, should establish an inquisitorial investigation, using all possible accuracy and all possible study to come to an understanding of the status of the lady and of her father and mother, so that not only the women included in the laws of 1422 and 1533 shall be excluded but also those who were born of fathers and grandfathers who have carried out arte meccanica et manuale, or are of another status similar to this.[13]

It is easy to see what opportunities there must have been for individual witnesses to destroy the reputations of families with aspirations to ally themselves by marriage with members of the Venetian patriciate. On the other hand, as far as can be seen from an analysis of numerous seventeenth-century cases, these opportunities were rarely taken up. Only a small minority of applications were turned down by the *Avogadori*, and this usually took place after exhaustive enquiries which were notable for the restraint of many witnesses who held back what they knew for reasons of their own, rather than speaking of matters which might damage those under investigation. Allegations of doubtful sexual morality were made from time to time, but much of this fell into the category of gossip repeated among servants rather than of deliberate attempts to blacken the reputation of an applicant family.[14]

The two exceptions to this pattern examined in this essay are of particular interest because the use of scurrility or calumny by close relatives in each case illustrates on the one hand something of the value systems among the upper levels of Venetian society, and on the other the powerful motives which drove men to try to prevent others from rising up in society. They also demonstrate the way in which factual information which was widely known could be given a negative twist with the greatest of ease.

The first case relates to Cecilia Torre di Mattio, a widow, and the daughter of a Venetian notary, whose petition to be allowed to marry a Venetian patrician was presented to the *Avogadori di Comun* in 1663.[15] The second case relates to a petition in favour of patrician status for a boy born of a marriage between a patrician and a non-patrician woman which had not been officially recognised by the *Avogadori*.[16] Marina Crivelli, the widow of the patrician Zuanne Domenico Cicogna, came forward in 1648 to advance the claim of Francesco, their eleven-year old son, to be allowed to take up his seat in the *Maggior Consiglio* when he reached the age of majority at twenty-five.[17] The responses of those around them to each petition are revealing.

There was little about Cecilia Torre's petition to distinguish it from those of dozens of other women in the seventeenth century, who hoped to convince the *Avogadori di Comun* that they and their mothers had lived an honest and modest life, free from all taint of infamy (all stock phrases echoing the criteria laid down by legislation), and that her father and paternal grandfather were men of high status, free from any association with the vile and mechanical arts. As the first witness to speak on her behalf, the Franciscan Bonaventura Zambelli, stated :

> I know Cecilia. Her paternal grandfather was a silk merchant. I have known her father for forty years because his father brought him to our monastery in his youngest years, and later he went away and applied himself to legal work at the Palazzo. His father spent hours in the Church and the monastery.[18]

The inferences are clear: the Torre family had shown two generations of devotion to the Church. The son of a merchant, whose social status was relatively highly valued in Venice, had been educated as a notary, an occupation with an even greater social *éclat*.[19] Another witness, a lawyer, noted that Mattio Torre 'lived well and honourably'.[20] He had placed Cecilia in the convent, to be educated by the nuns.[21] Another daughter had married a respected merchant.

The regular procession of character witnesses attesting to the validity of individual points in Cecilia's petition was then interrupted by her sister-in-law Giulia Gattamarin, the widow of Domenico Pizzati. She was clearly unhappy about the consequences if Cecilia were given permission to marry a patrician and bear his sons.

> This woman thinks that by marrying into a patrician family, she will be supported by relatives of the highest status who will gain advantage for her own pretensions by marrying the Illustrious Nicolo Marin Magno. This marriage should be censured according to those laws which wish to maintain the blood of Nobles free from contamination . . . it would be simple for the said Cecilia with the support of such kin to violate the power of those laws to universal scandal and with the most damaging precedents.[22]

Giulia's strategy was quite straightforward. She appeared to be playing the game by all the rules. By emphasising her concern for the purity of the blood of the patriciate as enshrined in the law, as a non-patrician she demonstrated her loyalty to the Republic and to the concerns of its ruling families. What is more, by drawing the magistrates' attention to the social dangers of allowing non-patrician families to derive personal advantage from their new connections with the patriciate, she articulated some of the unspoken anxieties among members of the Venetian nobility about the implications of any of their number becoming associated with those who were their social inferiors.[23]

The *coup de grâce*, however, came in Giulia's claim that Mattio Torre, Cecilia's father, was not the respectable notary which he had claimed to be. Instead, she declared, Mattio was the illegitimate son of one Bambara, who worked at the Ridotto di San Moise, a gambling house not far from St Mark's, and in other gambling houses, selling playing cards, snuffing out candles, and doing other jobs. Mattio, until he was of an age to serve, went to the Piazza San Marco and carried out jobs of the lowest kind. He subsequently worked as a servant in the house of one Franceschi, Notary at the anti-blasphemy magistracy, who taught him to read and write. Mattio then built the foundations of his later good fortune by marrying a certain Greghetta, a wealthy prostitute.[24]

It is almost as if Giulia had sat down to list every calumny which could possibly damage Mattio's reputation. It is not easy to see what else could have been included. As the bastard son of Bambara, Mattio would have been the product of an unorthodox sexual liaison. As the husband and eventual heir of a prostitute,[25] he was guilty of sexual impropriety himself. Both Bambara and Mattio had worked in jobs which excluded them from consideration as 'civil and honourable men', both essential criteria for the family of a woman permitted to bear patrician sons. Mattio, indeed, was guilty of having hidden his origins when joining the ranks of the notaries, a post usually reserved for *cittadini*, who were only permitted to attain this status after their reputation had been investigated by the *Avogaria di Comun*.[26] He had been a servant, and worse.

Cecilia's petition was eventually approved. Long and careful questioning of many witnesses had demonstrated that Giulia's claims were calumny, not disinterested evidence, but it is easy to see how close she was to factual accuracy, and how shrewd was her strategy. Several witnesses assured the magistrates that Mattio was legitimate. One of them was Father Donà Bontempio, second priest of the parish of San Geremia, who confirmed that both Mattio and his father had been born in his parish.[27] An illegitimate birth would have been known to the parish clergy. Very little passed them by. On the other hand, the ranks of the notaries and other government officials were sprinkled with the illegitimate sons of the Venetian nobility, who were only too pleased to publicise this connection, even if this meant revealing that their parents had not been married.[28] Giulia's revelation of Mattio's illegitimacy was, of course, intended to send rather different signals.

Mattio Torre's father was certainly called Bambara. In a society in which lineage counted for a great deal, it was easy to suggest that when father and son did not share the same surname, there must have been a whiff of scandal. On the other hand, it was not unknown for men to take on other names. As Zuanne Sfuogher, the jeweller explained, 'Mattio was the son of a man called Bambara or Torre. His family is supposed to have been originally called Bambara, but Mattio's father called himself Torre.' Other witnesses knew him as Bambara. Everyone, though, spoke well of him.[29] He was a man without an occupation, whose only connection with gambling houses was that he went there to gamble. The magistrates were told by a patrician witness that Bambara could not have been to the Ridotto di San Moise, because at the time it had not yet opened. (It opened in 1638.) On the other hand, he was a frequent visitor to the Ridotto di San Marcuola (now the site of Venice's winter casino).[30] Under government supervision, these gambling houses were frequently visited by members of the Venetian nobility.[31] They would indeed have seen men selling playing cards, snuffing candles and carrying out other menial tasks. Why, then should they not have believed that Bambara, long since dead, had been among them?

It was also true that Mattio Torre married twice, latterly to Cecilia's mother, and that his first wife had been called Greghetta. She remains something of an enigma. This was almost certainly not her real name, but a nickname alluding to her Greek origins. As Francesco Erizzo, a member of the secular clergy, stated, 'Mattio Torre's first wife was one whom they called "La Greghetta", who may have been a signora.' Another witness could not positively identify her social status, but knew that she had 'quite a lot of money'.[32]

There is no proof that la Greghetta was a prostitute. What is important in the context of Giulia's calumny, though, is Greghetta's description as una *meretrice*. Venetian society made a distinction between *meretrici* (ordinary prostitutes) and *cortegiane* (courtesans).[33] There is no legal definition of the courtesan, but Venetian law as clear about which women were considered as prostitutes. In a law of 1542, they stated that

> Prostitutes are to be considered those women who, while unmarried, have commerce and intercourse with one or more men. Furthermore, those married women are to be considered as prostitutes who do not live under one roof with their husbands, but live apart from them and have intercourse with one or more men.[34]

The accusation that Mattio had married a prostitute and benefited as her heir effectively made him a pimp at one remove. Such behaviour only emphasised the case that a notary who was the illegitimate son of a gambling house employee and had been a servant did not belong to those whose social reputation permitted them and their descendants to be associated with the Venetian elite.

Giulia's strategy failed. Before we consider why she undertook to blacken the reputation of Mattio Torre in the first place, it would be useful to examine a second attempt at calumny associated with patrician status. Marina Crivelli had come to the notice of the magistrates of the *Avogaria di Comun* in 1648, when she petitioned for the right of her son, Francesco, to be listed as a member of the patriciate, with the right to sit in the Great Council when he came of age. She had married the nobleman Zuanne Domenico Cicogna at the age of thirty-four in 1634. Just like Mattio Torre, her father, Zuanne Francesco Crivelli, was a notary, as was his father before him.[35] Marina's case differs from that of Cecilia Torre in the sense that while Cecilia was asking for patrician status to be granted to her upon marriage to a noblemen so that she could bear sons who had the right to sit in the Great Council, Marina had already married and was now the widow of a patrician. When she had married Cicogna, she had not applied to have patrician status. It was not uncommon for Venetian patricians to marry with the blessing of the Church but without the blessing of the state, and often of their own families, in the knowledge that their sons would not be counted as patricians.[36] In Marina's case, changing circumstances led her to ask for the retrospective registration of her son's birth by the *Avogaria di Comun*. Once again, these requests were not uncommon, and many were granted patrician status retrospectively.[37]

As in the case of Cecilia Torre, the scurrilous statement which was introduced into the case in an attempt to block the petition, came from a close relative, the nobleman Francesco Cicogna, Marina's brother-in-law. He explained that his brother Zuanne Domenego had married twice. His first wife, a patrician, had borne him a son, Nicolo, who was registered in the Golden Book as a patrician. After her death, Zuanne Domenego had married Marina Crivelli, and their son Francesco was born in 1637. Seven years later, Zuanne Domenego died of dysentery at the age of sixty-three, leaving two sons, one with patrician status, and one without. The real problem arose when Nicolo, the patrician son, also died, and a petition was made to recognise his half-brother as a patrician.[38]

Like Cecilia Torre's sister-in-law, Cicogna turned to calumny to reinforce his case that his nephew Francesco had no right to patrician status. He asserted that Marina Crivelli was illegitimate, that when her parents Francesco Crivelli and Bianca Osello had published their marriage banns in the church of San Marcilian, the marriage had been opposed and that it had been stopped on the orders of the Church. The marriage did not take place, and the couple had lived in covert concubinage.[39] There was no record of the marriage in either the registers of San Marcilian, where the banns had been published, nor in the church in Villa Zonigo.

To the social crime of illegitimacy was added one which was intended to be even more damning. Supposing Crivelli and Bianca Osello had somehow married in secret, no patrician magistrate would respect a petition on behalf of a boy whose maternal grandmother had been a peasant of the lowest condition. Bianca Osello's sister had married a peasant named Marco Patron. Her brother, Beltrame, was a journeyman furrier, a man who worked with his hands. With such close family associations, there could be no doubt that Bianca Osello was a peasant.[40]

Once again, the strategy of scurrility mixed factual accuracy with innuendo. It was not difficult when so many people below the elite in Venetian society were of ambiguous status. An inhabitant of Villa Zonigo, Santo Santello, confirmed that he knew about Bianca Osello. She was the wife of Francesco Crivelli. She belonged to 'Cha Osello'. In other words she belonged to a family whose identity was so clear that it could be expressed in collective terms, a collectivity that was both linear and lateral. Venetian patrician families were referred to as Ca' Grimani, or Ca' Contarini. They had genealogies to prove it. So did the Oselli. Marina Crivelli submitted an Osello family tree in evidence which spanned five generations. Santo Santello had heard from his father that Bianca was of low social condition but he could not say if she were peasant or citizen. Other witnesses had heard that the Oselli were Venetian citizens, and that Bianca's father was rich and lived from his properties. Her marriage contract dated August 1594 does not value her dowry. On the other hand it included a house and a shop in Venice close to the Rialto. Significantly, this property had been placed under mortmain (*fideicommissum*) and was due to pass to her from her childless brothers, Alvise and Beltrame.[41] Only the wealthy went to the trouble of protecting their property by mortmain.[42] She may have been a wealthy peasant, but there was enough about her wealth and the family into which she married, for the accusation of low birth to be taken with a pinch of salt. It may even have been that the *Avogadori* were prepared to ignore this socially damaging circumstance in order to ensure that the Cicogna family line remained in existence. But that thought opens up a very large can of worms indeed.

Francesco Cicogna's calumny failed. Four years after the initial petition was submitted to the *Avogaria di Comun*, Marina Crivelli's marriage was registered, and her son was given patrician status. With hindsight, one wonders why either Francesco Cicogna or Giulia Gattamarin should have placed their own reputations on the line by attempting to subvert the reputation of the families who were petitioning for patrician status. The answer is fairly straightforward. While each of them claimed to be acting in the interests of the purity of the elite by demonstrating the moral and social threats posed by the applicants and their families, their prime objective was to protect their family patrimony, something with which the magistrates could be expected to sympathise.

Francesco Cicogna was very clear about this. The death of his nephew Nicolo had enabled him to unite the two halves of an inheritance first transmitted by his grandfather, Girolamo Cicogna in a will dated 1565. The property had been subjected to the twin requirements that it should a) be placed under mortmain, and b) it could only be inherited by the donor's legitimate male descendants if they were members of the Great Council. The property had been divided between Francesco and his brother Zuanne Domenego. The latter passed his share to his patrician son Nicolo. On Nicolo's death, Francesco would normally have inherited it from his nephew, since his other nephew was not a member of the Great Council.[43] Marina Crivelli's petition consequently represented as much of a material threat to Francesco Cicogna, as a moral one. The loss of one half of the patrimony to his nephew meant a loss of income, a loss of face, and above all the loss of the potential to make effective marriage alliances or to fund a political career of some importance.

Giulia Gattamarin's opposition to Cecilia Torre might be described as a fight between two widows. We do not know anything about Giulia's material condition, nor if she had any children. What we do know is that Cecilia had inherited the property of her first husband, Zuanne Gattamarin, and that her proposed marriage to Nicolo Marin Magno would transfer this property to her new husband. It is very probable that Giulia did have sons, who stood to inherit a considerable sum from Cecilia if she remained unmarried and therefore without children of her own. Giulia was driven above all by the thought that as patricians, the Magno family were both in an influential position to prevent the Gattamarin patrimony from passing to his sister, and were motivated by strong feelings of self-interest. By bringing her late husband's property into a new marriage, Cecilia offered the Magno family renewed possibilities of gaining prestige within the patriciate.

But where do these two cases really leave us? By engaging in calumny, Giulia Gattamarin and Francesco Cicogna help us to understand the significance of patrician status as a prize to be won, both for the general social privileges which it offered to those who were associated with it, and the very specific prizes to be won, such as the property under mortmain which could only be passed on to a legitimate male descendant of a patrician family, or the support of a powerful family in a bitter family feud. It is important to remember that all magistrates in Venice and its empire were drawn exclusively from the ranks of the patriciate, and that they were open to persuasion from friends and quite distant relatives with whom they shared some kind of affinity.

The kind of calumny used, however, also tells us something about what divided and what united Venetian society. The rigid statutory barriers between the elite and the rest of society were reinforced by the rhetoric of honour which was designed to ensure that only those men and women who shared its characteristics could be permitted to become associated with the patriciate. Smearing potential members with the stigma of illegitimate birth, or sexual immorality, servile birth or menial occupations was a way of reinforcing these barriers and playing on the elite's collective fears. On the other hand, they were particularly potent forms of scare-mongering not because they referred to a world unknown to the elite, but because they belonged to a world which was all too familiar to patricians. Everyone had servants. Many engaged in short-term or long-term illicit sexual liaisons. Far from living apart from the rest of Venetian society, members of the elite were in contact with it all the time and consequently understood its complexities and ambiguities, even though they preferred to explain everything in terms of black and white. Perhaps this is the answer to the riddle of why individuals were ready to lie and twist facts in the hope of being believed, and why, in the end, their strategies nearly worked.

Notes

1   J.G. Peristiany 'Introduction', in Peristiany (ed.), *Honour and Shame* (London: Weidenfeld and Nicholson, 1965) 9–18.

2   P. Preto, 'Le "paure" della società veneziana: le calamità, le sconfitte, i nemici esterni ed interni', in *Storia di Venezia*, vol. VI, (Rome: Istituto dell' Encyclopedia Italiana, 1994), 215–38; R. DeRosas, 'Moralità e giustizia a Venezia nel '500–'600. Gli esecutori contro la bestemmia', in G. Cozzi (ed.), *Stato, società, giustizia nella Repubblica Veneta* (sec. xv-xviii), (Rome: Jouvence, 1980), 433–528; A. Vizziano, 'Giustizia, disciplina e ordine pubblico', in *Storia di Venezia*, VI, 825–61. B. Pullan, *The Jews of Europe and the Inquisition of Venice. 1550–1670*, (Oxford: Basil Blackwell, 1983), 92–116, provides a parallel study of denunciations before the Inquisition.

3   See James Fenimore Cooper's novel *The Bravo*, for an example of the former. Thomas Otway's *Venice Preserv'd* enjoyed considerable success on the London stage in the early seventeenth century because of the way in which it reinforced stereotypes of the brutality of the Venetian state.

4   A.F. Cowan, *The Urban Patriciate: Lübeck and Venice, 1580–1700* (Cologne and Vienna: Böhlau, 1986), 51–7; see O.T. Domzalski, *Politische Karrieren und Machtverteilung im venezianischen Adel (1646–1797)* (Sigmaringen: Jan Thorbeke Verlag, 1996), for an excellent analysis of patrician office-holding at the end of the period.

5   A. Zannini, *Burocrazia e burocrati a Venezia in età moderna: i cittadini originari* (sec. xvi–xviii), (Venice: Istituto Veneto di Scienze, Lettere ed Arti, 1993); A. Bellavitis, ' "Per cittadini metterete . . ." La stratificazione della società veneziana cinquecentesca tra norme giuridici e riconoscimento sociale'), *Quaderni Storici*, 89, (1995) 359–83; M. Cassini, 'La cittadinanza originaria a Venezia tra i secoli xv e xvi. Una linea interpretativa', in *Studi Veneti offerti a Gaetano Cozzi* (Venice: Il Cardo, 1992), 133–50.

6   R. Mackenney, *Tradesmen and Traders. The World of the Guilds in Venice and Europe, c.1250–c.1650* (Beckenham: Croom Helm, 1987); R. Davis, *Shipbuilders of the Venetian Arsenal* (Baltimore: The Johns Hopkins University Press, 1991).

7   This essay is part of a long-term study of marriage and social differentiation in early modern Venice. The *Prove di Nobiltà* are stored among the papers of the magistracy of the *Avogaria di Comun* in the *Archivio di Stato di Venezia* (hereafter ASV).

8   J.C. Davis, *The Decline of the Venetian Nobility as a Ruling Class* (Baltimore: Johns Hopkins University Press, 1962), 54–5.

9   G. Bacco (ed.), *Relazione sulla organizzazione politica della Repubblica di Venezia al cader del secolo decimo settimo* (Vicenza, 1846), 44, 86.

10   Stanley Chojnacki argues that the legislation which refined the definition of a male patrician in the fifteenth and early sixteenth centuries developed out of a need to accommodate tensions between families of differing income levels. Chojnacki, 'Social identity in Renaissance Venice: the second Serrata', *Renaissance Studies*, 8 (1994), 345–6.

11   For Venetian attitudes, see U. Tucci, 'The Psychology of the Venetian merchant in the Sixteenth Century', in J.R. Hale (ed.), *Renaissance Venice* (London: Faber, 1973), 346–7; for Italy in general, see C. Donati, *L'idea della nobiltà in Italia* (Bari: Laterza, 1988), 247–65.

136   Subversion and Scurrility

12 Copies of this legislation are available in several collections in Venice: ASV, *Compilazione Leggi*, 277, 'Matrimoni'; ASV, *Avogaria di Comun* (hereafter *AdC*), 108, 'Nozze, Denuncie et parti prese in materia di matrimonio, 1478–1663' ASV, *AdC*, Reg.16; Venice, Biblioteca Marciana, It. VII 196 (8578), 'Raccolte di parti e Ordine in materia della Nobiltà veneziana'. See also S. Chojnacki, 'Nobility, women and the state: marriage regulation in Venice, 1420–1535', in T. Dean and K.J.P. Lowe (eds), *Marriage in Italy 1300–1650* (Cambridge: Cambridge University Press, 1998), 128–51; S. Chojnacki, 'Marriage Legislation and Patrician Society in Fifteenth-century Venice', in B. Bachrach and D. Nicholas (eds), *Law, Custom and the Social Fabric in Medieval Europe* (Kalamazoo: Western Michigan University Press, 1990).
13 ASV, *AdC*, 108.
14 See A. Cowan, 'Love, Honour and the Avogaria di Comun in early modern Venice', *Archivio Veneto*, 5th ser., 144, (1995), 12–14.
15 ASV, *AdC*, 221, 17.
16 ASV, *AdC* 211 (no fascicolo number given).
17 For the mechanisms by which men could enter the council at the age of twenty rather than twenty-five, see Domzalski, *Politische Karrieren*, 29–35.
18 ASV *AdC*, 221, 17.
19 For the high status of notaries and their work, see M.P. Pedroni Fabris, *"Veneta auctoritate notarius"*. *Storia del notariato veneziano (1514–1797)* (Milan: A. Guiffre Editore, 1990), 47–52, 149–51.
20 ASV, *AdC*, 221, 17.
21 For the increase in convent education, see V. Hunecke, 'Kindbett oder Kloster', in G. Bock (ed.), *Lebenswege von Frauen in Ancien Regime*, special edition of *Geschichte und Gesellschaft*, 18, (1992), 451–7.
22 ASV, *AdC*, 221, 17. By naming Cecilia's future husband, Giulia breached the convention that all petitions to the *Avogaria* requested permission in principle to marry into the patriciate.
23 Many of these anxieties had already surfaced during the debates in 1645 and 1646 about the wisdom of allowing non-patricians to buy their way into the nobility. See D. Raines, 'Pouvoir ou privilèges nobiliaires. Le dilemme du patriciat vénitien face aux agrégations du xviie siècle', *Annales: économies, sociétés, civilisations*, 46 (1991), 827–47; A. Cowan, 'New families in the Venetian patriciate, 1646–1718', *Ateneo Veneto*, 23 (1985), 55–75.
24 ASV, *AdC*, 221, 17.
25 M.F. Rosenthal, *The Honest Courtesan. Veronica Franco, Citizen and Writer in sixteenth-cetury Venice* (Chicago: University of Chicago Press, 1992), 21–3; A. Barzachi, *Donne o cortigiane? La prostituzione a Venezia : Documenti di costumi del xvi al xvii secolo* (Verona: Bertani, 1980).
26 Zannini, *Burocrazia*, 103.
27 ASV, *AdC*, 221, 17.
28 Zannini, *Burocrazia*, 108–18.
29 ASV, *AdC*, 221, 17.
30 ASV, *AdC*, 221, 17.
31 C. Biliotti, *Il Ridotto. Cenni Storici* (Venice: Naratovich, 1870).
32 ASV, *AdC*, 221, 17.
33 Rosenthal, *Honest Courtesan*, 67.
34 Idem.

35 ASV, *AdC*, 211 (no fascicolo given).
36 See my comments on the reasons for secret marriages by patricians in A. Cowan, 'Patricians and Partners in early modern Venice', in E. Kittell, and T. Madden (eds), *Medieval and Renaissance Venice. Studies in Honor of Donald E. Queller* (Chicago: University of Illinois Press, 1999). 276–93.
37 See, for example, the cases of Zuanna Negri, wife of N.H. Bartolomio Semitecolo di Giacomo. ASV *AdC*, 214; Margarita Varisco, wife of N.H. Andrea Catti. *AdC* 236, 78; and of Cattarina Alberti, wife of N.H. Antonio Querini di Andrea. *AdC* 237, 96.
38 ASV, *AdC*, 211 (no page number given).
39 For patrician familiarity with concubinage, see Cowan, 'Patricians and Partners'; G. Martini, 'La donna veneziana del '600 tra sessualità legittima ed illegittima: alcune riflessioni sul concubinato', *Atti dell'Istituto Veneto di Scienze, Lettere ed Arti*, 145 (1986–87), 301–39.
40 ASV, *AdC*, 211 (no page number given).
41 ASV, *AdC*, 211 (no page number given).
42 See the wills of Franceschina Badoer Gradenigo (1618) Venice, Biblioteca Querini Stampalia IX. Cod VII, doc. 49; and of Francesco Giustinian di Angelo (1665), ASV, *AdC, Misc. Civ.*, 397, 25.
43 ASV, *AdC*, 211 (no page number given).

9
The last Austrian–Turkish war (1788–91) and public opinion in Vienna

Gerhard Ammerer

The Enlightenment encouraged the emergence and acceptance of a plethora of new ideas; regrettably, however, opinion research institutes and demoscopic polling were not among them, and it is much more difficult to reconstruct anything resembling a 'public opinion' or 'popular opinion' for this period than for the twentieth century.[1] Indeed, the lenient censorship laws of Joseph II's reign promoted such a diversity of views that for Austria during the late eighteenth century the task is harder still. Yet as Jürgen Habermas has observed, it is precisely at this time, with the emergence of bourgeois society, and the development of the press as a new factor in politics, that a coherent, independent 'public opinion' began to form.[2] The press very quickly became the 'servant of two masters'. On the one hand, it was systematically made to serve the official interests of the political authorities, as was clearly illustrated by a press regulation issued in March 1769 by the Vienna government:

> In order that newspaper writers may be informed as to domestic ordinances, undertakings and other matters that may arise which are suitable for public dissemination, the aforementioned are to be summarised on a weekly basis by government officials and handed over to the newspaper publishers.[3]

On the other hand, during the first half of the eighteenth century, reasoned editorial consideration began to make an appearance in the daily press. By articulating the interests of the subjects of the realm, newspapers introduced a counterweight to official power. The press, once the handmaiden of the authorities, was transformed into their adversary; and one of the high points of this process in Austria is to be located during the last Austrian war against the Turks (1788–91), which took place during the reign of Joseph II.

Indeed, there were already conflicting views in the Vienna of Joseph II about who were the actual carriers of public opinion. It is clear from an examination of early definitions of the term that, in German-speaking countries at least, this function was initially ascribed to the 'intelligentsia' and the 'educated classes'.[4] Yet the observations of contemporaries suggest that in reality the constituency of public opinion was much broader and more complex in its make-up. Commenting on the state of affairs in Vienna during the Turkish war, Johann Pezzl reports, not without a certain irony, that:

> Despite the seriousness of the situation, it is great fun to discuss these matters with people of various social classes, to hear their blather and disputation. Most of them have thrown in their lot with some newspaper columnist or other, whose rantings and ravings they blindly follow. . . In pubs, these notions are advocated with the utmost vigour, not just with words but with fists as well.[5]

This quotation makes two points clear. Firstly, public opinion is to be regarded as a complex of consistent as well as contradictory views and expressions on a particular issue voiced by a range of individuals and social groups. Secondly, its formation was only partly spontaneous; for the most part, it emerged as the result of journalistic manipulation. In performing historical research on such 'public opinion', then, we can investigate the views expressed in the contemporary media, the reception these were accorded, and their effect. I should like here to present a small sample of public opinion relating to Austria's last Turkish War, an event which was obviously considered a matter for prolonged and heated discussion. The material ranges from the semi-official accounts of those close to the government to the highly critical views of its opponents. Moreover, the war prompted not only a copious amount of written opinion but also found its expression in music and the graphic arts, and the ways in which these both influenced and reflected public opinion will also be taken into account in the discussion which follows.

The war and its repercussions

In 1781, Catherine the Great and Joseph II concluded an agreement whose primary aim for Russia was a war against the Turks.[6] This not unproblematic alliance was immediately subjected to fierce criticism by Prussia, France and England and at the same time became a target of Austrian caricaturists as well (see Figure 9.1).[7]

The war was eventually triggered by a joint journey undertaken by the emperor and the czarina in 1787 to Sevastopol, where a naval port was under construction. With some justification, the Turks perceived this event as a threatening gesture and launched a preventive war.[8] Then, instead of merely dispatching the agreed auxiliary corps of 30,000 men, Joseph II moved

Figure 9.1 'Politische Spazierfahrt' (Going for a little political spin). Satire of the 1781 alliance concluded between Joseph II and Catherine the Great

against the Ottomans in 1788 with an army of almost 300,000. The campaign was tantamount to a catastrophe; Count Lacy, the aged and incompetent Austrian field marshal, dispersed his troops along the entire 825-mile border separating the two empires, thus severely diminishing their military striking power.[9] And despite the great vote of confidence given to the newly-appointed commander-in-chief, Ernst, Baron of Laudon, he also proved to be extremely cautious in his military engagements. Nevertheless, he succeeded in taking Belgrade on 8 October 1789. The following year, Austria and Turkey agreed to a cease-fire. And whereas Russia ended hostilities only in early 1792 after achieving major territorial gains, those regions conquered by Austria were relinquished by Joseph II's successor, Leopold II, on 4 August 1791.[10]

The hardships which the population had endured in the meantime were enormous. The war took a heavy toll of human lives, above all as a result of diseases and epidemics, the chief cause of which was the swampy terrain in the region of Semlin, site of the army's main encampment. Within a single year, 172,000 soldiers took sick, of whom 33,000 died.[11] This was a substantially higher number than that of battle casualties, and was certainly an essential factor contributing to the continually increasing number of deserters. Indeed, after spending a few months with his army in the field, the emperor himself returned to Vienna critically ill.[12]

As a consequence of all this, Joseph II – it was asserted – was 'not loved by his people';[13] and this unpopularity was compounded by further factors. One of the most important was the new system of military conscription, which introduced the compulsory enlistment of all men who were not indispensable by virtue of their occupations. In 1788 the demand for recruits rose with no end in sight, and large numbers of young men performed acts of self-mutilation, committed felonies or simply fled in order to escape military service.[14] A further hardship borne by the population was the massive number of sick or crippled soldiers who returned from the war. A veritable horde of war veterans, invalids and deserters swarmed, across the land, begging and stealing.[15]

The Turkish War also had a deleterious effect on the otherwise buoyant economy, and gave rise to symptoms of economic stagnation which then persisted for many years. The brunt of the damage was suffered by Austria's commercial trade with Turkey, which had only just begun to make substantial progress.[16] Above all, however, the enormous costs of conducting the war, amounting to over 220 million Florins, ripped a gaping hole in the state's purse which could hardly be patched up by further increases in the quantity of money in circulation.[17] New sources of income were feverishly sought. What usually happens in such cases is familiar to each of us as a result of painful personal experience. 'When the coffers are empty, new taxes are imposed' was the laconic and prophetic formulation in an anti-Turkish War pamphlet which appeared during the summer of 1788.[18] The reference here is to the War Tax Decree, which was enacted on 13 November 1788 and raised tax revenues considerably. Above all, however, the most direct impact on the vast majority of the population came from the declining value of real wages, a situation caused to no small extent by a doubling of the price of foodstuffs in Vienna.[19] Finally, alongside the dissatisfaction caused by these very real material hardships, there were also more general, ideological objections to the war, which arose as a consequence of the ideological influence of Enlightenment thinking. The ideas of Voltaire and Rousseau in particular were broadly disseminated to great effect in Austria, and opposition to war had become a prominent theme of writers at this time.[20]

Journalism as maker and mirror of public opinion

With his relaxation of the censorship, Joseph II laid the groundwork for a 'press with a mind of its own'. From 1781, there was rapid growth in newspaper and pamphlet publishing.[21] Accounts by travellers visiting Vienna repeatedly remark on the hunger for reading matter on the part of the city's population, even among the 'lower classes'; and the latest issues of periodicals were to be found not only in the exclusive salons and coffeehouses, but in simple beer halls and wine bars as well.[22] For months during 1788, the Turkish War was the most important topic of conversation in Vienna, and this was reflected in the burgeoning press. The discussion below is based on a representative sample of the public prints of the day, ranging from the *Wiener Zeitung* (then as now, the official organ and mouthpiece of the government), to those publications which made an effort to report objectively on events, and other publications which were cuttingly satirical.[23]

The heated debate about the war was organised around a number of positions. Circulating initially there were arguments about the justification for the war. The war reporting of those 'loyal' newspapers otherwise concerned chiefly with affairs at court, based their pro-war stance on two principal arguments: the 'just war' and the assertion that the Turks were Europe's arch-enemy and had to be destroyed.[24] Thus, Johann Rautenstrauch proceeded from what was actually not an especially eccentric variant of 'natural rights':

> Any people which has advanced itself beyond others in matters of custom, enlightenment and insight and which, through a form of government both well-founded and wise, has been placed in the position to carry out great undertakings, is to a certain extent justified by nature in vanquishing . . . barbaric nations . . . If I am not mistaken,

then, these are the very reasons which justify the neighbours Austria and Russia driving the Turks into a corner. To repress a barbaric government which had plagued Europe for centuries is equivalent to avenging the rights of humanity.[25]

This completely ahistorical disparagement of the Turks by no means corresponded to their image among the Austrian population in 1788. Indeed, the hostile perception of the cruel, bloodthirsty and tyrannical Turkish dog continued to slumber in the collective subconscious, and several authors attempted to reactivate it; these efforts obviously met with scant success. The barbarian myth, as well as the newspapers' fairy-tales of Turks who 'shipped whole sacks full of Christian ears back to Constantinople',[26] was set straight in a number of pamphlets. Even J.M. Schweighofer, a proponent of the war, pointed out that the firm resolve to wage war – the official line – had no resonance among the people generally; there was little animosity towards the Turks on the part of the emperor's subjects, who had come to regard them as friends during the preceding fifty years.[27] There had been a shift in mentalities during the decades before the war, a development particularly marked among the educated upper classes, where there was a growing interest in the Ottoman Empire, not least among scholars. The 'oriental fashion' was also well-established in the art world.[28] Indeed, the topos of tyrant had been transformed into the topos of caring and enlightened sultan; the cruel Oriental consumed by lust and drink (Osmin) was now contrasted with the magnanimous and merciful monarch (Selim Bassa) as, for example, in Mozart's opera 'Die Entführung aus dem Serail' (The Abduction from the Seraglio).[29]

A few Viennese dailies offered extremely detailed war coverage marked by a conspicuous sense of loyalty to Joseph II. As early as February 1788, *Das Wienerblättchen* had reported on the drafting of the still top-secret Austrian declaration of war, a scoop which indicates an especially close relationship between the paper and the government. Thoroughly positive reportage could also be found in the *Neuester Rapport von Wien*. The efforts of this paper to convince its readers of the authenticity of its published descriptions went so far that they appear rather curious. In December 1789, for example, in a proud reminiscence of the capture of Belgrade two months previously, it cited a manuscript, only recently discovered, of a Turkish speech said to have been prepared for delivery at a 'session of the council of state at Constantinople' shortly thereafter.[30]

Fictitious reports and letters are also to be found in the *Neueste Wiener Nachrichten*, though here they are pressed into the service of a critical point of view. The failing fortunes of the war, disease statistics, unfitness for service and inflation are a few of the central topics in this paper's efforts to provide objective coverage. At the same time, following Turkish military successes, it criticised the one-sided positive reporting by others authors.[31] One of the pamphleteers who displayed total loyalty to the government and completely supported the war effort was Johann Rautenstrauch. His *Exhaustive Diary of the Current War Between Austria and Turkey*, published as a series of individual volumes, promised its readers 'a comprehensive depiction of the events of this war'.[32] On the book market, however, it proved to be a flop, so that publication had to be halted after a few issues due to lack of consumer demand.[33] The reading public obviously had little interest in such semi-official reportage and preferred to read articles more critical of the war.

In 1788, one pamphlet caused a particular stir. The anonymous author imparted to the people of Austria 'A Word in Strictest Confidence on the Subject of the Turkish War'.[34] On every page of this slim volume, no matter which one is selected, the reader finds catchwords such as 'peril . . . murderous weaponry . . . enemies . . . weeping . . . crutch . . . blood . . . evil demon . . . plague' (in this case on page 6). The fierce discussion which raged about this text, however, does not seem to stem from its drastically formulated prose; it is to a much greater extent due to the unprecedented nature of this work, in which an author dared to deny a emperor (and a czarina for that matter) the fundamental right to commit an abuse of power and, through the conduct of a foolish war, to decide the lives and deaths of human beings: 'Who can order: you must die so that I may become great and my realm prosper? . . . To do this requires a dreadful audacity, to commit such an injustice before the eyes of the entire world . . . You enemies of humanity!'[35] The conclusion, consistent with these considerations, climaxed in the call for revolution:

> There is a feeling which lies within each of us – the feeling of right and wrong; when reason and courage are aligned with this feeling, humanity can provide for its own deliverance. In some places, they have done so already. Stirred by living feelings of injustice, they have brought down the despot. The history of England proves only too well what human beings – a united people – can do! It shows that the prince without the forbearance of those under his subjugation is like a bee without a stinger . . . What, then, would be the best form of government? The limited monarchy. Leave to the monarchs the power over a certain portion of the estates of their subjects, but wrest from their hands only the power over human life.[36]

This work presented the Glorious Revolution and the English parliamentary system as models for the subjects of the Habsburg Monarchy to imitate, and the reception accorded it was enormously far-reaching.[37] Indeed, not all reviewers knew quite how to handle radical ideas of this sort. Some newspapers reprinted a few short excerpts without commentary and left it up to the public to decide for themselves. In Schubart's *Chronik*, however, the following lines appeared: 'There has recently appeared in Vienna a book entitled *A Word in Strictest Confidence on the Subject of the Turkish War*, written in a tone which would compel even the boldest and most candid Briton to express amazement.'[38]

Songs, satires and plays

Despite all the interest in Turkey which had recently manifested itself both in economic and intellectual life, the clichéd images portraying the Ottomans as the destroyers of Christendom continued to be purveyed in song.[39] Such clichés and stereotypical characterisations were particularly conspicuous in the folk-songs sung of the Turkish War. During the first year of the war, ridiculing the Turks and singing the praise of Joseph II were favourite themes:

> How heavenly does Joseph's realm
> extend through God's great might,
> and the strong arm of the Lord
> is with him in each fight.[40]

Evoking an historical mental image which was still quite deeply rooted, the former conqueror of Belgrade was simply replaced with, or compared to, the city's conqueror of 1789:

Song of Praise to Laudon, the Hero on the Taking of Belgrade.

> On distant honour's field, old man
> you nobly joined the fray,
> to crown with glorious laurel wreath
> your head, already grey . . .
>
> Praise of you is loudly sung
> by every man and boy,
> comparing you, most properly
> with Eugene of Savoy . . . [41]

The great number of poems and songs written in honor of Laudon in 1788–89, as well as the two biographies which then appeared in Vienna, show that, at least for a short time, Austria once again had a hero to celebrate.

Collections of war songs were published in Vienna as early as 1788. As in the case of the newspapers and pamphlets, the orientation here was resolute loyalty to the government, with titles such as *The Voice of Nobility to the Emperor in the Campaign against Turkey* or *War Songs for Joseph's Heroes in the Campaign against the Turks*:

146   Subversion and Scurrility

Song of the Soldiers, before Joseph, their emperor.

Our Kaiser, all the best to him,
His fame we warriors sing.
So fill our tankards to the rim
Let the happy chorus ring:
Kaiser Joseph, shout his praise!
To his health and length of days! . . . [42]

On the other hand, there also appeared collections such as *Austrian and Turkish War Songs*, which were opposed to the emperor. The 'Fantasy of a Misanthrope upon the Outbreak of the Turkish War', for instance, draws a stark picture of the catastrophe:

To war! This joyous celebration
In your honour we put on.
Now take your plague and your starvation
And from this place begone!
. . .
Set castles, cities, huts ablaze
Tear wall and fortress down,
Man and woman, dig your graves
In this rubble-strewn ground.
. . .
What have I then from Fatherland
To pay the ultimate price?
My life! – gone to a Turkish band!
Say, brother, ain't that nice? . . . [43]

Here we once again encounter the spirit of rebelliousness against a form of politics that the people absolutely rejects, which it finds oppressive and in which it can see no real sense. In the case of one prominent song of the Turkish War, musicology has encountered some problems which have persisted to this day. This has to do with a poem written by the literary dilettante Johann Wilhelm Ludwig Gleim.[44] It was set to music by Wolfgang Amadeus Mozart, who was also a pre-publication subscriber of the anti-war songs quoted above. In this song in four verses entitled 'Ich möchte wohl der Kaiser sein' (I'd like to be the emperor),[45] Otto Biba, for example, discovers 'rousing patriotism'.[46] Mozart composed the melody on 5 March 1788 for Friedrich Baumann, a popular comedian at the Leopoldstädter Theater, who performed the song in a concert two days later. However, a mood of unanimous, euphoric bellicosity corresponding to the mood depicted in the song's text seems not to have prevailed in Vienna, not even a month after Austria's declaration of war against Turkey. Moreover, as a patriotic song, when sung by a comedian, it would certainly have been accorded scant applause by the audience. The melodic progression, though, points toward another possible interpretation. Since the young Mozart and the considerably older Haydn were on friendly terms, and since Mozart not only meticulously studied Haydn's music but also took every opportunity to hear his works, one may proceed from the assumption that Mozart had attended a performance of the German-language version of the Haydn opera 'La vera costanza' by the theatrical company of Kumpf and Schikaneder in Vienna in 1785 or 1786. [47] As in several other works, Mozart seems to have modified a melody from Haydn here in this war song as well. A segment of Mozart's composition is reminiscent of a sequence in an aria by Masino in this opera.[48] The German title of Haydn's aria might be translated as 'Keep your long ears open wide!' The text of Haydn's work alone, which Viennese music aficionados would surely have had in mind, would have made very clear to them Mozart's opinion of the Turkish War: 'Nor does stupidity like to be alone, everything goes better by twos . . . Listen, dear people, listen to what I'm telling you: it's the same today as it ever was, the world is full of foolishness . . .'[49] By thus reaching into an ironic bag of musical tricks, Mozart and Baumann could apparently be assured of appealing to the taste of the public.[50] In this interpretation the song is to be understood as a pure parody.

Joachim Perenet's satiric pamphlet *The Lilliputian Tax Return* was aimed directly at the war taxes passed in November 1788.[51] In over a hundred pages, people of various different social classes and occupations submit their tax returns and expound their arguments as to why they regard themselves as being in no position to pay their share of the pointless 'Frog Tax'. Among its many targets, the humour plays on reforms introduced by Joseph II:

> Tax return of an executioner.
> Since the highly acclaimed Enlightenment, there are no more heads to be lost in Lilliput and my business is completely dead.
> . . .
> Tax return of a recruit.
> As the citizen of a state currently at war, the signatory is exempt from the Frog Tax because he may soon be assessed the Head Tax for which he is liable to the fatherland.
> . . .
> Tax return of a Freemason
> My wealth is a secret.[52]

A considerably more complex treatment of this subject was presented in the play *The War Tax*.[53] It attests, among other things, to a general receptiveness in Vienna to Enlightenment ideas such as those of Lessing or Herder.[54] These are given expression especially by the character of Marianne, the daughter of the Hofrat von Lamberg. Like Rousseau, she detests human bloodshed and is horrified as her brother, serving as a lieutenant in the Turkish War, recounts his heroic deeds.[55] Marianne is fond of Lessings 'Emilia Galotti'; however, due to the financial burden caused by the war taxes, her rich uncle reneges on his promise to provide the dowry for her wedding. Appearing as the rescuer of this 'damsel in distress' is Dorsuffi, a Turk who had been brought to Vienna as a captive along with his valuable Walachian gelding. Like Selim Bassa in Mozart's 'The Abduction from the Seraglio', he proves to be a man of great generosity; through the sale of the horse, he makes possible the couple's wedded bliss. In the face of this human kindness and the obvious lack of a legitimate *casus belli*, all agree by the end of the play that 'War does no one any good!'[56]

Graphic reportage

In the wake of the flood of pamphlets appearing in the 1780s in Vienna, engravings, allegorical prints and caricatures also became best-sellers. From 1781 on, it was above all the engraver and publisher Hieronymus Löschenkohl who, along with his staff, produced hundreds of prints with themes taken from current events, and thus became known as the 'graphic reporter of the Age of Joseph II'.[57] 'His chief consideration was to take advantage of the moment, the present,' wrote Löschenkohl's contemporary, the bookseller Franz Gräffer, 'and most of these pictures were absolutely devoured by the public'.[58] Löschenkohl himself, in an announcement in the *Wiener Zeitung*, spoke of 'contemporary history in pictures'.[59] Thus, the Turkish War also sold well in graphic format. By the signing of the peace treaty, Löschenkohl had produced well over 200 prints and had risen to become the darling of the Viennese public.[60] Like the newspaper correspondents, he also made every effort to prove, or perhaps rather to fake, the authenticity of the depictions by means of references to the fact that the sketches were drawn at the very scene of the event portrayed. Indeed, Löschenkohl's graphics depicted the victories of the Austrian and Russian troops, while negative events such as military setbacks remained completely out of the picture.[61] The propagandistic agenda in the caricatures is especially clear. Here, Löschenkohl exposes the Turks to gleeful ridicule, such as in the engraved burial scene of Sultan Abdul Hamid in April 1789 or the illustrations in the 'Turkish Heroes' Calendar of the Year 1790', in which the enemy is depicted as a bunch of comical gnomes in the style of the popular Callot figures (see Figure 9.2).[62]

**Figure 9.2 Caricatures from 'Turkish Heroes' Calendar for
the Year 1790 by Hieronymus Löschenkohl**

Public opinion

Literary and graphic sources such as these can provide us with little more than
a fragmentary insight into the broad range of public opinion. Contemporary
accounts of the reception of these works and the discourse initiated by them,
along with the few instances of eyewitness testimony to the mood prevailing
in Vienna, offer an additional approach to the questions initially raised here.
The intensity of these discussions is repeatedly mentioned by contemporary
observers.

Löschenkohl's Turkish engravings were not the only best-sellers; many
pamphlets and articles penned by correspondents critical of the war also did a
brisk business. Rautenstrauch, whose *War Diary*, as we have seen, went out
of print due to lack of reader interest, worked himself up into a veritable
frenzy over the success enjoyed by a competitor, the *Impartial Geographic-
Historical War Guide*:[63]

> Can this be? Is it possible, I ask, that in the enlightened city of Vienna
> a rag like this, a conglomeration of the most pathetic nonsense jumbled
> together in the clumsiest and most confusing language, can find so
> many eager purchasers that its publisher is even in the position to set
> up his own expedition bureau?[64]

The passion for the printed word which manifested itself in the Habsburg
imperial capital is also described by Rautenstrauch in an anonymous
pamphlet entitled 'Recollections Concerning the Special Supplements to the
Vienna Newspapers which have thus far Appeared during the Current War':
how impatiently 'the citizens of Vienna, representing all classes and stations,
now wait . . . No sooner has the day begun, and thousands are already
inquiring at the bureau whether a supplement will appear.'[65] He repeatedly
emphasises that the readership is made up of 'people of all sorts', even
'servants from outlying rural areas', who would read the paper though they
were barely capable of comprehending the contents.[66] Patriotism and
Enlightenment, Rautenstrauch concludes, are to blame for the fact 'that even
the lowliest types of persons, with views taken from the war journalism which
has appeared here to date, deliver their verdicts upon these events in unison
with the more refined elements of the population'.[67]

The author thus offers a hint as to who, in his opinion, would justifiably
be entitled to hold an opinion on matters of public interest: not the mob of
common folk, but rather the 'refined elements of society', that is to say, the
nobility and the educated elite. At the same time, he takes note of the fact that
public opinion on the subject of the Turkish War was held by all social classes.
That this opinion was overwhelmingly negative particularly during the first

year of the war, is made more than clear by newspaper reports, pamphlets and private correspondence. In the words of one writer: 'Prayers are offered up rather on behalf of the Turks than for Joseph II. This war is unjust and proves the ingratitude of Austria, for which it will never be forgiven.' And a foreign envoy reported from Vienna that 'the rabble even took veritable pleasure in the Austrian defeat that day'.[68]

In October 1788, the young Archduchess Elisabeth characterised popular opinion in the following terms: 'Lacy dare not show his face in Vienna since everyone here is bitterly opposed to him.'[69] Poems ridiculing the field commander were already making the rounds then, and in that same month, the 'rabble' gathered in front of his country estate and pelted it with stones. A nightcap is said to have been placed upon the marble bust of Mars which stood in his garden.[70]

Similar derision also had to be borne by the emperor following his return to Vienna. In his biography of Joseph II, Groß-Hoffinger even mentions a demonstration against the Turkish War taxes in front of the gates of the imperial palace.[71] Police reports filed in 1788–89 were also unanimous in describing the unpopularity of both the war and the emperor.[72] The taking of Belgrade seems to have been the one and only event which gave rise to a temporary shift in attitudes.[73] Nevertheless, it did not take long for this glowing Belgrade euphoria to subside and for the barometer of the mood in Vienna to sink back to its former low.

In the final analysis, the Turkish War cost Joseph II not only his physical health but the last remnants of his popularity as well.[74] The emperor, however, who was known for the mildness of his censorship policies, by no means underestimated the power of public opinion. This was clearly illustrated by the ban he placed on a handbill entitled 'A Few Words Concerning the Current War'. Here, the author sketches a vision of a future in which the costs of the Turkish War have left Austria totally bankrupt: 'In the aftermath of squandering the treasures of the Church, they now clutch greedily at the property of their subjects, in order to make the entire country a doss house for beggars.'[75]

Notes

1   On the discussion of the term see: Arlette Farge, *Subversive Words. Public Opinion in Eighteenth-Century France* (Cambridge: Polity, 1994), first published in France as *Dire et mal dire: L'opinion publique au XVIII siecle* (Paris: Éditions du Seuil, 1992); Melvin Small (ed.), *Public Opinion and Historians. Interdisciplinary Perspectives* (Detroit: Wayne State University Press, 1970); Andreas Ernst, 'Öffentlichkeit – das unsichtbare Wesen mit der großen Wirkung.

Konzeption und Anwendung für die schweizerische Parteiengeschichte', in *Schweizerische Zeitschrift für Geschichte*, 46 (1996), 60 ff.; Lucian Höscher, *Öffentlichkeit und Geheimnis. Eine begriffsgeschichtliche Untersuchung zur Entstehung der Öffentlichkeit in der frühen Neuzeit* (Stuttgart, 1979).

2   Jürgen Habermas, *Strukturwandel der Öffentlichkeit. Untersuchungen zu einer Kategorie der bürgerlichen Gesellschaft* (Darmstadt: Luchterhand, 1984), 15 ff. and 33 ff. In recent years his theory has been criticized above all on two grounds: that he is restricting 'public opinion' to verbal communication; and that he leaves the upper classes completely out of consideration. See especially: Andreas Gestrich, *Absolutismus und Öffentlichkeit. Politische Kommunikation in Deutschland zu Beginn des 18. Jahrhunderts (Kritische Studien zur Geschichtswissenschaft 103)* (Göttingen: Vandenhoeck & Ruprecht, 1994), 12–33.

3   Quoted by Habermas, *Strukturwandel*, 36.

4   Elisabeth Noelle-Neumann, 'Die Träger der öffentlichen Meinung', in Martin Löffler (ed.), *Die öffentliche Meinung. Publizistik als Medium und Faktor der öffentlichen Meinung* (Munich and Berlin: C.H. Beck'sche Verlagsbuchhandlung, 1962), 26.

5   Johann Pezzl, *Skizze von Wien*, 5 (Vienna and Leipzig, 1788), 635.

6   There is little recent literature on this last Austrian–TurkishWar. See Karl Teply, 'Das österreichische Türkenkriegszeitalter', in Zygmunt Abrahamowicz et al. (eds), *Die Türkenkriege in der historischen Forschung* (Vienna: Franz Deuticke, 1983), 48; Erich Donnert, 'Joseph II. und Katharina II. Ein Beitrag zu Österreichs Rußland- und Orientpolitik 1780–1790', in Georg Plaschka, Grete Klingenstein *et al.* (eds), *Österreich im Europa der Aufklärung. Kontinuität und Zäsur in Europa zur Zeit Maria Theresias und Josephs II. Internationales Symposion in Wien 20.–23. Oktober 1980*, 1 (Vienna: Österreichische Akademie der Wissenschaften, 1985), 576–80; Karl Gutkas, 'Kaiser Josephs Türkenkrieg', in Karl Gutkas *et al.* (eds), *Österreich zur Zeit Kaiser Josephs II. Katalog der Niederösterreichischen Landesausstellung im Stift Melk 1980* (Vienna, 1980), 271–3.

7   Helmut Rumpler, *Eine Chance für Mitteleuropa. Bürgerliche Emanzipation und Staatsverfall in der Habsburgermonarchie* (Vienna: Ueberreuter, 1997), 22.

8   Claus Scharf, *Katharina II., Deutschland und die Deutschen (Veröffentlichungen des Instituts für europäische Geschichte Mainz, Abteilung Universalgeschichte 153)* (Mainz: Philipp von Zabern, 1995), 426 f.; Reinhold Neumann-Hoditz, *Katharina II. die Große mit Selbstzeugnissen und Bilddokumenten* (Reinbek bei Hamburg: Rowohlt, 1988), 185.

9   Hanns Leo Mikoletzky, *Österreich. Das große 18. Jahrhundert* (Vienna: Österreichischer Bundesverlag für Unterricht, Wissenschaft und Kunst, 1967), 366; Adolf Beer, *Die orientalische Politik Oesterreichs seit 1774* (Prague: F. Temsky; Leipzig: G. Freytag, 1883), 96; Edith Kotasek, *Feldmarschall Graf Lacy. Ein Leben für Österreichs Heer* (Horn: Verlag Ferdinand Berger, 1956), 170 ff.

10   Teply, *Türkenkriegszeitalter*, 48; Christian Friedrich Daniel Schubart, *Chronik 1791*, 1 (Stuttgart: Verlag des Kaiserl. Reichspostamts, 1791), 575–9.

11   A.J. Groß-Hoffinger, *Lebens- und Regierungsgeschichte Josephs des Zweiten und Gemälde seiner Zeit* (Stuttgart and Leipzig: L.F. Riger & Comp., 1836), 473 f.

12   Mikoletzky, *Österreich*, 365 f.

13 See the famous pamphlet: (Joseph Richter,) *Warum wird Kaiser Joseph von seinem Volke nicht geliebt?*, Vienna 1787.

14 Donnert, *Joseph II*, 590; Johann Carl Hauckh, *Leitfaden zu dem Kenntnisse der gefürsteten Graffschaft Tyrol für die Zuhörer der politischen Wissenschaften entworfen* (Innsbruck, 1789), 56; Paul von Mitrofanov, *Joseph II. Seine politische und kulturelle Tätigkeit*, 1 (Vienna and Leipzig: C.W. Stern, 1910), 371, 387.

15 See, for example, Tiroler Landesarchiv, Handschrift 1223 (Decree on Beggars).

16 Hans Halm, *Habsburgischer Osthandel im 18. Jahrhundert. Österreich und Neurußland* (II): *Donauhandel und -schiffahrt 1781–1787* (Veröffentlichungen des Osteuropa-Institutes München), (Munich: Isar Verlag, 1954), 185.

17 Gustav Otruba, 'Wirtschaft und Wirtschaftspolitik im Zeitalter des aufgeklärten Absolutismus', in Institut für Österreichkunde (ed.), *Die Wirtschaftsgeschichte Österreichs* (Vienna: Hirt, 1971), 121; Roman Sandgruber, *Ökonomie und Politik. Österreichische Wirtschaftsgeschichte vom Mittelalter bis zur Gegenwart* (Vienna: Ueberreuter, 1995), 222.

18 *Ein Wort im Vertrauen über den Türkenkrieg* (Vienna 1788), 31.

19 *Vaterlandschronik*, 12 Dec., 1788, 816; Pezzl, *Skizze*, 636.

20 Ernst Wangermann, 'Nulla salus bello. Zu einigen Auswirkungen der Aufklärungsliteratur in Österreich', *Literatur und Kritik*, 1/5 (1966), 348 f.

21 Leslie Bodi, *Tauwetter in Wien. Zur Prosa der österreichischen Aufklärung 1781–1795* (*Schriftenreihe der Österreichischen Gesellschaft zur Erforschung des 18. Jahrhunderts* 6), (Vienna, Cologne and Weimar: Böhlau, 1995) 2nd edn, esp. 43 ff., 176 ff.; Lucia Franz, 'Die Wiener Realzeitung. Ein Beitrag zur Publizistik der theresianisch-josefinischen Epoche', (Phil. Diss., Vienna, 1966); Eduard Beutner, *Aufklärung versus Absolutismus? Zur Strategie der Ambivalenz in der Herrschersatire der österreichischen Literatur des josephinischen Jahrzehnts*, in Gerhard Ammerer and Hanns Haas (eds), *Ambivalenzen der Aufklärung. Festschrift für Ernst Wangermann* (Vienna: Verlag für Geschichte und Politik, 1997), 241–53.

22 Marianne Lunzer, 'Josephinisches und antijosephinisches Schrifttum', in Erich Zöllner (ed.), *Öffentliche Meinung in der Geschichte Österreichs* (Vienna: Österreichischer Bundesverlag, 1979), 54.

23 See for example (Franz Xaver Huber,) *Herrn Schlendrians, Oberster Richter zu Tropos, Erklärung der Tropsanischen Kriegsvorfälle* (Vienna, 1788).

24 (J.M.) Schweighofer, *Betrachtungen über die Ursachen und Folgen des Türkenkriegs* (Frankfurt and Vienna, 1788); Kaspar Pilat, *Christliche Betrachtungen über den gegenwärtigen Krieg des Erzhauses Oesterreich mit der Ottomanischen Pforte. An meine Landsleute in Böhmen* (Prague, 1788).

25 (Johann) Rautenstrauch, *Ausführliches Tagebuch des itzigen Krieges zwischen Oesterreich und der Pforte*, 1 (Vienna: Joseph Stabel, 1788), 8; also see Klaus Hildebrandt, 'Johann Rautenstrauchs publizistischer Beirag zur Aufklärung', (Phil. Diss., Vienna, 1966).

26 *Ueber den National-Charakter, die Sitten und Militair-Verfassung der Türken, nebst Bemerkungen über den Türkenkrieg*, 1, 1788, 6 f.

27 Schweighofer, *Betrachtungen*, s.p.

28 Maximilian Grothaus, 'Zum Türkenbild in der Adels- und Volkskultur der Habsburgermonarchie von 1650–1800', in Gernot Heiß and Grete Klingenstein (eds), *Das Osmanische Reich und Europa 1683–1789: Konflikt, Entspannung und Austausch* (Vienna: Verlag für Gesellschaft und Politik, 1984), 87; Pezzl, *Skizze*,

710–14; several articles in Christine Wessely (ed.), *Die Türken und was von ihnen blieb* (Vienna: Verband der wissenschaftlichen Gesellschaften Österreichs, 1978); Monika Kopplin, 'Turcica und Turquerien. Zur Entwicklung des Türkenbildes und Rezeption osmanischer Motive vom 15. bis 18. Jahrhundert', in *Exotische Welten – Europäische Phantasien*. *Katalog zur Ausstellung des Instituts für Auslandsbeziehungen und des Württembergischen Kunstvereins* (Stuttgart, 1987), 150–63; Gerhard Ammerer, ' "Türkenkopfstechen". Deckenfresko von Christoph Lederwasch und Johann Michael Rottmayr', in *Salzburg Edition*, Loseblattsammlung (Vienna: Archiv Verlag, 1994), s.p.

29   Maximilian Grothaus, 'Toleranz und Schwärmerei. Mozarts Orientalismus in mentalitätsgeschichtlicher Sicht', in *Zaubertöne*. *Mozart in Wien 1781–1791, Ausstellungskatalog* (Vienna: Eigenverlag der Museen der Stadt Wien, 1990), 431; Cornelia Kleinlogel, *Exotik – Erotik. Zur Geschichte des Türkenbildes in der deutschen Literatur der frühen Neuzeit (1453–1800)*, (Frankfurt am Main, Berne, New York and Paris: Peter Lang, 1989), 358 ff.; Roland Wurtz, *Das deutsche Singspiel im 18. Jahrhundert. Colloquium der Arbeitsstelle 18. Jahrhundert der Gesamthochschule Wuppertal und der Universität Münster* (Heidelberg, 1981), 125–37.

30   'Eine Rede gehalten, nach eingetroffener Nachricht vom Verluste der Festung Belgrad, in der ersten darauf gehaltenen Versammlung des Divans zu Konstantinopel', in *Neuester Rapport von Wien*, 9 December 1789, 134–9.

31   See, for example, *Neueste Wiener Nachrichten*, 23 October 1788, 330.

32   Rautenstrauch, *Ausführliches Tagebuch*, 3.

33   Kurt Strasser, *Die Wiener Presse in der Josephinischen Zeit* (Vienna: Verlag Notring der wissenschaftlichen Verbände Österreichs, 1962), 92.

34   Anonymous [Josef Judmann?] *Ein Wort im Vertrauen über den Türkenkrieg* (Vienna, 1788).

35   Ibid., 13–17.

36   Ibid., 25.

37   'Diese Schrift hat viel Aufstehen gemacht', *Allgemeine Deutsche Bibliothek*, 93/2, 1790, 592.

38   Christian Friedrich Daniel Schubart, 'Gang des Türkenkriegs', *Gesammelte Schriften und Schicksale*, 8 (Stuttgart, 1840), 163. On the Austrian image of England, see Ernst Wangermann, 'England und die Aufklärung. Zum österreichischen England-Bild', *Uni-aktuell*, October 1985.

39   Helene Patrias, 'Die Türkenkriege im Volkslied' (Phil. Diss., Vienna, 1947), 62; Senol Özyrt, *Die Türkenlieder und das Türkbild in der deutschen Volksüberlieferung vom 16. bis zum 20. Jahrhundert* (Munich: Wilhelm Fink, 1972), 387–9.

40   'Kriegslied' (1788), in Özyrt, *Türkenlieder*, 379.

41   'Loblied an den Helden Laudon auf die Einnahme der Stadt Belgrad. Gedruckt in diesem Jahr', in Özyrt, *Türkenlieder*, 386.

42   *Kriegslieder für Josephs Helden. Bey den Feldzügen gegen die Türken*, 1, 1788, 12.

43   'Phantasie eines Menschenfeindes beym Ausbruch des Türkenkriegs. Ein Fragment', in *Oesterreichische und türkische Kriegslieder* (Vienna, 1788), 74.

44   Josef Neubauer, *Weiss und Rosenfarb. Die Dichter der Mozartlieder. 16 Miniaturen* (Vienna: Brüder Hollinek, 1990), 28.

45 Wolfgang Amadeus Mozart, *Neue Ausgbe sämtlicher Werke. Serie II.:
    Bühnenwerke, Werkgruppe 7, 4* (Kassel, Basel, Tours and London: Bärenreiter,
    1972), IX f.; on this song see Gerhard Ammerer, ' "Ich möchte wohl der Kaiser
    sein" (KV 539) – ein patriotisches Kriegslied?', *Mitteilungen der Internationalen
    Stiftung Mozarteum*, 33 (1996), 33–46.
46 Otto Biba, in *Mozart-Martineen 1995, Programmheft* (Salzburg, 1995), 75.
47 Friedrich C. Heller, 'Joseph Haydn – eine Künstlerfreundschaft', in Peter Csobádi
    (ed.), *Wolfgang Amadeus. Summa summarum. Das Phänomen Mozart: Leben,
    Werk, Wirkung* (Vienna: Paul Neff, 1989), 56–60; H.C. Robbins Landon, 'Mozart
    und Haydn', *Zaubertöne*, 485 f.
48 Eva Badura-Skoda, 'Personal Contacts and Mutual Influence in the Field of
    Opera', in Jens Peter Larsen, Howard Serwer and James Webster (eds), *Haydn
    Studies. Proceedings of the International Haydn Conference* (New York and
    London: Norton, 1981), 420.
49 Joseph Haydn, *List und Liebe (La vera costanza)*, Nr. 5, Arie des Masino: 'Spann'
    deine langen Ohren . . . '
50 Ammerer, ' "Ich möchte wohl . . . " ', 46.
51 Joachim Perinet, *Liliputische Steuerfassion* (Vienna, 1789).
52 Ibid., 17, 21 and 27.
53 *Die Kriegssteuer. Ein Schauspiel in drei Aufzügen, nach einer wahren Geschichte
    gearbeitet, dem Willigen zum Vergnügen, und dem Murrenden zur Belehrung,
    während dem Winter-Quartiere aufzuführen* (Vienna 1789).
54 Wangermann, 'Nulla salus bello', 51.
55 *Die Kriegssteuer*, 46.
56 Ibid., 118.
57 Robert Waissenberger, 'Die Zeit, in der Hieronymus Löschenkohl wirkte', in
    Reingard Witzmann, *Hieronymus Löschenkohl. Bildreporter zwischen Barock
    und Biedermeier* (Vienna: Edition Tusch, 1978), 5.
58 Franz Gräffer, *Kleine Wiener Memoiren und Wiener Dorfstücke*, ed. Anton
    Schlossar, 1 (Munich: Georg Müller, 1918), 253 f.
59 *Hieronymus Löschenkohl. Ausstellungskatalog des Historischen Museums der
    Stadt Wien* (Vienna: Eigenverlag des Museums der Stadt Wien, 1959), 13.
60 Witzmann, *Löschenkohl*, 20.
61 Gerhard Ammerer, ' "Scherz und Ernst bey einem zwischen den Drey Kayser-
    Höfen, Rußland, Oesterreich u. der Ottomannischen Porte angestellten Triset
    Spiel" – Ein allegorischer Kupferstich zum Türkenjahr 1788 und die öffentliche
    Diskussion', *Homo Ludens. Der spielende Mensch*, V (1995), 288.
62 Hieronymus Löschenkohl, *Türkischer Helden Calender auf das Jahr 1790*
    (Vienna, 1790).
63 *Unpartheyisch geographisch-historischer Kriegsweiser* (Vienna, 1788).
64 Rautenstrauch, *Ausführliches Tagebuch*, 4, 381 f.
65 [Johann Rautenstrauch,] *Erinnerungen wegen der über die itzigen Kriegsvorfälle
    bisher erschinenen besonderen Beylagen zur Wienerzeitung* (Vienna, 1788), 5.
66 Ibid., 6 f.
67 Ibid., 13.
68 Mitrofanov, *Joseph II*, 212.
69 Kotasek, *Lacy*, 179.
70 Mitrofanov, *Joseph II*, 369 f.
71 Groß-Hoffinger, *Lebens- und Regierungsgeschichte*, 128.

72 Ernst Wangermann, *From Joseph II to the Jacobin Trials. Government Policy and Public Opinion in the Habsburg Dominions in the Period of the French Revolution* (Oxford, 1969), 30.
73 *Vaterlandschronik*, 13 October 1789, 693; 30 October 1789, 802; *Wöchentliche Beiträge zur Kriegs- und Staatsgeschichte*, 13 October 1789, s.p.
74 Friedrich Engel-Jánosi, 'Josephs II. Tod im Urteil seiner Zeitgenossen', *Mitteilungen des Instituts für Österreichische Geschichtsforschung*, 44 (1930), 324 f.
75 An original could not be found; quoted in *Vaterlandschronik*, 16 December 1788, 842.

10
Surrealist blasphemy

Malcolm Gee

'Surrealism', André Breton wrote in 1924, 'will usher you into death, which is a secret society.'[1] The surrealist group over which he presided functioned as an intellectual sect, dedicated to an elitist practice of literature and art. From this perspective, a study of their work may appear out of place in a collection dedicated mainly to popular scurrility and subversion. However, certain features of the surrealist 'project' do relate to this theme. In particular, their interest in the legacy of nineteenth-century 'decadence', their militant atheism, and their growing ambition to politicise their activity on their own terms, led them to a fascination with the power of the obscene and blasphemous as subversive devices in modern culture.

As Werner Spies has pointed out, the anticlericalism of Breton and his friends went hand in hand with their literary enthusiasms.[2] The body of nineteenth century literature they admired, from the Gothic novel to Lautréamont, linked the power of the imagination to defiance of conventional morality and its institutional basis in the Church; it explored the erotic charge of 'evil' and violence. The heroine of M.G. Lewis's *The Monk*, that Breton cited in 1924 as an example of the ability of the marvellous to salvage 'inferior' forms of literature (the novel), acquires sexual appetite and power over her lover (the monk in question) through a satanic pact. Maldoror, Lautréamont's monstrous alter ego, personified, Breton claimed, the principle that 'evil', based on the gratification of forbidden desires, is the driving force in history.[3]

The fascination with evil and its basis in the occult could give surrealist activity a somewhat quaint air of decadence. This was certainly true of one of their protégés, the Abbé Gengenbach, who wrote to them in 1925 suggesting that in his case suicide *was* a solution: he had been expelled from his traineeship with the Jesuits after an affair with an actress. Having failed to carry out this resolution he emerged as a troubled exponent of Satanism, and Breton provided his lecture 'Satan à Paris' with a guarded homage in 1927.[4] However, Surrealism had other, more virulent, aspects from the beginning, and these became more pronounced during the course of the decade, as the group sought to establish its revolutionary identity. At the end of 1926 the eighth issue of *La Révolution surréaliste* clearly laid out the different strands of their position. Literary texts were juxtaposed with contemporary comment, anti-religious tracts and images, and Breton's statement of principle, *Légitime défense*, in which he made the case for the distinctiveness and validity of a Surrealist 'politics'. This was in the face, on one hand, of the evolution of the French communist party and, on the other, of developments in society, including the literary and artistic circles with which the group were most familiar. Breton's violent critique of Henri Barbusse – now literary editor of *L'Humanité* – was partly prompted by the latter's indulgence towards the prominent catholic writer Paul Claudel and Jean Cocteau, who had recently announced his conversion. Georges Ribemont-Dessaignes contributed an exercise in blasphemous invective prompted by this phenomenon of high profile repentance and re-admission into the Church: a process he described in a characteristic image as 'The Holy Body opening up like a vulva on heat'.[5]

   'They say: all this is anticlericalism, and anticlericalism is an old bit of nonsense', Ribemont-Dessaignes commented. But the fashion for conversion that prompted his text was an indication that this traditional arena of republican struggle retained social and political significance. In fact the mid-1920s saw a revival of Catholic activism. The 'Cartel des Gauches' that came to power in 1924 threatened to pursue the doctrinaire secular policies of pre-war radicalism. The *Féderation Nationale Catholique* was founded in 1925 to organise mass protests in the light of this, and to co-ordinate catholic political activity in general. Its president, General Castelnau, was also head of the *Ligue des patriotes*, the anti-Dreyfusard nationalist movement that too revived in mid decade.[6] The return to power of Raymond Poincaré in 1926, in the context of the 'crisis of the franc', marked a conservative reorientation of national politics that comforted the Catholic movement and incensed the extreme left. Breton opened *Légitime défense* with an attack on 'le sinistre "Lorrain" ': 'we consider the presence of M. Poincaré at the head of the government as a grave obstacle in the realm of thought, a more or less gratuitous insult to the mind, and a savage, inadmissible joke'.[7] Violent anticlericalism was integral to the 'line' that Breton and Louis Aragon now sought to impose in the group and over which it split during 1927 and 1928. The necessary intransigence of himself and his remaining colleagues, Breton asserted in the second manifesto, published in the final issue of *La Révolution surréaliste* in December 1929, impelled them 'to laugh like savages at the French flag, to puke their disgust at *every* priest and to aim the long distance weapon of sexual cynicism at the proponents of "primary duties" '.[8] The issue of *Variétés* 'le Surréalisme en 1929' which, earlier that year, had first publicised the ruptures in the group, included a satirical text by Aragon and

Breton that manifested this spirit, in a humorous vein. The *Treasure of the Jesuits* was a 'surrealist' version of an established genre of popular boulevard theatre, a cabaret-type review of the year 1928. Using two topical incidents – a parliamentary debate on Church funds that split Poincaré's 'Union nationale', and the murder of the cashier of the Catholic foreign missions – Aragon and Breton constructed a scenario that drew on anticlerical traditions and identified a modern femme fatale as murderess and beneficiary of the Jesuit gold. The final scene parodied a Masonic ceremony, in which the discoverer of the treasure is promoted in the secret order and then receives the 'Very Sinister Illustrious Unknown Superior Authority'. This mysterious 'black pope' and 'anti-Christ' then unmasks 'himself' as the heroine, 'Mad Souri'.[9]

Etienne-Alain Hubert has noted that moments in *The Treasure of the Jesuits* are reminiscent of paintings by Giorgio de Chirico and Max Ernst. Several aspects of the piece, in fact, have affinities with Ernst's subversive, and humorous, use of found imagery. One of the sources for the final satanic dénouement appears to have been a book on *The Mysteries of Freemasonry* by Léo Taxil, that had contributed to Catholic scaremongering in the 1880s.[10] The illustrated magazines of that era became, at this time, Ernst's principal sources for the visual material of his collage novels. He shared Breton and Aragon's taste for the 'outmoded' and 'dark' remnants of nineteenth-century culture, and their intransigence in respect of religion. Blasphemy had figured in his work from the Dada period. Linked to eroticism, it was a recurring element in his output at the end of the decade, when his complicity with the Surrealists was reinforced. The anticlerical issue of *La Révolution surréaliste* included a reproduction of a painting that was a striking affirmation of this: *The Virgin chastising the infant Jesus in the presence of three witnesses –* Breton, Eluard and Ernst himself. His first collage novel *La Femme 100 Têtes*, published in December 1929 with a preface by Breton, opened on the theme of man's defiance of God, using a joking reference to the doctrine of the Immaculate Conception to introduce the specific poetics of collage.[11] These images, and this theme, were fresh in Breton and Eluard's minds when they composed *The Immaculate Conception* the following summer. Besides containing virtuoso exercises in the simulation of mental disorders, this text, as Marguerite Bonnet and Etienne-Alain Hubert point out, posits a 'poetic anthropology' within a framework that at key points parodies a Christian one.[12] The final section, 'The Original Judgement', included an image of 'beautiful women with their décolletage in the form of a cross' that Dalí drew on for his frontispiece to the luxury edition. The original project for the cover had been even more directly blasphemous: it reproduced a statue of the Virgin crowned with the words 'je suis l'Immaculée Conception' – those pronounced in a vision by the Virgin of Lourdes in 1858.[13] This satirical gesture is somewhat in the spirit of another blasphemous publication of 1930, Ernst's second 'novel', *The Dream of a Little Girl who wanted to enter Carmel*.

This book uses seventy-nine wood engravings from nineteenth-century illustrated books, adapted and captioned by the artist, to answer the question 'what do little girls dream of who want to take the veil?' An introductory text gives a precise, and lurid, portrait of the dreamer. Her name is Marceline-Marie. At the time of the dream – Good Friday 1930 – she is sixteen years old. She is a pupil in a convent in Lyon. At age seven she was raped, had her milk teeth knocked out by the perpetrator, and took first communion. At age eleven she experienced her vocation during a procession of relics; she levitated 'for several seconds' and cried out:

> Enter, dear knife, into the incubation chamber!
> The celestial bridegroom invites me to the feast!
> I sacrifice myself and I give myself!
> The earth is soft and white!

She has an 'irresistible tendency toward the practice of obstinate devotion and theatrical sacrifice' and, prompted by her double name, suffers from a problem of identity. In the 'dream' this is dramatised by 'Marceline' and 'Marie' appearing as 'two distinct but clearly related persons'.[14] It is not always easy to discern the distinctive roles and character of 'Marceline' and 'Marie' in the sequence of 'dream' images. However, the overall source of her confusion is clearly her relationship with her body and sexuality, experienced in itself and imagined via Christian doctrine. She 'dreams' of her parents, her confessor, the Pope, myriad animals and insects, the convent authorities, and finally her 'celestial bridegroom'. Praying to him, in the dream, leads to physical gratification: in the third section of the novel – 'the knife'- after 'propagating catastrophes with our flexible hands' (58), Marceline-Marie feels that the sky is 'falling into my heart'. She wakes up feeling dizzy, finds her nightie 'really indecent' and goes back to sleep smiling. However, when the bridegroom comes down to earth, he betrays her by disappearing and going mad: 'Even as an image I must die' (76). Marceline-Marie is left with her parents, as his ageless widow (77, 78).

'Marceline-Marie' was partly inspired by Ernst's wife, Marie-Berthe Aurenche. She had been educated in a convent and had a close friend in the Carmel at Lisieux. Her own relation to Catholicism was ambivalent. This led to a crisis in the mid-1930s, when her relationship with Ernst failed. However, as Werner Spies has observed, the 'Dream of a Little Girl' was not prompted just by personal circumstances: it was a contribution to the anticlerical campaign of the Surrealist group at the time.[15] The scurrilous presentation of

Marceline-Marie's relations with her 'celestial bridegroom' satirises Catholic doctrine, which combined a personalised, romantic conception of the relationship between the nun and her 'bridegroom', Christ, with violent denial of the body. 'Dirty as a carmelite' was, indeed, a common expression of the period.[16]

The visionary dramatisation of the nun's mystical 'betrothal' to Christ was most famously outlined in the writings of the founder of the reformed Carmelite order, Saint Teresa of Ávila. Marceline-Marie's experience of levitation may be a specific reference to this model of ecstatic religious behaviour – this was one of the ways in which Teresa revealed divine possession in public, to her embarrassment.[17] Marceline-Marie's religious ardour is explicitly linked to a more recent and topical exemplar – St Thérèse de l'Enfant Jésus, the 'little saint' of Lisieux. The 'dream' reads, indeed, in some respects as a parody of Thérèse's famous book, 'The History of a Soul', the autobiographical essays written at the end of her short life at the request of her two sisters who were with her in the convent. Thérèse decided that she had a vocation when she was nine. She persuaded her father, for whom she was his 'dear little Princess', to accept this when she was fourteen. Faced by the refusal of the authorities to accept her profession below the normal age, she travelled to Rome with her sister Céline to petition Pope Leo XIII directly. She was allowed to enter Carmel at fifteen in April 1888 and finally took the veil in November 1890. She died of tuberculosis in 1897. Her simple, and tragic, story was used as an element in Catholic propaganda from the turn of the century onwards. The book gradually became a best-seller and the French hierarchy initiated the beatification process in 1910. This involved abrogating normal rules, which required a fifty-year delay after the death of a postulate saint. The Vatican agreed to this in 1919 and the process of beatification followed by canonisation was completed in 1925, after verification of the requisite number of miracles. One of these took place as the relics of Thérèse were moved from the cemetery of Lisieux to the cathedral in 1923, where 50,000 pilgrims took part in the procession, and a 'perfume of roses' (Thérèse's favourite flowers) had emanated from the opened tomb.[18] 'Marceline-Marie's' vocation came to her (in 1925) during a service consecrating a statue of St Thérèse, and the cemetery of Lisieux figures directly in her dream (23). This, constituted in images from Thérèse's own time, presents a violent, erotic version of adolescent religious fantasy that mocks the saccharine piety of the 'History of a Soul' (see Figures 10.1 and 10.2).

A year after publishing 'Dream of a Little Girl' Ernst made an even more explicit attack on the Church's doctrine in respect of sexuality in the article 'Danger de Pollution' that appeared in the third issue of the group's new

Figure 10.1 Max Ernst, *Rêve d'une petite fille qui voulut entrer au Carmel*, plate 50

Figure 10.2 Max Ernst, *Rêve d'une petite fille qui voulut entrer au* *Carmel*, **plate 55**

journal *Le Surréalisme au Service de la Révolution*.[20] He had come across an anticlerical publication by Léo Taxil from the 1880s that reproduced (or claimed to) the secret textbooks used in Catholic seminaries to train priests for their duties as confessors. *Les Diaconales. Manuel des Confesseurs* was a comprehensive theoretical and practical discussion of the sins of the flesh ('luxure'), that categorised them according to type and degree.[21] Ernst presented this as a grotesque demonstration of the fact that because love is the enemy of Christian morality, the 'clerical police', through the 'droppings of the Church professors', had erected a complex system of repression, based on the confessional. Through the good work of the confessors

> the virtue of pride, that made man beautiful, has given way to the vice of Christian humility, that makes him ugly . . . There is no sight on earth more likely to arouse our circonspection than the sight of a confessor going about his disgusting business according to the precepts of St. Augustin, St. Thomas Aquinas, St. Alphonse of Liguori and Mgr. Bouvier [author of *Les Diaconales*], the obscene bishop of Le Mans and a Roman count.

André Breton considered *Le Surréalisme au service de la révolution* – of which six issues were published between 1930 and 1933 – to have been 'by far the richest, in our sense of the term,' of the Surrealist reviews, 'the most alive (an exalting and dangerous life)'.[22] After the disappointments and loss of momentum of the previous two years, the group reasserted its identity and its 'revolutionary' stance – albeit in a context that led in 1932 to a further violent split with Aragon and other partisans of an unconditional allegiance to the French Communist Party.[23] The vitriolic nature of Ernst's piece, and its subject, were characteristic of the tone and focus of the review, that set out to establish a surrealist position combining disdainful, violent critique of society, informed by Marxist-Leninism, with a continued appeal to the transforming power of imagination and desire. Hatred of Christianity was central to this position. Love, said Ernst, must be renewed by the collective unconscience: 'That is impossible under the rule of the capitalist and clerical police.' The first issue of *Le Surréalisme au service de la révolution* included images from Buñuel and Dalí's film *L'Age d'Or*, that articulated the same message with a similar savage humour. And four of the six issues of the review contained texts by, or about, the Marquis de Sade, whose work exemplified the transgressive force of the sexual imagination, defiance of society, and of God.

'Sade est surréaliste dans le sadisme': Breton had identified the eighteenth-century aristocrat as a precursor in the first manifesto of 1924. Following Guillaume Apollinaire's lead, he and his colleagues had set out in the 1920s to rediscover and re-evaluate the work of this most denigrated and suppressed of French authors. In an essay on eroticism written in 1923 Robert Desnos identified Sade's writing as the first manifestation of the modern spirit, because it placed sexuality at the core of human experience and dared to examine 'love and its performance (actes) from the point of view of the infinite'.[24] In 1925, in *La Liberté ou l'Amour* – a text that was itself prosecuted when it appeared in 1927 – he presented Sade with Robespierre as a hero of the revolutionary spirit,[25] as did Paul Eluard in 'D.A.F. de Sade, écrivain fantastique et révolutionnaire', that appeared in the eighth, anticlerical, issue of *La Révolution surréaliste*. Eluard pointed out that Sade was 'sovereignly unhappy' – his refusal of 'normality' and adherence to the principle of absolute liberty for his imagination, had led him to spend most of his life in prison.[26]

This admiration, and appropriation, of Sade as a model of extremism and defiance in the exercise of the (erotic) imagination was supported by a determined effort to disseminate and properly reassess his work. The new review carried a series of articles by Maurice Heine, who had dedicated himself to this task since the war and who was currently engaged in publishing *Les cent vingt journées de Sodome* – for the first time in France. Heine too emphasised the modernity of Sade's thought: 'an author who is so close to us that it takes a real effort of the imagination to realise that only ten years separate us from the bicententary of his birth.' In his introduction to *Dialogue between a priest and a dying man* (1926) he insisted on Sade's intransigent atheism, and contrasted it with the pantheist tendencies of his contemporaries. In another note in the review, in 1933, he cited an episode from *La nouvelle Justine* that demonstrated Sade's readiness to 'free sadism from its human prison' and defy nature itself. The chemist Almani declares himself to be nature's executioner, 'her murderous nets are thrown just over us; let us try to catch her in them herself by masturbating her if I can; block her in her creations to insult her better'. Heine went on to argue that Sade's significance had been distorted by the 'erroneous legend of a sadistic Sade'. In fact he was a philosopher who was the first thinker to have 'studied in an objective, methodical and comprehensive manner one of the great moral forces of mankind.' From this perspective Sade's materialism, and the primacy of instinct in his system, made him a precursor of Freud, another key point of reference for the Surrealists. Louis Aragon, retrospectively, noted the influence of both on Ernst's *Dream of a Little Girl*: 'in many respects [it is] a meditation on the relation of opposites – of Justine and Juliette'.[27]

The importance of Sade and Freud to the preoccupations of the surrealist group at this time was made evident in the programme-manifesto they drew up for the public screening of *L'Age d'Or* in December 1930. Breton presented the film as an exemplary demonstration of the possibility of understanding the process of sublimation, and of exposing the dual working

of the sexual and the death instincts in the individual and society. André
Thirion, under the heading 'social aspect – subversive elements' highlighted
the film's sacrilegious and political character: 'the struggle against religion is
also the struggle against the world'; love thwarted by society engenders
revolt, and so 'it is not by chance that Buñuel's sacrilegious film echoes the
blasphemies shouted by the divine marquis through the bars of his prisons'.[28]

L'Age d'Or, that Buñuel and Dalí originally planned together as a sequel
to Un Chien Andalou (to be called 'The Andalusian Beast' or 'Down with the
Constitution') was, like its predecessor, in many ways a very Spanish
concoction. However, it was also the product of interaction with the highly
specific Parisian milieu of the surrealist circle, that had greeted the first film
enthusiastically in the summer of 1929.[29] Over the next eighteen months the
two Spaniards became closely implicated in the reformulated surrealist group.
For Dalí the encounter with Surrealism, linked to his sexual liberation by Gala
Eluard, meant confirmation and encouragement of his capacity to formulate
visual expressions of his obsessive erotic fantasies, informed by his reading
of Freud. For Buñuel it meant an exhilarating engagement with a group whose
moral indignation at bourgeois society matched his own. He was fascinated
by their discipline and morality, based on 'passion, mystification, insult,
malevolent laughter, the attraction of the abyss'.[30] It was these qualities that
he sought to realise in L'Age d'Or. 'You can't imagine how I've changed and
the progress I think I've made', he wrote to his close friend Pepín Bello in
May 1930, 'especially in the field of morality and intransigence'.[31] His
discovery of Sade, through the Surrealists, was a key element in this
'progress'. 'I discovered in Sade a world of extraordinary subversion, in
which there is everything from insects to the customs of human society, sex,
theology . . . it really dazzled me.'[32]

In his response to L'Age d'Or – published in the same issue of Le
Surréalisme au service de la révolution as Ernst's 'Danger de Pollution' –
Maurice Heine referred to the 'evident freudo-sadism' of the film. The
representation of desire in the central 'narrative', and of the obstacles it
encounters, are clearly informed by Freudian notions of psychic motivation.
Buñuel and Dalí included some specifically sadist 'touches' – notably during
the climactic garden scene in the woman's voice-over 'What joy! What joy to
have murdered our children!' The male protagonist, indeed, is in a sense a
sadian figure: he pursues sexual pleasure with ruthless, criminal egotism. And
the epilogue of course makes a direct homage to the author of Les cent vingt
journées de Sodome, as the 'Duc de Blangis' leaves the château de Selligny
with his accomplices. The duke is dressed to resemble Christ – this
blasphemous alignment with Sade's scorn for religion was made explicit in
the programme notes. Heine reproached Buñuel for not following Sade's own

lead and condemning Mahomet, Moses and Confucius equally with Christ, but he was understandably enthusiastic at the overall gesture: 'With it, you have marked with real blood a screen too used to rose water or syrup' (see Figures 10.3 and 10.4).[33]

Removal of the phrase 'The Duke of Blangis is obviously Jesus Christ' was the one change that the Vicomte de Noailles asked to make to the programme published for the public screening of *L'Age d'Or*, which opened on 22 November 1930 at Studio 28, a small art cinema in Montmartre. The launch of the film had been carefully prepared: the Noailles had screened it to select audiences at their Parisian home in July, and hired the cinema *Le Panthéon* for another private screening (to about two hundred guests) on 22 October=. From the reception that some sectors of 'Le Tout Paris' gave the film, he probably realised that this blasphemous assertion was potentially dangerous. The *L'Age d'Or* 'affair' broke out properly after 3 December, when a group of right-wing militants vandalised the screen and the exhibition of paintings and photographs in the foyer. The authorities eventually used the 'pornographic' character of certain scenes as grounds for seizing the film and withdrawing its visa (granted on the basis of a somewhat misleading plot synopsis).[34] Its 'obscenity' was certainly a cause of offence, but it was its political and blasphemous features that were most frequently cited in the Press campaign that precipitated the ban.

Léon Daudet, with characteristic malevolence and awareness, suggested that the secret services had considered using a scandal over the film as a diversionary tactic from the failures of government foreign policy: 'This film cost 1,200,000 francs. Who paid for it? Sadism, the police, or both?'[35] The *Camelots du Roi*, linked to *L'Action Française*, did not in fact participate in the incident on 3 December, that was caused by members of the 'League of Patriots'. The sustained campaign, principally in *L'Ami du Peuple* and *Le Figaro* began shortly after, as screenings were resumed under police protection. The League itself described *L'Age d'Or* as 'bolshevik inspired' and 'obscene', 'attacking religion, country and family'. These aspects were highlighted in Richard-Pierre Bodin's open letter to the censor in *Le Figaro* of 7 December and in the right-wing councillor J. Le Provost de Launay's equally publicised letter to Jean Chiappe, the Prefect of Paris. Chiappe had the legal power to stop screenings of the film, which he exercised on 11 December. 'Country, Family and Religion are dragged in the dirt,' Bodin commented, citing the programme notes and the scene in which a monstrance is placed in the gutter while a society couple get out of a taxi to go to the reception. (It was at this point in the film that members of the League had thrown ink at the screen.) On 10 December, in an article that published de Launay's letter, Bodin again drew attention to the blasphemous and

Figure 10.3 *L'Age d'Or*: **The love scene in the garden**

Figure 10.4 *L'Age d'Or*: The Duc de Blangis and his accomplices leave the Château de Selligny

revolutionary character of the film: 'This is a bolshevik exercise of a very special kind , that sets out to corrupt us.' It recalled the worst passages of Huysmans' *Là-Bas*, and was, indeed, of satanic inspiration.[36]

On 14 December Charles de Noailles wrote to Buñuel, who was now in Hollywood, informing him of events. He pointed out that Buñuel's own name was played down in the publicity, that focused on the surrealist group and himself, since that lent itself better to scandal. The Surrealists published a brochure on the 'Affair', emphasising its political nature: the official reaction demonstrated the fascisisation of the regime, the incompatibility of Surrealism and bourgeois society, and the persecution of elements in society that opposed the coming war against the Soviet Union.[37] For Breton and his colleagues the affair was a welcome vindication of their claim that a surrealist position, and mode of expression, was political. They had succeeded in exposing, on their own terms, the limits of republican tolerance and the growing strength of 'fascist' forces in French society. Thanks to the power of the cinema, they had finally been perceived as a real threat to normal society.

Buñuel professed himself somewhat bemused by the turn of events: 'So that's the result of a film that I thought was tender over and above its violence', he wrote to Charles de Noailles. He noted that several of the incidents that had occurred – including the official Italian protest that it caricatured the King and Queen of Italy – were worthy of featuring as jokes in the film itself.[38] The blasphemous tone of *L'Age d'Or*, that triggered the scandal and the film's repression, encapsulated surrealist attitudes at the end of the decade, as did, in its way, Ernst's *Dream of a Little Girl*. The critics who took violent offence at the film did not generally comment on its humour. The film is, however, partly constructed around 'gags' and this aspect of the work, as is also the case with Ernst's 'novels', was equally attuned to surrealist thinking. Breton and Aragon placed Freud's recent essay on 'Humour' (1927) at the opening of their survey 'Surrealism in 1929': it was one of the key sources for the theorisation of the concept of 'black humour' that Breton was developing at the time. Freud explained jokes and humour in terms of the pulsional 'economy' of the psyche. Jokes allow the release of aggression and repressed desires; humour, which is the superior form of the comic sense, is a demonstration of the ego's ability, in exceptional cases, to isolate itself from the real ('Well, this week's starting well', says the condemned man on his way to the gallows on Monday morning). For the Surrealists black humour was a form of defiance in relation to a social world that incited despair.[39] Ernst claimed that it was central to his practice of collage: it was the necessary opposite to 'rosy humour' in 'an epoch that is not rosy'.[40]

In 'Danger de pollution' Ernst imagined a scenario that Buñuel might have enjoyed filming. Mgr Bouvier laid down in *Les Diaconales* that a robed priest who masturbates while celebrating mass, or descending from the altar afterwards, commits a double sacrilege because of the inherent insult to God, and the 'pollution' (useless dispensation of sperm) that ensues. Ernst invited his 'sympathetic male reader or charming female one' to enjoy themselves 'morosely' at the thought.

> This image can only be surpassed in beauty by that of *two* priests who, dressed in sacred robes and having held in their hands the immaculate lamb, masturbate *each other* while descending majestically the steps of the altar and who, having got to the bottom and come, mutually absolve each other of their *quadruple* sacrilege.

He was referring here not only to Bouvier's stipulations concerning sacrilege but also to the section on 'unconsummated sins of the flesh', one of the chief of which is 'morose or contemplative delectation. This, Bouvier says, is the remembering of a vile act that the imagination represents as real, without the desire to carry it out – such as 'imagining one is fornicating'.[41] The notion that the mere exercise of the imagination constituted a mortal sin was, in its way, an amusing one. Its elaboration formed one underlying thread in much of Ernst, Buñuel and Dalí's work. This contributed to what Walter Benjamin referred to as the 'profane illumination' of the Surrealists, which he argued allowed them to develop a concept of freedom that turned the 'romantic dummy' of late-nineteenth-century satanism to revolutionary use.[42] The Marquis de Sade's assertion of a sovereign right to imaginative excess, despite condemnation and imprisonment, represented a model of this notion. It was one that, Breton pointed out, included 'black' humour. Buñuel also recognised this: like the monster Minski's horrific all-human diet,[43] the Duke of Blangis/Christ's polishing off of his last victim, in the final scene of *L'Age d'Or*, is a joke.

Notes

1   'Le surréalisme vous introduira dans la mort qui est une société secrète. Il gantera votre main, y ensevelissant l'Ma profond par quoi commence le mot Mémoire.' *Manifeste du Surréalisme* (1924), quoted here from *André Breton. Oeuvres Complètes*, ed. Marguerite Bonnet (Paris: Gallimard (La Pléiade), I, 1988), 334. Henceforth *Breton, Oeuvres*. The masonic resonances of this passage are commented on by David Hopkins in *Marcel Duchamp and Max Ernst. The Bride Shared* (Oxford: Clarendon Press, 1998), 122. See note 10 below.
2   Werner Spies, *Max Ernst. Collages. The Invention of the Surrealist Universe* (London: Thames and Hudson, 1991), (original edn, Cologne: DuMont Schauberg, 1974), 232 and 265, note 782.

3   On *The Monk* (1795), see the 'Manifeste du surréalisme', *Oeuvres* I, 320. Breton cited Léon-Pierre Quint's characterisation of the role of 'evil' in *Les Chants de Maldoror* in his notice on Lautréamont for the *Anthologie de l'Humour Noir* (1940), *Oeuvres* II, 1992, 987.

4   Gengenbach's letter was published in *La Révolution surréaliste*, 5. For Breton's introduction to 'Satan à Paris', see *Oeuvres* I, 923–27. He cites Huysman's *Là-bas* with approval on the cult of the Devil: (it is) 'less insane than that of God. The cult of God stinks while the other is splendid.'

5   'La Saison des bains de ciel', *La Révolution surréaliste*, 8, 23–6.

6   See Serge Bernstein, 'La Ligue', in *Histoires des Droites en France*, Jean-François Sirinelli (ed.) (Paris: Gallimard, 1992), vol. 2, 65–104 and Eugen Weber, *The Hollow Years. France in the 1930s* (London: Norton, 1994), ch. 7, 182–206.

7   'Légitime défense', *La Révolution surréaliste*, 8, 30–36. In one of his contributions to this issue (illustrated by a photo in which he is seen insulting a priest in the street), Benjamin Péret gave an anticlerical gloss to 'La baisse du franc': 'Franc petit franc . . . jadis curé pansu tu officiais dans les couloirs des bordels', ibid., 13–14.

8   *La Révolution surréaliste*, 12, December 1929, 1–17. The issue included a violent text, 'Comment accommoder le prêtre' by Jean Koppen, ibid., 30–31, with further advice on the subject.

9   'Le Trésor des jésuites', *Oeuvres* II, 994–1014. Her name was an anagram of Musidora, the star of the 1917 film *Les Vampires*, who was meant to play the role in the benefit performance for which it was written. The piece was not performed in 1928 in the event.

10   Breton, *Oeuvres* I, 1746, 1754. Hubert suggests that Ernst on occasion used illustrations from Taxil's publications for his collage works. Ernst's use of masonic imagery, notably in his 1939 painting 'La Toilette de la Mariée' is analysed by David Hopkins, *Marcel Duchamp and Max Ernst*, 119–25. Taxil's book provided details of secret chapters of freemasons, including women, that supposedly demonstrated the satanic basis of the movement – *Les Mystères de la franc-maçonnerie dévoilés par Léo Taxil* (Paris: Letouzey & Ane, *c.* 1890). In fact much of this was a hoax, perpertrated by Taxil (Gabriel Jogand-Pagès) when he was acting as a Catholic propagandist, after the bankruptcy of his 'Librairie Anti-cléricale'. See *Satan franc-maçon: La Mystification de Léo Taxil présentée par Eugen Weber* (Paris: Julliard, 1964) and Elisabeth Ripoll, 'Léo Taxil ou le feuilleton de l'anticléricalisme' in *Le Populaire à l'ombre des clochers*, CIEREC Travaux XCI, St. Etienne, 1997, 55–66. See also note 21 below.

11   On the 'novels', see Spies, *Max Ernst. Collages*, 216–7, 223–34. Spies argues that the visual blasphemy found in the work of Ernst and Buñuel was qualitatively different from the 'enlightenment anticlericalism' of most Surrealist texts.

12   Breton, *Oeuvres* I, 1634.

13   Ibid., 1629–30.

14   *Rêve d'une petite fille qui voulut entrer au Carmel* (Paris: Editions du Carrefour, 1930). English quotations are from Dorothea Tanning's translation (New York: Brazillier, 1982).

15   Spies, *Max Ernst. Collages*, 231. On Marie-Berthe's character, see also Patrick Waldberg, *Max Ernst* (Paris: J.-J. Pauvert, 1958), 259–65; Jimmy Ernst, *L'Ecart absolu. Souvenirs d'un enfant du surréalisme* (Paris: Ballard, 1986), 50, 54–64,

123, 151–2 (original edn *A Not-so-still life* (New York: St Martin's, 1984)); Jean Aurenche, *La Suite à l'écran* (Institut Lumière/Actes Sud, 1993),17–37.

16 Eugen Weber, *The Hollow Years*, 182–3. The practice of shaving girls' heads when they took the veil is referred to recurrently in the 'dream', as David Hopkins observes – *Marcel Duchamp and Max Ernst*, 136–7.

17 *The Life of St Teresa of Avila*, London: Shead and Ward, 1979, 120–21.

18 *The Story of the Canonization of St Thérèse of Lisieux* (London: Burns and Washbourne Ltd), 1934. *Histoire d'une âme* was first published in 1898. An English translation appeared soon after under the title *The Little Flower of Jesus* (London: Burns and Oates, 1901).

19 For Thérèse's thoughts on her 'celestial bridegroom' see *The Little Flower of Jesus*, 72, 120–22, 126–7. Charlotte Stokes first pointed out the relationship between Ernst's *Dream* and *The History of a Soul* in 'Surrealist as religious visionary', in Donald E. Morse (ed.), *The Fantastic in World Literature and the Arts* (New York: Greenwood Press, 1987), 167–82. St Thérèse was so popular in the postwar era that she appeared in the cinema as an intercessor in the cause of marriage in *La Rose effeuillée* of 1926 (roses were her emblematic flowers). Georges Sadoul recalled the group's joy at Breton's anecdote of having seen, in a small boulevard cinema during the projection of this film, 'a woman take off her coat and pass from seat to seat, completely naked', *Rencontres* I (Paris: Denoël, 1984), 41.

20 December 1931, 22–35. The text is reproduced in Max Ernst, *Ecritures* (Paris: Gallimard, 1970), 174–85.

21 *Les Livres secrets des confesseurs dévoilés aux pères de famille* (Paris: chez M. Léo Taxil, 1883). This was one of numerous publications of Taxil's *Librairie Anti-cléricale* on the Rue des Ecoles (many of the others were semi-pornographic.) Ernst mentioned the *Librairie* in his text.

22 *Entretiens* (Paris: Gallimard, 1969 (1952)), 154-5. On the overall characteristics of the review, see Dawn Ades, *Dada and Surrealism Reviewed* (London: Arts Council of Great Britain, 1978), 250–65.

23 On this period, see Sarah Wilson, 'Art and the Politics of the Left in France, c1935–1985' (PhD, University of London, 1991), ch. 3.

24 'De l'érotisme', written for the collector Jacques Doucet, cited in Annie Le Brun, 'Les surréalistes, Sade et Minotaure', *Sade, aller et détours* (Paris: Plon, 1989), 113–45. On this general topic see also Raymond Jean, 'Sade et le surréalisme', in Centre Aixois d'études et de recherches sur le dix-huitième siècle, *Le Marquis de Sade* (Paris: Colin, 1968), 241–51.

25 Marie-Claude Dumas, *Robert Desnos ou l'exploration des limites* (Paris: Klinsieck, 1980), 439–47.

26 *La Révolution Surréaliste*, 8, (December 1926), 8–9.

27 'L'essai Max Ernst' (1975), in *Louis Aragon. Ecrits sur l'art moderne* (Paris: Flammarion, 1981), 312–47, here 333.

28 'L'Age d'Or', 8–19 of the programme. Presented as a collective text, but each section had been drafted by individuals. Taken here from facsimile published as an insert to 'L'Age d'Or. Luis Buñuel – Charles de Noailles. Lettres et Documents (1929–1976)', *Les Cahiers du Musée National d'Art Moderne, Paris. Hors-série/Archives* (Paris, 1993). Henceforth, *Cahiers*.

29 See: Agustín Sánchez Vidal, 'De l'Age d'Or à la ruée vers l'or', in *Cahiers*, 11–27; idem, 'The Andalusian Beasts' in Michael Raeburn (ed.), *Salvador Dalí:*

174   Subversion and Scurrility

the early years (London: Thames and Hudson, 1994), 193–207; idem, *Buñuel, Lorca, Dalí: el enigma sin fin* (Barcelona: Planeta, 1988), 183–252. The latter reproduces the original texts of key correspondence between Dalí and Buñuel and between Buñuel and Pepín Bello. On 17 February 1929 Buñuel sent Bello a long letter referring to his and Dalí's discovery of and enthusiasm for the writing of Benjamin Péret. He included a cutting from *La Révolution surréaliste* 8 with the photograph of Péret insulting a priest.

30 Luis Buñuel, *Mi Ultimo Suspiro* (Barcelona: Plaza, 1982), 106.

31 *Buñuel, Lorca, Dalí*, 246–7.

32 José de la Colina and Tomás Pérez Turrent, *Luis Buñuel. Prohibido Asomarse al interior* (Mexico: Planeta, 1986), 27. He had been lent a rare copy of the German edition of the *cent vingt journées* by Robert Desnos. Maurice Heine had very recently purchased the manuscript for Buñuel's patrons Charles and Marie-Laure de Noailles. She was descended from Sade on her mother's side.

33 *Le Surréalisme au Service de la Révolution*, 3, 12–13.

34 *Cahiers*, 94–101, 120. Chiappe was able to ban screenings by invoking the responsibilities of municipal authorities to maintain order. For the censorship issues raised by the incident, see Jean-Pierre Jeancolas, *15 ans d'années trente* (Paris: Stock, 1983), 38–41 and Paul Leglise, *Histoire de la politique du cinéma français. Le Cinéma et la IIIe République* (Paris: Librairie Générale de Droit et de Jurisprudence, 1970), 1, 27–33.

35 'Un Nouveau Panama', *L'Action Française*, 28 November 1930, 1

36 Buñuel's press cuttings with articles from *Le Figaro, l'Ami du peuple* and *l'Humanité* are reproduced in *Cahiers*, 173–6. See also Elyette Guiol-Benassaya, *La Presse face au surréalisme de 1925 à 1938* (Paris: CNRS, 1982).

37 Noailles to Buñuel, *Cahiers*, 104–5; the brochure *L'Affaire de l'Age d'Or* is reproduced 111–6.

38 *Cahiers*, 107–8.

39 'Le Surréalisme en 1929', *Variétés* (Brussels), special issue June 1929; André Breton, *Anthologie de l'humour noir* (1940, 1945), *Oeuvres* II, 895–1176, 1692–1735.

40 'Au-delà de la peinture', in *Cahiers d'Art*, 1937, 6/7, 40.

41 *Les Diaconales. Manuel des Confesseurs*, ch. IV.

42 'Surrealism: the last snapshot of the European intelligentsia' (1929), in *One-way Street and other writings* (London: New Left Books, 1992), 225–39.

43 Breton, *Anthologie*, *Oeuvres* II, 890–9.

11
The policing of popular opinion in Nazi Germany

Tim Kirk

Despite all its shrill nostalgia for a half-timbered Teutonic past, the main domestic aim of the Nazi Party (NSDAP) was a quintessentially modern one: that of nation-building. Arguably the first truly national party in German history, at least in so far as it attempted to direct its appeal in one way or another to all sections of society, the NSDAP repeatedly professed its intention to create the single German nation that eluded its predecessors. It would reconcile the differences that arose from the disorderly multiplicity of German identities based on class, regional loyalties, gender and confession, and unite all citizens – *Volksgenossen* ['national comrades'] in the tortured vocabulary of Nazi 'newspeak' – in a single transcendental national community: the *Volksgemeinschaft*. The Germans were to have not just greatness thrust upon them, but unprecedented national unity as well.

Yet the reality was somewhat different. Even in its best electoral performance the party could only muster the support of a third of the electorate, and these supporters were disproportionately concentrated in the north and east, in the countryside and among the middle classes: in short, among the disorientated electorate of the collapsing political parties of the Protestant bourgeoisie. Moreover, the reality of Nazi rule belied the propaganda of the *Volksgemeinschaft*: class differences were reinforced by Nazi policies, even if they were to some extent obscured by populist rhetoric and isolated gestures towards egalitarianism. Regional loyalties also remained strong, and enthusiasts in newly incorporated irredenta such as the 'Alpine and Danubian *Gaue*' quickly overcame their euphoria, became rapidly disillusioned and eventually distanced themselves from the Reich altogether. Above all, it has been argued, the party never succeeded in breaking down the persistent 'immunity' of the two socio-ideological camps it needed to break into most of all: the organised industrial working class, and the community of practising and politically conscious Roman Catholics.[1]

This is not to say that the Nazi regime did not achieve something of a consensus between 1933 and 1945. The party was instinctively populist, and was only too aware that while a dictatorship could be established by force, other methods would also be necessary in order to achieve sufficient domestic stability to wage a war. National unity was essential, both for its own sake, and in order to avoid the divisions which many on the German right believed had been responsible for Germany's defeat in 1918.[2] The regime expected resistance and suppressed it ruthlessly, above all by means of the terror visited on the labour movement and working-class communities in the months immediately before and after Hitler's appointment. The threat of organised resistance was largely broken with the destruction of the underground Communist movement during the early 1930s, and there would be no fundamental political threat to the regime until there was an attempted coup from within the German establishment in 1944. Opposition persisted, however, even in the absence of resistance leaders, and was expressed in symbolic gestures of defiance and protest. Even such apparently trivial details of everyday behaviour as the use of 'Good morning' instead of the 'German greeting' (Heil Hitler!) were noted with concern or irritation by the police – especially when such neglect of the new proprieties was more common among the working class.[3]

Ultimately the regime expected the problem of internal dissent to be resolved by propaganda and the education of future generations. In the meantime it required censorship, tight control of the news media and the effective suppression of any form of free public opinion, objectives which were achieved relatively quickly by Goebbels and the Ministry of Propaganda. But people also very quickly became sceptical about what they heard from official sources. In the spring of 1934 the local authorities in Hanover reported the 'most unbelievable rumours' as a result of news not being published in the press about events people were aware of; and the police made a similar observation a few weeks later: 'The common complaint about press reporting is that it never tells the whole story, and that it talks things up [schönfärbe]. The close surveillance of the press is not understood by large sections of the population, and is seen as the cause of all kinds of rumours.'[4] The problem for the regime was twofold. On the one hand it needed to monitor carefully the 'popular opinion' that could not be suppressed.[5] The party's rise to power had, after all, been assisted by an ability to articulate popular concerns; Nazi leaders had subverted the public discourse of Weimar republicanism by voicing not only popular anxieties but bar-room bigotries as well. On the other hand, the Nazis' instincts were plebiscitary: they sought to mobilise support and elicit acclamation for their actions rather than engage in discussion and persuasion; but in order to do that it was useful to know the temper of popular feeling.

To this end the Nazis eavesdropped on the German people at every opportunity, and as a result they have bequeathed a more extensive, thorough and complete record of popular opinion than almost any other political regime in modern European history. We already know a great deal about the concerns and attitudes of ordinary Germans, and about popular responses to the regime and its policies from studies based on the reports smuggled out of Germany during the 1930s to the exiled leadership of the Social Democratic Party in Prague (the 'Sopade' reports).[6] But there were also similar reports from all manner of government agencies, which were required not merely to report problems or incidents as they arose, but to provide the regime with on-the-spot analyses of popular morale and the political situation.

The monitoring of popular opinion was not new in Germany. The origins of a modern political police force have been located in the time of Joseph II, the first regular reports by the Prussian political police were submitted in the years following the 1848 revolutions, and the practice was continued during the empire and the Weimar Republic.[7] In addition to the police, the local government authorities in Germany had long performed the function of reporting to the appropriate ministries on a range of issues, including political developments, police matters, and social and economic problems. Thus the new regime was able from the outset to take advantage of intermediate agencies of the state which had both a grass-roots presence in local government offices and a long tradition of 'observing' the population.[8] From February 1933 the Prussian criminal police (*Landeskriminalpolizei*) was instructed to report twice a month on measures taken in connection with the Decree for the Protection of People and State of February 1933.[9] From the end of 1933 the Gestapo was required to submit more general reports on the mood of the population every month, including commentaries on the impact of economic and social policy. A separate section, reporting a 'general overview of domestic political developments', appeared from July 1934.[10]

Finally, from the late 1930s, the regime was able to rely on regular and comprehensive reports supplied by the security service (SD) of the SS. The so-called 'reports from the Reich' were comprehensive digests compiled on the basis of information supplied by reporters at the local and regional level.[11] These reports, like those from the political authorities and the police, had their beginnings in the years before the Nazis came to power, although this time they originated within the party rather than the state. Before 1933 the SD had had the job of monitoring and reporting on the activities of the party's political opponents. After 1933, however, when the police effectively became an adjunct of the regime and, as we have seen, the Gestapo took over the surveillance of the 'enemies of National Socialism' (now redefined as enemies of the state), it became unnecessary for the party to compile its own reports on domestic opponents. For some time, therefore, the SD concentrated its efforts on political intelligence from abroad, and on academic studies of the opponents of Nazism. But eventually, during the late 1930s, it became involved again in the systematic reporting of popular and recorded responses to political events, new government policies, statements by leading public figures, the contents of wartime newsreels, and even commented on the reception of feature films. As the SD resumed this function there was the potential – not for the first time – for a counter-productive rivalry within the machinery of the police state, and in July 1937 Heydrich sought to regulate the relationship between the SD and the Gestapo with a secret decree determining the division of labour between them. The two organisations were neither in competition, he maintained, nor was one subordinate to the other; instead they were to see their work as mutually complementary. The SD would concentrate on education, science, and the arts, on racial matters, and on party and state. The Gestapo was to be responsible for the left, for treason and for emigrants. In a number of other areas (religious groups, Jews, pacifists, the economy, the press) the SD was to take care of 'general questions', while the Gestapo would deal with individual questions which involved police measures. In practice the relationship remained tense and difficult.[12] Nevertheless, SD reports on the 'general situation' began in 1937, and from September 1939 digests were compiled daily in SD regional offices; then, from October of that year there appeared the 'reports on the domestic political situation', which comprise one of the most frequent, regular and comprehensive sources on the political situation in the Reich and the mood of the population.[13]

Similar assessments of the popular mood were compiled by a range of other institutions apart from the police, such as the judiciary, the German Labour Front (*Deutsche Arbeitsfront*, DAF) and not least local functionaries of the party itself. The Defence Economy Inspectorates (*Wehrwirtschafts-inspektionen*) reported on the mood and morale of the workforce and on local political problems. The Reich Ministry of Economics and Reich Labour Ministry also received 'economic' situation reports directly from subordinate offices and organisations ranging from regional 'chambers of economics' (*Wirtschaftskammern*) and chambers of commerce to employment offices and Reich Trustees of Labour.[14] Most of these reports can be regarded as reliable, if not in the detail then in the general indications they provide of the mood of the day. They were, after all, intended for internal circulation, and not for propaganda purposes.

Even in peacetime, then, Germans were – in principle – under an unprecedented degree of surveillance: at work, while shopping or travelling on public transport, and in social situations such as pubs and restaurants. Dissent was effectively criminalised and, even where there was no directly seditious intent, outspokenness might attract a disproportionately severe punishment. In March 1933 a presidential decree was issued which made an offence of 'malicious attacks' on the government. It provided for up to two years' imprisonment for anybody making or passing on an 'untrue observation', or one which grossly misrepresented the government, and up to three months for those who passed on such remarks innocently or unwittingly.[15] This decree was superseded in December 1934 by a more comprehensive law against malicious attacks on state and party, and for the protection of party uniforms. The number of people arrested under this legislation rose steadily during the 1930s. In Munich, for example, 425 people appeared before the 'special court' (*Sondergericht*) dealing with such cases in 1933, and 1,445 in 1939; the recorded expressions of 'non-conformist' opinion followed a similar pattern in Düsseldorf.[16] The intensity of surveillance was stepped up when war broke out in 1939, and regional Gestapo headquarters were issued with new guidelines for the policing of popular opinion, Any attempt to undermine the unity and fighting spirit of the German people was to be ruthlessly suppressed: 'In particular, anybody who makes any remark which questions the victory of the German people or the justness of the war is to be arrested immediately.'[17]

The war both extended the range of opinion which was considered seditious or impermissible, and at the same time increased the authorities' sensitivity. At the beginning of October the SD reported that a number of people had been arrested on 'malice' charges and for similar kinds of subversive behaviour, and in particular for spreading atrocity stories (*Greuelpropaganda*) and listening to foreign radio stations. There were thirteen such arrests in Berlin, the report went on, twelve in Dortmund, nine in Graz, five in Kiel, four each in Düsseldorf, Karlsruhe, Stuttgart and Vienna, and three each in Chemnitz, Cologne and Schwerin: a handful each, in other words, in many of the most important cities in the Reich. The following week the number of such cases had increased almost fourfold, and it was simply reported that 245 people had been arrested on similar charges in the course of a couple of days.[18] Yet the impression of an omnipotent police state shared by contemporaries and many historians is misleading. Although the Gestapo seemed to be everywhere, it had in fact nothing approaching the resources or personnel to police the whole country in the way the regime would have liked. In practice there were not nearly enough secret policemen to contemplate such a 'totalitarian' project; and the Nazi regime, like other authoritarian dictatorships, relied on fear, self-policing and denunciation to back up its system of political control. Nobody ever quite knew whether they were being watched, and people adapted their behaviour accordingly.[19] They were also assisted in their endeavours by 'social co-operation', the readiness of people to police each other and to work for the objectives of the police state, what Robert Gellately has called 'the key relationship between the Gestapo, German society, and the enforcement of policy' which was constituted by the 'volunteered provision of information by the population at large about instances of disapproved behaviour'.[20] They did so by working as spies for the Gestapo, often reporting on the very persecuted communities to which they belonged;[21] or they denounced their neighbours, colleagues, and even friends and family to the police, sometimes because they were afraid of the consequences for themselves if they failed to do so; but often because they had a grievance against an acquaintance, or might benefit materially from the arrest or disappearance of a colleague, neighbour or business rival. Reinhard Mann has calculated that of some 200 denunciations in Düsseldorf eighty were related to private disagreements and fifty were politically motivated.[22] The police had to assess the reliability of denunciations, and although they were alert to such motives, they might suspend their disbelief if there were other good reasons for pursuing the ostensible culprit. False denunciations, however, could be punished with a spell in a concentration camp.[23]

The motives for such false denunciations doubtless afford interesting insights into the social history of an unusual political situation, but genuine denunciations are perhaps more significant. Over a quarter of Gestapo proceedings in Düsseldorf between 1933 and 1944 had their origins in denunciations by local people, almost twice as many as the number uncovered by the Gestapo's own observations and reports from police spies.[24] People denounced neighbours often simply because they shared at least some of the Nazis' values and or prejudices. Historians of denunciation have described it as a 'fundamental political act which stigmatised those perceived as an internal or external enemy offending against norms, regardless of what historical forms authority . . . had taken'.[25] And indeed the effective function of denunciation was more than merely to provide the police with information or help them locate subversive activity: it was at the heart of the Nazi project. *Volksgenossen* who denounced their fellow citizens were thereby mobilised, however passively or indirectly, for the work of constructing the *Volksgemeinschaft*, and were drawn into a complicity with the regime. This may be seen as a collusion by many German people in their own repression, or it may be interpreted as a continuing willingness to reinforce that order which the party's supporters had hoped it would restore, against the forces which threatened it. This complicity, evident not only in acts of explicit collusion, but also in ostensible gestures of defiance, in the kind of insults that were used against party bigwigs and prominent figures themselves. The most scurrilous of anti-Nazi remarks were often also the ones which reflected the party's own prejudices: leading politicians (including Hitler) were said to be Jewish or queer; their wives were promiscuous, fat, unattractive, haughty or extravagant. Sometimes it is possible to discern a principled ideological objection to the Nazis among such scurrility, but bad temper, bigotry and self-pity are just as likely.[26]

The fragile political stability of Nazi Germany, then, did not rest on repression and the threat of coercion alone. The government continued to build on the support it had won before 1933 by further stigmatising the dwindling numbers of its outspoken opponents. During the 1930s it was able to create a limited consensus on a number of issues as the economy recovered and Germany's greatness was ostensibly restored. Yet the limits of that consensus were clear from the outset. Gestures of defiance and statements of dissent were reported regularly by all the regime's surveillance agencies throughout the short history of the Third Reich.

The most latently oppositional group remained the industrial working class. Despite the destruction of the KPD as an effective underground political organisation, the possibility of subversion from this quarter was never entirely eliminated. Activists persisted and switched their attention increasingly to the dissemination of propaganda. Printed material was smuggled into the Reich from abroad, principally from German-speaking comrades in Austria and the Sudetenland. By 1938, however, the annexation of both these territories by the Reich meant new sources of material had to be found in northern and western Europe – and much to the irritation of the SD the progressive Scandinavians even sent Braille material in Esperanto.[27] These sources would also dry up during the war; but in any case the import and dissemination of printed matter had always been dangerous and susceptible to detection by the police, and was often supplemented by more informal methods: graffiti, which was widespread in large factories, or home-made flysheets and stickers with simple slogans or symbols. In October 1939 'Heil Moskau' and hammer-and-sickle signs were painted in white on briquettes of coal by miners in Halle; in Berlin leaflets were found with the inscription 'Long live the Soviet Union! Down with Hitler!'; and in Jena, a few weeks later, stickers with hammer-and-sickle symbols appeared during the night on shop windows displaying pictures of Hitler. Such avowals of support for Stalin and the USSR had always been among the most frequent anti-regime slogans used by German Communists, and they seem to have persisted after the outbreak of war in Poland despite the Hitler-Stalin pact. In fact rumours circulated that the prohibition of the KPD was about to be lifted.[28] (Churchmen disappointed by the apparent Nazi-Soviet rapprochement were among the keenest promoters of such rumours.)

By the later 1930s such 'whispering propaganda' – the 'unwritten newspaper' was being used as a substitute for printed material: 'Flysheet propaganda is on the wane', the Gestapo commented in July 1936. 'The main substitute is oral propaganda.'[29] In 1938 the SD reported that it was the most important form of oppositional subversion in Germany and that it was used 'above all in discussion groups in factories, pubs, at home, with the family and in the street.' Apart from topical political themes – including the 'Jewish question' – the main subject of conversation was pay. Despite the foreign policy triumphs and the anxieties about the approaching war, and despite the pogrom, people were still primarily concerned about everyday matters.

Much of the material for 'oral propaganda' came from Radio Moscow and other anti-German stations, which broadcast regularly in German, especially at times of domestic political tension.[30] The regime knew that such 'disinformation' was being spread, but nobody could be sure whether those spreading it were genuinely political opponents or merely the 'careless talkers' that all the belligerent governments came to warn against. Oral propaganda was virtually indistinguishable from the 'innocent' rumour and gossip that form the background noise of any community. Workers' leaders certainly recognised the importance of such informal talk, and emphasised the 'maintenance of contacts' for the survival of political consciousness in working-class communities. Among the overwhelming majority who were never involved with the underground resistance such contacts were easily maintained, whether at work, where an old shop steward would find himself still the spokesman – formal or informal – for his workmates; or in the neighbourhood, where the same people were to be encountered in shops, on trams and in bars. In most districts communities were generally close-knit, and there was little need at the 'Stammtisch' (regulars' table) for any explicit acknowledgement of political loyalty. Nevertheless there were easy pickings here for officious Nazi functionaries and vigilant police informers, especially at the end of the evening when, in the phrasing of the Gestapo's bureaucratic euphemism, people were 'in angeheitertem Zustande', cheered a little, that is, by a few drinks, and inclined to relax.[31] As tongues became looser a relatively specific grievance might prompt more general criticisms of the government, party leaders, the army, the war, or whatever occurred to the speaker next. Jokes were told, songs were sung, and the leaders of party and state, from Hitler down to local functionaries were cursed and maligned, often in very offensive language. Hitler was, variously, a dog, a swindler, a megalomaniac, an idiot, a scoundrel (ein Lausbub) and – significantly – 'queer' or Jewish.[32] On the whole, however, Hitler himself was generally absolved from blame, and the severest criticism was for other leading Nazis and local functionaries. So many people were arrested for inviting members of the regime to 'kiss their arses' that the Gestapo came to used the abbreviated, euphemistic term 'Götz quotation'. (A similar expression had been used in Goethe's play Götz von Berlichingen.)

These were precisely the 'malicious attacks' that ended in arrest and appearances in the regime's 'special courts'.[33] Such incidents scarcely constituted a threat to the regime, but they did reveal the superficiality of much outward compliance. Thus on one occasion, when somebody struck up an old socialist song on the accordion and everybody sang along, the 'strong influence of alcohol' was taken into account by the Gestapo, and only two people were arrested, such behaviour was taken as evidence that there had been no real political conversion among these people, although the accordionist himself was after all now a member of the SA. In the words of a police observer, these were people 'into whose flesh and blood Marxist ideas [had] penetrated so deep that they [would] not allow themselves to be persuaded of the opposite'.[34]

The survival of such inner convictions, the tenacious hold of a prior ideological authority, was an insurmountable obstacle to the construction of the *Volksgemeinschaft*, and one which was also found among other sections of the population. The authorities monitored all kinds of groups and found them wanting, including their own former allies from the *völkisch* movement, Stahlhelm veterans, the so-called Tannenberg or Ludendorff movement and Strasser supporters.[35] Of all the potential sources of opposition on the conservative right, however, the regime kept a particular eye on the activities of the 'political churches'. Although the churches had been prepared to compromise with the Nazis, and had established an uneasy *modus vivendi* with the regime, there were also open conflicts over a number of issues, and there were rumours among the Catholic clergy in 1939 that the regime would crack down harder after the war.[36] In addition many Christians were involved in resistance movements, and many more, clergy and laity alike, were critical of the regime and its policies.

The most extreme case in this respect were the Jehovah's Witnesses, whose response to the regime was far more uncompromising than that of the mainstream churches. They continued to proselytise despite persecution and imprisonment in concentration camps, and were equally adamant in their conscientious objection to military service (which was introduced in 1935). By 1938 they were the only minor sect still active, although their activities had been much curtailed by police crackdowns, and despite the fact that, like the Communists, they found it difficult to get their propaganda material over the border. They too turned to oral propaganda, and hundreds were tried for 'malicious attacks'.[37] Gestapo and SD alike regularly reported their persistent activity and the frequent arrests which followed: from Upper Styria, for example, where 'intense activity' was reported in industrial areas in December 1939, part of a general upsurge in activity after the Anschluss.[38] Almost all the death sentences for conscientious objectors during the first year of the war were Jehovah's Witnesses, and by 1945 the sect had suffered by far the highest proportion of persecutions, imprisonments and deaths of any oppositional group.

Among the clergy and congregations of the mainstream churches attitudes to the regime inevitably reflected those of German society as a whole. Both confessions produced conscientious resisters, but there was also a measure of co-operation from Protestants and Catholics, and many individuals had mixed feelings about the regime. Much of the churches' resistance was pragmatic opposition to government interference. Throughout the 1930s the essentially secular Nazi regime sought to extend state control in areas over which the churches were jealous and a number of local conflicts arose between church and state.[39] After the outbreak of war in 1939 priests and pastors came under renewed attack for their 'defeatism'.[40] At the beginning of the war, for example, a priest from Pirmasens remarked during a graveside oration that although Germany had experienced much, there was much worse to come because millions of people had been dechristianised and corrupted. Similarly, a Protestant pastor in Frankfurt attracted the attention of the Gestapo for suggesting that Germany would lose the war because the English had stronger nerves and attended church.[41] A few weeks later a Catholic priest in Fulda preached a 'defeatist' sermon which painted such an apocalyptic picture of the future that it left the congregation 'extraordinarily depressed': German technical, scientific and industrial achievements (for which, it was suggested, there was an idolatrous respect) would be annihilated; towering city blocks would be reduced to rubble, electrical networks would be in shreds; trains would rust, and dead birds and would lie beside the remains of railway lines.[42] In Austria, where -after the first flush of enthusiasm – opposition from all quarters was stronger than in the '*Altreich*', the Catholic opposition used similar homespun propaganda techniques to those of the Communists: flysheets, stickers, graffiti and scratched symbols.[43] Moreover, clerical opposition in Austria was associated with an incipient sense of separate Austrian nationality, and both the symbol of Schuschnigg's Austrofascist movement and the graffiti of the Habsburg legitimists were also frequently found in Vienna.[44] In those recently 'incorporated' parts of the Reich where a majority of the population was not German, – such as Slovenia – such protest was much stronger.[45]

After the fall of France there was less defeatist talk; in fact there seemed for a time to be less opposition to report from any quarter, and the Gestapo became increasingly occupied with resistance not from Germans but from the foreign slave labourers who were being brought to Germany to solve the labour shortage problem. The regular section on the regime's opponents in SD reports gave way to less regular and less frequent special reports. The regime's drive to control what was being said in Germany did not stop at dissent, however, but covered all unlicensed speech. In a telling criticism of the Catholic clergy in the summer of 1941, priests were accused of exploiting the regime's popularity by appropriating Nazi terminology and by 'associating the church with respected National Socialist figures'; while at the same time a couple of Evangelical publishing houses were ticked off for trespassing on the territory of Nazi racism. They had used German heroes past and present to illustrate the compatibility of 'Christian and German values', and asserted the affinity of Protestantism and 'Nordic' man with reference to examples of great Scandinavians, thereby earning the pedantic rebuke from an SD reporter that not all that was Scandinavian was also 'Nordic'.[46]

Ultimately, the regime set out to control not merely dissent, but all popular discourse. Reporters not only noted the hundreds of thousands of daily grumbles and seditious jokes, they plotted the course of political gossip from its origins in Communist pamphlets or Allied radio broadcasts as part of a broader project. The regime set out consciously to manufacture consensus, and that meant not merely mobilising support for the regime and raising morale – although as the tide of the war turned, that became the primary consideration. It also meant determining the shape of popular discourse. Like all modern governments the Nazis wanted to replace rumour and speculation with informed debate – and to control that debate at the same time. Throughout the history of the Third Reich anxieties were expressed by regime functionaries about the uncontrollability or irrationality of rumour and gossip.

The same travelling salesmen who had been so important in spreading the word to the remotest villages when the Nazis themselves were the subversives were, by the end of 1934 the carriers of 'sensational rumours'. (In fact they were merely hoping to put pressure on business people with stories of raw materials shortages.)[47] In November 1939 an upsurge in rumours about the imminent end of the war was linked to the activities of 'Soothsayers, clairvoyants and gypsies . . . particularly in rural districts'.[48] Towards the end of the war there were rumours of new weapons developments which would save Germany from defeat. The reversal at Stalingrad and the Allied aerial bombardment of western Germany intensified such rumours, and in July 1943 the SD reported that they had 'reached such a scale throughout the Reich that almost every national comrade is touched by them in some way'. There were extraordinarily detailed accounts of the rumoured weapons, and they were discussed openly in public places. People were convinced – especially in those places that suffered the heaviest bombing – that the ring of enemies was tightening around Germany, and that only a miracle – the discovery of new weapons – could change the course of the war. This miracle would enable Germany to mount a successful aerial assault on British cities, reducing them to rubble, at which point the United States would leave the war, and Germany would be able to direct all its military resources against the Soviet Union.[49]

More disturbing than such wishful thinking were the 'rumours' being spread about the effects of Allied bombing. Firms with their head offices in the Ruhr were transmitting news to customers in other cities less affected by the bombing: 'In Wuppertal there are only odd houses or streets left standing' wrote one firm. Another, in Hamburg, sent out detailed mimeographed reports to its customers: 'The extent of the destruction is unimaginable and indescribable. We cannot estimate the number of human lives that have fallen victim to this terrible attack. Without access to further details we believe it would have to be between ten and fifteen thousand'. As the state propaganda machine attempted to reassure people, play down the devastation and talk up any positive news, uncontrollable rumours were increasingly undermining morale. They also reflected a growing scepticism about the government. Ministers were rumoured to have fled abroad, and state and party leaders to have used their positions for all kinds of advantage.[50]

Such rumours could not be suppressed, of course, because there was a great deal of truth in them. Moreover, as morale plummeted people's priorities and perspectives began to change. It was realised increasingly that the government and the party had more to fear from defeat than anybody else, and the notion of a stark choice between victory and total annihilation was increasingly seen as an anxiety peculiar to the regime's leaders. 'If we lose the war' according to popular opinion as early as November 1943, 'it won't be half as bad as our leadership would have as believe'.[51] In the end it was clear that popular opinion in Germany, indeed German society, had dissociated itself from the Nazis; it was sceptical, resigned and the focus of its attention was increasingly what would become of Germany after defeat, after the Nazis had gone. Many people were already thinking themselves into the post-war frame of mind which would make it difficult to find any Nazis in Germany at all. It was this dissociation between people and government that finally prompted the Nazis to stop listening. Towards the end of the war situation reports became increasingly irregular, and in the end they were considered so depressing or difficult to produce that they were wound up altogether.

Notes

1   See Martin Broszat 'Resistenz und Widerstand. Eine Zwischenbilanz des Forschungsprojekts', in Martin Broszat, Elke Fröhlich and Anton Grossmann (eds), *Bayern in der Ns-Zeit IV. Herrschaft und Gesellschaft im Konflikt. Teil C* (Munich: Oldenbourg, 1981), 691–709.

2   See Tim Mason, *Social Policy in the Third Reich. The Working Class and the 'National Community'* (Providence and Oxford: Berg, 1993), 19–40.

3   'Lagebericht der Staatspolizeistelle Hannover an das Geheime Staatspolizeiamt Berlin für den Monat Mai 1934', reprinted in Klaus Mlynek (ed.), *Gestapo Hannover meldet . . . Polizei-und Regierungsberichte für das mittlere und südliche Niedersachsen zwischen 1933 und 1937* (Hildesheim: Lax, 1986), 167.

4   Ibid., 173. 'Lagebericht des hannoverschen Regierungspräsidenten an den Reichsminister des Innern Berlin für den Monat Juli 1934', also in Mlynek, *Gestapo Hannover Meldet*, 194.

5   Ian Kershaw, *Popular Opinion and Political Dissent in the Third Reich. Bavaria 1933–1945* (Oxford: Oxford University Press, 1983), 4.

6   The party's summaries of these reports have been republished as *Deutschlandberichte der Sozialdemokratischen Partei Deutschlands (Sopade) 1934–1940*, 7 vols (Frankfurt: Verlag Petra Nettelbeck, 1980). Kershaw, *Bavaria*, was based to a large extent on the Sopade reports. For a discussion of the origins of the party's reporting and the uses of the reports as historical sources see Bernd Stöver, *Volksgemeinschaft im Dritten Reich. Die Konsensbereitschaft der Deutschen aus der Sicht sozialistischer Exilberichte* (Düsseldorf: Droste, 1993), 55–114.

7   See Wolfram Siemann, *'Deutschlands Ruhe, Sicherheit und Ordnung', Die Anfänge der politischen Polizei 1806–1866* (Tübingen: Max Niemeyer Verlag, 1985), esp. 389 ff.: 'Innerpreußische Konzentration der politischen Polizei seit 1851: die "Wochenberichte Inland" '. See also Richard Evans, *Kneipengespräche im Kaiserreich. Die Stimmungsberichte der Hamburger Politischen Polizei 1892–1914* (Reinbek: Rowohlt, 1989) and 'Proletarian mentalities: pub conversations in Hamburg', in *Proletarians and Politics. Socialism, protest and the working class in Germany before the First World War* (New York: Harvester Wheatsheaf, 1990), 122–91.

8   Günter Morsch, *Arbeit und Brot. Studien zu Lage, Stimmung, Einstellung und Verhalten der deutschen Arbeiterschaft 1933–1936/37* (Frankfurt: Peter Lang, 1993), 14–18.

9   The Decree of the Reich President for the protection of the People and State was passed after the Reichstag fire, and effectively suspended civil liberties. See J. Noakes and G. Pridham, *Nazism. 1919–1945. A Documentary Reader*, 4 vols (Exeter: Exeter University Press, 1983–98); here Vol. 1, 141–2.

10   Mlynek, *Gestapo Hannover*, 15–17; Morsch, *Arbeit und Brot*, 19–21.

11   Heinz Boberach (ed.), *Meldungen aus dem Reich. Die geheimen Lageberichte des Sicherheitsdienstes der SS 1938–1945*, 17 vols (Herrsching: Pawlak, 1984).

12   Ibid., vol. 1, 12–14.

13   Ibid., vol. 1, 18–21. See also Lawrence Duncan Stokes, 'The Sicherheitsdienst (SD) of the Reichsführer SS and German Public Opinion September 1939 – June 1941' (PhD, John Hopkins University, 1972).

14   Morsch, *Arbeit und Brot*, 26–7.

15   Verordnung des Reichspräsidenten 'Zur Abwehr heimtückischer Angriffe gegen die Regierung der nationalen Erhebung', 21 March 1933, in Wolfgang Michalka (ed.), *Deutsche Geschichte 1933–1945. Dokumente zur Innen-und Außenpolitik* (Frankfurt: Fischer, 1993), 22.

16   Peter Hüttenberger, 'Heimtückefälle vor dem Sondergericht München 1933–1939', in Martin Broszat et al. (eds), *Bayern in der Ns-Zeit IV*, 435–526;

here 444–5; Reinhard Mann, *Protest und Kontrolle im Dritten Reich. Nationalsozialistische Herrschaft im Alltag einer rheinischen Großstadt* (Frankfurt and New York: Campus, 1987), 241.
17 'Grundsätze der inneren Staatssicherung während des Kriegs', Chef der Sicherheitspolizei, Berlin, 3. September 1939 an die Leiter aller Staatspolizeileitstellen. Captured German Records microfilmed at Alexandria T-175 Roll 280 774107–774108. (hereafter, Grundsätze).
18 Bericht zur innenpolitischen Lage, 9 October 1939, *Meldungen*, vol. 2, 332–3; 13 October 1939, ibid., 347.
19 Cf. Sheila Fitzpatrick and Robert Gellately, 'Introduction to the Practices of Denunciation in Modern European History', *Journal of Modern History*, 68 (1996) 747–67.
20 See Robert Gellately, *The Gestapo and German Society. Enforcing Racial Policy 1933–1945* (Oxford: Oxford University Press, 1990), 130. See also Klaus-Michael Mallmann and Gerhard Paul, 'Omniscient, Omnipotent, Omnipresent. Gestapo, Society and Resistance', in David Crew (ed.), *Nazism and German Society 1933–1945* (London: Routledge, 1994), 166–96.
21 See Walter Otto Weyrauch, *Gestapo V-Leute. Tatsachen und Theorie des Geheimdienstes* (Frankfurt: Fischer, 1992).
22 Mann, *Protest und Kontrolle*, 295.
23 Grundsätze: 'Action is to be taken immediately against denouncers who file either unwarranted or exaggerated accusations against fellow citizens (*Volksgenossen*) for personal reasons, either a firm warning or in malicious cases imprisonment in a concentration camp.'
24 Mann, *Protest und Kontrolle*, 292
25 See the report of the project 'Denunziationspraxis am Oberrhein. Eine Analyse von Machttechniken innerhalb des Entwicklingsprozesses moderner Staatlichkeit und der Wende vom 18. zum 19. Jahrhundert', Christiane Kohse-Spohn, 'Denunzianten und Denunziationen', *Werkstattgeschichte*, 15 (1996).
26 Cf. Tim Kirk, *Nazism and the Working Class in Austria. Industrial Unrest and Political Dissent in the National Community* (Cambridge: Cambridge University Press, 1996), 112–128.
27 Meldungen aus dem Reich, 8 March 1940, *Meldungen*, 3, 855.
28 Bericht zur innenpolitischen Lage, 13 October 1939, *Meldungen*, vol. 2, 348–9; 16 October 1939, ibid., 357; 15 November 1939, ibid., vol. 3, 449–50; 6 November 1939, ibid., 422.
29 Monatsbericht über Linksbewegung, July 1936, in *Gestapo-Berichte über den antifaschistischen Widerstand der KPD 1933 bis 1945*, vol. 1, *Anfang 1933 bis August 1939* (Berlin: Dietz, 1989), 500.
30 Jahreslagebericht 1938, *Meldungen*, 2, 56
31 The term was used as a routine formula in the Gestapo's regular reports.
32 Gestapo 'day report', Vienna, 14–16 October 1939, Dokumentationsarchiv des österreichischen Widerstands, Film 78.
33 Hüttenberger, *Heimtückefälle*; Mann, *Protest und Kontrolle* (Croom Helm).
34 'Lagebericht der Statspolizeistelle Hannover an das Geheime Staatspolizeiamt Berlin für den Monat Juni 1934', in Mlynek, *Gestapo Hannover*, 169–71.
35 Jahreslagebericht 1938, *Meldungen*, vol. 2, 55–7; 74–79; 'Lagebericht der Staatspolizeistelle Hannover an das Geheime Staatspolizeiamt Berlin für den Monat Juni 1934', in Mlynek, *Gestapo Hannover*, 170.

36   See, for example, Jeremy Noakes, 'The Oldenburg Crucifix Struggle of
     November 1936: a case-study of opposition in the Third Reich', in P. Stachura
     (ed.), *The Shaping of the Nazi State* (London, 1978); Bericht zur innenpolitischen
     Lage, 25 October 1939, Meldungen, 2, 390.
37   Two hundred and seventy four in Munich between 1936 and 1939. See F.L.
     Carsten, *The German Workers and the Nazis* (Aldershot: Scolar, 1995) 114–21.
     Here 218.
38   Bericht zur innenpolitischen Lage, 4 December 1939, *Meldungen*, 3, 525.
39   See for example Reich Interior Minister Wilhelm Frick on the 'deconfession-
     alisation of all public life', reported in the *Völkischer Beobachter*, 8 July 1935, in
     Michalka, *Deutsche Geschichte*, 89. The development of relations between
     regime and churches from the point of view of one province is thoroughly
     documented in Ian Kershaw's study of Bavaria: Kershaw, *Bavaria*, 156–223.
40   'Kriegserfolge und Gegnertätigkeit' Meldungen aus dem Reich, 24 June 1940,
     Meldungen, 4, 1305-6; 'Kirche und Krieg', *Meldungen aus dem Reich*, 4 July
     1940,; *Meldungen*, 5, 1350.
41   Bericht zur innenpolitischen Lage, 16 October 1939, *Meldungen*, 2, 357.
42   Bericht zur innenpolitischen Lage, 1 December 1939, *Meldungen*, 3, 515–16.
43   Bericht zur innenpolitischen Lage, 24 November 1939, ibid., 492.
44   Bericht zur innenpolitischen Lage, 1 December 1939, *Meldungen*, 3, 515–16.
45   USNA T-175 Roll 84; Tim Kirk, 'Limits of Germandom: The Resistance to the
     Nazi annexation of Slovenia', *Slavonic and East European Review*, 69 (1991).
46   Meldungen aus dem Reich, 13 August 1942, *Meldungen*, 11, 4070–71; 14 July
     1941; ibid., 7, 2517–20.
47   'Lagebericht der Staatspolizeistelle Hannover an das Geheime Staatspolizeiamt
     Berlin für den Monat Oktober 1934', Mlynek, *Gestapo meldet*, 250.
48   Bericht zur innenpolitischen Lage, 20 November 1939, *Meldungen*, 3, 475.
49   SD-Berichte zu Inlandsfragen, 1 July 1943, *Meldungen*, 14, 5414–5; 18 October
     1943, *Meldungen*, 15, 5885–6.
50   SD-Berichte zu Inlandsfragen, 4 October 1943, *Meldungen*, 15, 5833–4.
51   SD-Berichte zu Inlandsfragen, 22 November 1943, *Meldungen*, 15, 6050.

12
Subversion and squirrility in Irvine Welsh's shorter fiction

Willy Maley

Whether as the product of a damaged masculinity, an impoverished sense of community, or a persistent spirit of radicalism and resistance, the language of urban working-class Scots raises problems of articulation and authenticity that have wider implications when it comes to defining a literature of subversion. In this essay I aim to look at the ways in which the shorter fiction of Irvine Welsh raises vexed issues of choice and voice, fragmentation and formal experimentation, locality and liminality, that ought to impinge upon any discussion of subversion and scurrility. Welsh has made his name as a merciless chronicler of Edinburgh's underside. The short stories from *The Acid House* collection on which this essay concentrates reveal the depths and lengths to which Welsh is willing to go in order to ground his texts in the multiple realities and fantasies of Scottish culture. Welsh's writing is remarkably rich in verbal texture. Its author's commitment to a vibrant oral culture rather than to any specific political project or party means that it is hard to see it as subversive in any conventional sense.

Recent developments in cultural theory offer useful ways of thinking about Welsh's work, but it is less a question of applying theory to contemporary Scottish fiction than of seeing how the fiction reflects and even anticipates intellectual currents. As Gilles Deleuze once observed, theory is local, and in two senses. On the one hand, it ought to engage intimately with particular places and people. On the other hand, it is local precisely because it applies itself to specific passages of texts and terrains. In both cases it avoids claims to totalisation.

One recent approach to culture based on the idea of theory as local is the concept of 'minority discourse', which draws on the category of 'minor literature', elaborated by Deleuze and Guattari.[1] According to David Lloyd and Abdul JanMohamed, 'minority discourse is, in the first instance, the product of damage – damage more or less systematically inflicted on cultures produced as minorities by the dominant culture'.[2] The fiction of Irvine Welsh comes into this category. The difference between a literature of commitment and a minor literature of damage is that while the former lays claim to the universality of the dominant discourse the latter acknowledges its limitations. Committed writing is often merely oppositional, and thus risks mirroring mainstream political values. Minority discourse cannot be so easily accommodated. bell hooks has rehearsed a view of radical popular culture as resisting representations rather than merely constructing alternatives that threaten to become doubles.[3] Her account of 'outlaw' or 'resistant' culture finds an echo in Welsh's entry into literature through the agency of Rebel Inc., a magazine devoted to publishing subcultural material. Finally, the idea of local points of resistance rather than a 'great Refusal' is upheld by Michel Foucault, who speaks of 'a plurality of resistances . . . spread over time and space at varying densities, at times mobilising groups or individuals in a definitive way'.[4]

In his ground-breaking study *Scott and Scotland*, Edwin Muir, writing against Hugh MacDiarmid's defence of dialect, famously declared that 'Scotland can only create a national literature by writing in English'. Muir insisted that 'until Scottish literature has an adequate language, it cannot exist. Scotland will remain a mere collection of districts'.[5] What for Muir was a negative image – 'a mere collection of districts' – is for Welsh and the new generation of Scottish writers something to be celebrated. Scotland is best laid out in schemes rather than gathered under one national heading.

The short story is a form that lends itself perfectly to the view of theory as a local activity, and literature as a local intervention. Where the novel has as one of its central aims the narration of the nation, the short story unfolds somewhere in the region of marginality, inarticulacy, eccentricity. Mary Louise Pratt has spoken of 'the short story being used to introduce new regions or groups into an established national literature, or into an emerging national literature in the process of decolonisation'.[6] Pratt mentions Joyce's *Dubliners*, Alice Munro's *Lives of Girls and Women*, and Sherwood Anderson's *Winesburg, Ohio* as examples of the short-story cycle establishing a sense of context and community. *The Acid House*, I would argue, belongs firmly within the same tradition. In its twenty-one short stories and closing novella Welsh can be seen to be mapping a linguistic and geographical domain hitherto disregarded or disenfranchised.

I want to offer several key examples of the short story as a specific literary form that reveals the limits of scurrility and subversion. Welsh's novels have attracted most critical attention, but I aim to examine aspects of the shorter fiction which I think go beyond the scope of the novel. Indeed, it could be argued that Welsh's strengths as a writer lie in spiky vignettes and swift explosive scenes, and that *Trainspotting* itself is a loosely connected sequence of short stories stitched together, not just by common characters, but by a common language, a patchwork quilt of colloquialisms, criss-crossed by catch phrase, cliché, and cursing. Its acceptance as a novel, despite its many voices and broken form, is due to a new 'postmodern' sensibility that no longer looks to the novel as a reassuring site of unity and cohesion. Though it could be argued that the figure of Mark Renton acts as an anchor in *Trainspotting*, a breakdown of narrative perspectives in the novel reveals the extent to which Welsh disperses viewpoints and voices and favours heteroglossia and polyphony, essential markers of subversion.[7]

It is significant that Welsh established himself initially through small publishing ventures such as Rebel Inc (now a major imprint of Canongate) and Clocktower Press (recently anthologised by Jonathan Cape), though it could be argued that he launched them as much as they launched him.[8] These fringe ventures afforded Welsh the freedom to explore the fanzine format at which he now excels, characterised by cartoon violence, endlessly inventive sloganeering, and increasingly intricate typographical experimentation. If the 'bittiness' of Welsh's writing, its episodic quality, is due in part to its origins in the pamphlet culture of small presses, it can also be seen to reflect the actual fragmentation of the culture at large. Where an earlier literature might have perceived its aim as inventing or proclaiming 'Scotland' in the singular, and a more recent writing may have regarded its mission as debunking the myths of an idealised Scotland, the new fiction is concerned with the proliferation of 'Scotlands', plural and diverse.

There is an argument for seeing in the short story a literary form that offers an insight into post-colonial resistance. The civic and social specificity of Welsh's shorter fiction undermines the claims to inclusiveness of larger narratives of nation and empire, and sets up counter-narratives of regional dissent. Welsh's style – sampling, streetwise, synthesising – is implicitly anti-colonial. Welsh is more inclined than his predecessors to sift through the junk and pulp of Scottish culture, hence his cult status. Welsh's influences, or effluences, range across contemporary film, music and television rather than resting on the canon. He excels at that potent blend of the excremental and existential, 'keech and Kierkegaard', that is all the rage in new Scottish writing, a social surrealism that takes its cue from cinema and dance as much as literature. The pop video, the club, and the fanzine are its archives. It is this openness to the most basic elements of society, as well as its most commodified culture, that marks Welsh out from James Kelman, rather than the endorsement of the myth of individualism, which, as Alan Freeman has ably shown, both writers share.[9] They also share a contempt for the conventional, conforming, and collaborationist working class, who appear as 'draftpaks', 'schemies', or 'straight pegs' in Welsh's work, and are charac-terised by one of Kelman's protagonists as 'a bunch of bastarn imbeciles'.[10]

Prolific, polemical and provocative, Welsh has staked his place at the forefront of the new wave of Scottish writers. He has been called 'the poet laureate of the chemical generation', but his appeal is much broader than the drug and youth culture he depicts so trenchantly. The devil is in the detail, and in the vitality of the local idioms, but there are big issues at stake too: cruelty, revenge, cycles of violence, crime and punishment, responsibility and guilt. Like Zola, Welsh is on the side of the vanquished, and arguably to a greater extent than his contemporaries and predecessors in a Scottish context. The social realist tradition stood in the way of the downtrodden, representing them without lending an ear and giving voice. A moralistic and patronising approach to representations of the working class has also been present in Marxist thought. Leon Trotsky railed against scurrilous speech, seeing it as a product of oppression rather than a means of resistance: 'Abusive language and swearing are a legacy of slavery, humiliation, and disrespect for human dignity – one's own and that of other people.'[11] Trotsky went so far as to argue for the imposition of fines upon those who swore in factories. The new Scottish writers not only fly – or fart – in the face of this old Left response to scurrility, but also refuse to be confined within the factory gates, gates that are in any case closed to the unconventional working-class characters who people their fiction. That those same factory gates are increasingly closed to their own workers is a contributory factor in the shift from 'workerist' fiction to a literature of unemployment.

Duncan McLean, the writer behind Clocktower Press, characterises the new Scottish fiction precisely in terms of a commitment to voice: 'a commitment to the voice as the basis of literary art, rather than some supposed canonical "officially approved" language'.[12] Welsh is engaged in this kind of commitment as distinct from political activism as it is conventionally perceived. Of course, Kelman is also committed to voice, but there is, on his part and that of his characters, a residual commitment of a more orthodox nature to individual morality.[13] Welsh is more linguistically subversive, more in touch with the contemporary moment, and he takes us down a step lower on the social ladder, to the bottom rung, in fact. Sometimes he takes the ladder away altogether, suggesting immobility and entrapment at the lowest levels of society.

Welsh's subjects are marginal or fringe figures, migrant and vagrant. Like the 'Eurotrash' of the story that bears that title, they are not part of any mainstream movement, but elements of a subculture who move within an informal economy, surviving by stealing and stealth. The users and abusers who inhabit his fiction are not the proletariat as traditionally conceived, nor can they be dismissed as lumpen or as an underclass. Rather, because they defy easy categorisation, and upset accepted notions of who is radical and who repressed, Welsh's characters are best described as 'subaltern', a term whose original meaning, 'next in line', is entirely appropriate since Welsh, as Kelman's tanist, takes his cue from the back of the queue. The meaning of subaltern status as a concept within postcolonial criticism has been defined by Gayatri Spivak:

> Subalternity is the name I borrow for the space out of any serious touch with the logic of capitalism or socialism . . . Please do not confuse it with unorganized labour, women as such, the proletarian, the colonized, the object of ethnography, migrant labour, political refugees, etc. Nothing useful comes out of this confusion.[14]

The space of subalternity is the natural habitat of Welsh's spivs – who are clearly 'out of any serious touch with the logic of capitalism or socialism' – and critics have noted the ways in which Welsh attacks both Romantic Scotland and Radical Scotland, kailyard and Clydeside.[15]

Where Kelman writes grittily and wittily of Glasgow, Welsh's narratives harness the apathy and abjection of his native Edinburgh, specifically the outlying 'schemes' of Leith, Muirhouse, Pilton and Wester Hailes. A rhetoric of resistance yields to a grammar of the grotesque, a magic and tragic realism that can strike the reader as surreal. Welsh's language is in some ways even more uncompromising than Kelman's, his characters' consciousnesses more disordered. 'The kind of language that a pejorative criticism would call 'strong' or 'bad' is a familiar feature, and the use of Scots makes fewer concessions to the reader brought up on a diet of standard English. But where in Kelman there is always the minimal, never the maximal violence in terms of grammar and lexis – a bit of backfronting (for example, placing 'but' at the end of a sentence), a few phonetic transcriptions, and some 'fucking insertion' – Welsh goes to town on the tongue, taking liberties and risks along the way. Where Kelman is a writer of commitment and integrity, Welsh is an author of anarchy and disintegration. One example will suffice to indicate a key difference between the two writers in terms of individuality and morality. In *How Late It Was, How Late* the bold and blind Sammy senses that drug addicts – 'junkies' – are hanging around beside the elevator in his block of flats. They present a threat to him, these 'fucking junky fucking shooting-up bastards'.[16] Sammy shares the dominant culture's fear and loathing of addicts. This is the same Sammy who later cautions his son, who has alluded to 'darkies', against using racist epithets: 'All I'm saying son if people dont want ye to call them a name, ye shouldnay call them it' (345). There is a question here of political consistency and hypocrisy. Such unthinking antipathies, authorial intrusions, and professions of political correctness are rare in Welsh's work. Where 'respect' in the literature of commitment might have meant respect for one's self, or for one's elders or betters, boiling down to deference, in the context of the new writing it means respect for other cultures, in other words, difference. In Kelman's novel, we follow Sammy's progress and share his perspective: that of a man who survives with integrity. Welsh's writing lurks with the 'junkies', rather than loiters with the disaffected, such as the fundamentally decent and humane Sammy.

In 'A Smart Cunt', the nerve-jangling novella that brings the curtain down on *The Acid House*, two young drug-users rob and kill a blind man. The story is told through the eyes of one of the assailants, Brian, and sets out to place the violence and intolerance he feels in several contexts – familial, social, vocational, national, political. The reader of Welsh's fiction is carried along with the perpetrators, until the lines blur, and it slowly dawns that behind every perpetrator is a victim. It's a strong moral stance that seeks to understand rather than condemn, and to comprehend first and foremost by entering the world and words of the individual and their community. Welsh's immersion in the idiom and outlook of his characters is similar to Kelman's, but the crucial difference lies in the absence of a moral centre and of a controlling consciousness. Renton is clearly the key figure in *Trainspotting*, but other characters are given a fair hearing in a way that is lacking in Kelman's fiction. Where Kelman can be seen to keep in place a distinction between the good working-class individual – conscientious, progressive, and resistant – and the bad guys who hover on the periphery – the addicts, hedonists, and time-servers – Welsh champions not only the socially excluded but the politically inarticulate and even the morally reprehensible. Which is not to say that he is amoral, merely that his subjects are not the deliberately dissenting individuals that a certain radical criticism finds it all too easy to countenance and indeed support, but a less palatable rabble whose unspeakable hatred and violence is shown to have a source and a referent, an objective correlative, in the shape of a complacent political culture. Critics who see Welsh's writing as a product of the logic of late capitalism, a symptom of capitalist decay, or just another commodity in a postmodern culture that shelves resistance, fail to take seriously his revolution in language, and his sense of outrage at injustice. Welsh gives us a constructive moral address within apparently hopeless situations. The difference is that his characters do not have to be good or sorry to earn our respect. According to Kelman: 'Good art is usually dissent; I want to be involved in creating good art.'[17] 'Good art' and 'dissent' go hand-in-hand for Kelman, but for Irvine Welsh, as for Mae West, goodness has nothing to do with it.

Welsh, like Kelman, directs his anger and energies at authorities and bureaucracies, but it is less a question of the individual versus the state – an opposition that can always come down to a bourgeois tautology – but more a matter of exposing the extent to which institutions and communities are structured by the very forces they seek to exclude. In *The Acid House* there is a tale of two cities and two cultures that takes as its premise a social encounter between two professors in Glasgow's West End. 'The Two Philosophers' features Lou Ornstein, an American Professor of Metaphysics at Edinburgh University, and Gus McGlone, Professor of Moral Philosophy at Glasgow University. The Conservative McGlone is a bourgeois Glaswegian from a wealthy suburb, while Ornstein is a working-class Chicago Jew. Ornstein believes in the inexplicable and the unexpected, what he terms 'unknown science'. As a reconstructed Marxist he clings to the possibility of social change, and a belief in a future emancipation, though less through the working class organised as the ruling class than by way of some unforeseen departure in rationality. McGlone holds firmly to the facts, and is a hardened 'refutenik'.

On this particular day, ensconced in a University bar, they lament the fact that their conversation always turns inevitably to logic versus magic. They decide to test their differing theories of knowledge and reality in a less 'intellectual' location, or at least one far removed from the informed eavesdropping of colleagues and students. Seeking a spot closer to reality, they take the subway south of the river to a rough neighbourhood where they enter a notoriously tough bar with the intention of airing their ideas within earshot of an unschooled audience, and thus establishing once and for all who has the clearest arguments in lay terms. They concede that this will prove nothing beyond the clarity and precision of their competing rhetorics, but it will provide some sport – more than they bargained for, it transpires.

In the event, they locate a pair of elderly men playing dominoes, and decide to impose themselves on one patron who 'seemed to have a view on everything'.[18] The two philosophers order drinks, commandeer a table, and commence their set-piece quarrel. Ornstein rehearses his familiar argument about the limits of existing scientific wisdom; McGlone holds firmly to his line of Popperian provability and soon, surrounded by a crowd, they have takers on either side whilst the argument becomes increasingly heated. Unbeknown to them, a posse of young soccer supporters is tuning in to their discourse. Eventually, one of the football fans has had enough: enough of fighting talk that never comes to blows, and enough of what is obviously a patronising effort to let the proletariat judge a patrician feud. The youth is especially angry at the pair of intellectuals for treating a friend of his father's 'like a fuckin monkey'. McGlone's protests are silenced with a sneer and he is told that the only way to resolve this dispute is by way of a 'squerr go', a roundtable discussion having failed to deliver a clear verdict. The youth orders the two professors to go outside and settle their differences there man to man. The Scot is somewhat reluctant to see conceptual *frisson* translated into kerbside fisticuffs. Conversely, Ornstein, recalling an undergraduate slight on McGlone's part, is willing to comply with subaltern ethics, and so they step out into the sun. The two philosophers are taken to a deserted car-park behind a nearby shopping centre. McGlone again demurs, but Ornstein starts boxing clever and McGlone is soon bested, the fight ending with the memorable line: 'The Chicago materialist, urged on by the crowd, put the boot into the prostrate classical liberal' (115). The police intervene, and both brawling scholars are apprehended. McGlone tries to assert himself during questioning. By contrast, Ornstein is tactful and polite, and so gets off scot free. The Glasgow police, predictably enough, manifest more sympathy for the amiable American than they do his supercilious and objectionable counterpart. The result is that McGlone is detained on a charge of breach of the peace (and roughed up a little for good measure). As he leaves the police station and heads for the subway, Ornstein is spotted by one of the young men from the bar who witnessed the earlier altercation:

> – Ah saw you fightin this efternin, big man. Ye were magic, so ye wir.
> – No, Ornstein replied, – I was unknown science (117).

We have come a long way for the sake of this joke, but it has revealed the hypocrisy of McGlone's posturing in the furnace of the very factuality to which he has so often had recourse. This little story engages with class, culture and varieties of violence, literal and linguistic, as well as with different ways of knowing. It makes manifest the latent violence and hierarchical structure of academic debate and exposes what was carefully hidden in the academic institution, namely aggression and exclusivity. The entrenched resistance to Irvine Welsh within the Scottish education establishment, especially in departments of English and Scottish literature, can be read in terms of the kind of macho posturing that 'The Two Philosophers' locates within an apparently civil intellectual discourse. It is less a question of the Scottish version of native inferiorism – the famous 'cultural cringe' – than of blatant social snobbery, and this tale lays bare the connection between fictional strategies and situations of discrimination and exclusion. It is appropriate that the last word goes to an 'outsider', an American, a Jew, and an Edinburgh-based academic. Welsh's love affair with American culture, antipathy towards Glasgow, and sympathy for the underdog, not to mention his rigorous class politics, makes him the scourge of Gus McGlone.

As this story indicates, Welsh's treatment of politics, sexuality, and violence, is utterly uncompromising, or, rather, it is completely compromising in its capitulation to the brutal realities arising from cultures of poverty and despair. Where others might gloss over and editorialise the meaner aspects of society, Welsh deals with them directly in a manner so cool and dispassionate as to seem cold and distant. In interviews he is quick to rebut any claims that he revels in violence. Instead, he argues that his writing shows things as they are, not as he would like them to be. As with most writing that cuts across the popular/cerebral divide, there are inevitably readers who are on a package holiday to hell as well as those who live there, natives and tourists. Welsh is aware of his mixed readership, and in a recent interview in the homeless magazine *The Big Issue* he maintained that the film version of *The Acid House*, which he has scripted himself, would be more disturbing than *Trainspotting*:

> It will be more inaccessible, more hard-core. The accents will be harder, so spoiled middle-class brats who want to shop around for their next cultural fix will find it more impenetrable. And those lazy, wanky critics who don't quite get it can f**k off – it was nothing to do with them in the first place.[19]

The problem is that the two constituencies Welsh wants to turn his back on – 'spoiled middle-class brats' and 'lazy, wanky critics' – are often one and the same. Moreover, his hybrid style, with its highs and lows, acts as a magnet for those he wishes to ward off. Far from repelling such readers by proliferating profanity or intensifying idiolect, Welsh is likely to win new readers of the same type. After all, if one wants to live vicariously then the lower the language the better. The lure of a 'cultural fix' is too great for those addicted to scurrility and subversion to be put off by more of the same.

If, in one critical account – the conventional one – scurrility is not necessarily subversive, then, from another perspective, subversion may simply be a stage or a phase, an allowable period of transgression ultimately controlled and corralled by the authorities, an overturning that leaves things exactly as they are. While some critics complain that recent approaches to text such as New Historicism, following on from Foucault, tend to see all forms of subversion as ultimately contained by the state – circumscribed rather than proscribed – Jacques Derrida has always been suspicious of subversion as such, acutely wary of predictable and programmatic forms of resistance, believing that:

> the responsibility of the writer is not first of all to put forward revolutionary theses. These are defused as soon as they present themselves in language and according to the existent devices of culture. It is the latter that must *also* be transformed. And that is very difficult, the very definition of 'difficult'.[20]

Welsh's work is not just cult fiction, but diffi-cult fiction. It questions commitment, redefines radicalism. While subversion suggests explicit political engagement of the kind that Welsh's writing generally avoids, scurrility implies shock tactics rather than reasoned opposition to political authority. Welsh is better known for his subversion of the stomach than for any obvious radicalism, but it is precisely this fusion and profusion of nausea and nous that marks him out as a true contemporary, a writer of (the) moment. Welsh's writing negotiates the twin pitfalls of earnest social comment and individualist apathy. Where Gayatri Spivak uses 'subaltern', a more slippery term than proletarian, to supplement Marxism, I would like to deploy another 'radical' term, a word with deep roots, in order to problematise any stable notion of subversion or scurrility. The word 'squrrility' or 'squirrilitie' is an obsolete variant form of scurrility, perhaps a subversion of normative understandings of scurrility. 'Squirrel' comes from the Greek for 'shade' and 'tail', and my particular focus is on some shady tales by Irvine Welsh. To squirrel is also to secrete and Welsh's writing is also replete with squirrellings of one kind or another. In a nutshell, squirrility is the term I am using in order to point up the ambivalence at the heart of the subversion and/or scurrility debate, where things are not black and white but grey and read. I am taking as a key text a bizarre tale entitled 'Snowman Building Parts for Rico the Squirrel', a story that marks the intersection of two kinds of Welshian narrative: the Scottish encounter with American culture and the manic metamorphoses of social surrealism.

One can instructively compare the treatment of a certain small furry rodent in a crucial passage in *Trainspotting* with what happens in 'Snowman Building Parts for Rico the Squirrel'. In the section of *Trainspotting* entitled 'Strolling Through The Meadows', Spud, the narrator in this instance and the 'cool cat' character, defends a squirrel against the evil intentions of Renton and Sick Boy:

> Rents starts shoutin and pointin.
> – Si! There's a fuckin squirrel at yir feet! Kill the cunt!
> Sick Boy's nearest tae it, n tries tae entice it tae him, but it scampers a bit away, movin really weird, archin its whole boady likesay. Magic wee silvery grey thing . . . ken?[21]

When Renton makes to stone the squirrel Spud intervenes:

> Leave it man. Squirrel's botherin nae cunt likesay! Ah hate it the way Mark's intae hurtin animals . . . it's wrong man. Ye cannae love yirsel if ye want tae hurt things like that . . . ah mean . . . what hope is thir? The squirrel's likes fuckin lovely. He's daein his ain thing. He's free. That's mibbe what Rents cannae stand. The squirrel's free, man (159).

Two women pass and look down their noses at Spud, Renton and Sick Boy. 'Rents gits a glint in his eye':

> – GIT A HAUD AY THE CUNT! he shouts at Sick Boy, but makin
> sure that the wifies kin hear um. – WRAP IT IN CELLOPHANE SO'S
> IT DISNAE SPLIT WHIN YE FUCK IT! (159)

Renton and Sick Boy then hurl abuse at the women, before turning on one another and trading sexual insults. Spud muses once more on the squirrel's innocence, 'that squirrel, like free n botherin naebody . . . n they wid jist kill it, like that ken, n fir what? It makes us feel really sick, n sad, n angry . . .'. He tries to leave the others' company but is restrained by Renton, whom he reproaches for intending harm on an innocent creature. Self-absorbed, Renton does not share Spud's concern for animals and others:

> – S only a fuckin squirrel, Spud. Thir vermin . . . he sais. He pits his
> airm roond ma shoodirs.
> – It's mibbe nae mair vermin thin you or me, likesay . . . whae's tae
> say what's vermin . . . they posh wifies think people like us ur vermin,
> likesay, does that make it right thit they should kill us, ah goes (160).

Renton gets upset, blaming his life, the drugs, the hard man syndrome epitomised by Begbie. Overcome by emotion, he hugs Spud warmly. This fleeting moment of intimacy is rudely breached by Sick Boy's homophobic outburst: 'You two fuckin buftie-boys. Either go intae they trees n fuck each other, or come n help us find Beggars n Matty' (161). In this episode and elsewhere, Spud voices Welsh's concern with cycles of violence, and with the politics of displacement.

Whereas the squirrel in *Trainspotting* serves the function of drawing attention to a common humanity and class consciousness, the one in 'Snowman Building Parts for Rico the Squirrel' is a different species altogether. This squirrel talks back, and inhabits close-knit hermeneutic circles, running rings round readers in a way that would baffle its near namesake Paul Ricoeur. The beast that speaks is a familiar motif in Welsh's fiction. *Marabou Stork Nightmares* has a talking bird at the heart of it, and *Filth* features a wordy tapeworm, whose speech squirms its way through the stomach of the eponymous policeman. Rico is, as the All-American mother Sarah Cartwright tells her son Bobby, 'a very special little squirrel' (137). Bobby finds it hard to accept that his little Rico has to go, despite his mother's assurances that 'it's Rico's mission to spread love all over the world'. Rico may just be sick of the snowman building parts he gets stuck with in the Midwest.

We are presented with a split screen, the doings of a working class family in Edinburgh being watched on TV by a sugary sweet American family, who have tuned into *Skatch Femilee Rabirtsin*, a clear favourite with the kids but evidently adult-oriented. The first line of the framed and italicised Scottish section of the story gives the flavour: 'Switch that fuckin telly oaf!' (138). It's no surprise that Bobby's mother disapproves: 'Listen Babby . . . The *Skatch Femilee Rabirtsin* is a horrible programme and your father and I agree that it's not good for you' (143). In the 'Strolling Through the Meadows' episode of *Trainspotting*, the squirrel functions as an image of corny kailyard cuteness, a pretext for hippy Spud to draw an analogy between himself and his friends as outcasts, and to depict their persecution and scapegoating of the squirrel as a mirror image of the disdain they elicit from the senior citizens of Edinburgh. The squirrel in this short story defies any possibility of salvation or solidarity. Rico is there in TV-land to help 'Babby', but can do nothing for the stereotypical small-screen Scots that he is watching: *Skatch Femilee Rabirtsin* are beyond the pale. Not even the army of squirrels with whom Rico returns, 'their eyes glowing with love', can rescue the Robertsons from their proletarian purgatory:

> – I wonder if one of those squirrels will go and help the little Skatch boy n girl on the television, Bobby junior thought out loud.
> – I'm sure one of them will, Babby, Sarah simpered.
> – Don't hold your fuckin breath on that one honey, Rico the squirrel muttered, but the family failed to hear him, as they were so consumed with joy (144).

Rico's pessimism ricochets off the glass wall that separates the wonderful world of Bobby Cartwright from the dark domesticity endured by Sean and Sinead Robertson; painful realities are not waved away by pat resolutions. Scottish subalterns cannot be represented by the magic eye in the corner of the room, only distracted by it. Culture and technology have failed them. This world of failures and consumers is marked by pessimism, but also, paradoxically, by a realism that is much more acute and accurate than the old stereotypes of masculine workerism and principled opposition that we find in the fiction of William McIllvanney. Welsh's characters seldom have recourse to officially sanctioned forms of political resistance, or even wildcat actions such as strikes or sit-ins. Instead, they practice a subtle and pervasive guerilla warfare, blocking rather than tackling its moral agents and servants of power.

I want to conclude with a brief examination of what is arguably Welsh's most explicitly political tale, 'A Blockage in the System', one of his most effective realist narratives, an absurdist, anarchist, obstructionist account of recalcitrant plumbers caught between two bosses and two local authorities and seduced by the siren call of a card game that represents a triumph of leisure time and social desire over the work ethic. 'A Blockage in the System' is a piece of straight realist fiction in which a group of city council plumbers debate whether or not to tackle a job that involves a blockage at a block of flats, whose source may be internal, in which case it is their province, or external, in which case it comes under the jurisdiction of the Regional Authority. Again, as with many of Welsh's stories, there is an old joke at the heart of it: 'Well, as one anarchist plumber sais tae the other: smash the cistern' (78). Paradoxically, the blockage is outside the system: 'Wir talkin aboot an ootside joab here. Defo' (79). But it is also inside the system, insofar as the plumbers themselves block the attempts of their boss to have them investigate it. In refusing to get their hands dirty and showing a clean pair of heels, the workers draw on the existing division of labour within local government, and their own rich rhetorical reserves, in order to defy the state. This is an important story because it sums up a kind of politics of refusal, of blockage, of hoarding, a cultivated indolence that impedes the progress of the system, chokes its passage. In terms of class and the cause of labour, to be obstructive, in this context, is constructive. What we have here is a highly localised conflict that will never go as far as an industrial tribunal, or even involve the union, since it is a matter of the boss disregarding the professional advice of his workers. The narrator remarks:

> Whit's it the gadge thit took us fir the ONC at Telford College sais?
> The maist important skill in any trade is accurate problem diagnosis.
> Ah goat a fuckin distinction, ah pointed at masel (81).

The workers who quibble on the source of the blockage are themselves the blockage. The phrase 'accurate problem diagnosis' may be allowed to stand as the final demand of Welsh's writing. The versions of squirrility I have identified in these tales – hoarding and hybridity – attest to the resourcefulness of Welsh's literary language. As with all subversives, there is a risk that the poet laureate of the chemical generation will not fulfil his end of the bargain, will sell out, welsh on the deal, and there are already signs of a backlash.[22] But Welsh's writing arguably offers a more subtle challenge to the state and the *status quo* than is provided by a traditional literature of subversion. Welsh's writing forms part of an emerging literature of abuse. Where an earlier culture would have blamed the victims and tried to teach them a new language, the new generation of writers are exploring, on their own terms, and in their own voices, the violence and values of subaltern states. True subversion transforms both form and content and, for Welsh, squirrility is that indispensable supplement which allows counter-discourses to operate successfully: language itself has to be turned over in order for subversion to take place. This conforms to the deconstructive idea of reversal and displacement, where the act of opposition and overturning has to be accompanied by a process of displacement that alters the terms of the debate. Derrida advises us to proceed according to a 'double gesture', a 'double writing that is, a writing that is in and of itself multiple'.[23] Welsh's writing is multiple and marginal, in this manner, rather than singular and central. It may not be subversive in hackneyed, stereotypical or dogmatic ways, but it does undermine unity and authority in its use of voice(s), and in its mixing of forms, genres, modes, and registers.

Notes

1   See Gilles Deleuze and Felix Guattari, *Kafka: Toward a Minor Literature*, trans. Dana Polan (Minneapolis and Oxford: University of Minnesota Press, 1986).
2   David Lloyd and Abdul R. JanMohamed, 'Introduction: Toward a Theory of Minority Discourse: What is to be Done?', in Abdul R. JanMohamed and David Lloyd (eds), *The Nature and Context of Minority Discourse* (Oxford: Oxford University Press, 1990), 4.
3   bell hooks, *Outlaw Culture: Resisting Representations* (London: Routledge, 1994).
4   Michel Foucault, *The History of Sexuality: Volume 1*, trans. Robert Hurley (New York: Vintage, 1990), 95–6.
5   Edwin Muir, *Scott and Scotland: The Predicament of the Scottish Writer* (Edinburgh: Polygon, 1982), 111–12.
6   Mary Louise Pratt, 'The Short Story: The Long and the Short of it', in Charles E. May (ed.), *New Short Story Theories* (Athens: Ohio University Press, 1994), 104.
7   The seven sections comprising forty-six chapters break down as follows: Renton appears twenty-one times in the first person; Begbie twice in the first person; Sick Boy twice in the first person; Spud four times in the first person; Tommy once in the first person; Kelly twice in the first person; Rab McLaughlin (Second Prize) once in the first person; Davie Mitchell once in the first person; Johnny Swan appears once in limited third person; Nina once in the third person (limited); Stevie once in the third person (limited); Billy Renton and friends once in the third person; Renton and Spud twice in the third person; Davie once in the first person; Renton once in third person (limited); Begbie, Spud, Renton Laura McEwan, Matty and Sick Boy appear once in the third person; Kelly, Spud, Gavin Temperley, Renton, and Sick Boy appear once in the third person; Alison, Anthony, Begbie, Mrs Connell and Lisa Connell, Renton, Shirley, Spud and Sick Boy appear once in third person; Begbie, Renton, Sick Boy, and Spud appear once in the third person.
8   See Duncan McLean (ed.), *Ahead of Its Time: A Clocktower Press Anthology* (London: Jonathan Cape, 1997) and Kevin Williamson (ed.), *Children of Albion Rovers* (Edinburgh: Canongate, 1996).
9   Alan Freeman, 'Ghosts in Sunny Leith: Irvine Welsh's Trainspotting', in Susanne Hagemann (ed.), *Studies in Scottish Fiction: 1945 to the Present* (Frankfurt: Peter Lang, 1996); 'Realism Fucking Realism: The Word on the Street – Kelman, Kennedy and Welsh', *Cencrastus*, 57 (1997), and 'Ourselves as Others: Marabou Stork Nightmares', *Edinburgh Review*, 95–96.

10   James Kelman, *The Busconductor Hines* (Edinburgh: Polygon, 1992), 180.
11   Leon Trotsky, *Problems of Everyday Life and Other Writings on Culture and Science* (New York: Pathfinder, 1973), 52.
12   McLean, *Ahead of Its Time: A Clocktower Press Anthology*, xii.
13   Willy Maley, 'Swearing Blind: Kelman and the Curse of the Working Classes', *The Edinburgh Review*, 95 (1996).
14   Gayatri Spivak, 'Supplementing Marxism', in Bernd Magnus and Stephen Cullenberg (eds), *Whither Marxism?: Global Crises in International Perspective* (London: Routledge, 1995), 115.
15   Gill Jamieson, 'Fixing the City: Arterial and Other Spaces in Irvine Welsh's Fiction', in Glenda Norquay and Gerry Smyth (eds), *Space and Place: The Geographies of Literature* (Liverpool: Liverpool John Moores University Press, 1997).
16   James Kelman, *How Late It Was, How Late* (London: Secker and Warburg, 1994), 156.
17   Cited, Kirsty McNeill, 'Interview with James Kelman', *Chapman*, 57 (1989), 3.
18   This and all subsequent quotations, Irvine Welsh, *The Acid House* (London: Jonathan Cape, 1994), 114.
19   Dominic Cavendish, 'Irvine Welsh: I'm Sorry Everybody!', *The Big Issue in Scotland* (1998), 158.
20   Jacques Derrida, in Elizabeth Weber (ed.), *Points . . . Interviews, 1974–1994*, trans. Peggy Kamuf and others (Stanford: Stanford University Press, 1995), 124.
21   This and all subsequent quotations, Irvine Welsh, *Trainspotting* (London: Secker & Warburg, 1993), 159.
22   Joseph McAvoy, 'Now the Drugs Don't Work', *Cencrastus*, 60 (1998) and 'Irvine's Amazing Talking Tapeworm', *Cencrastus*, 62 (1999).
23   Jacques Derrida, *Positions*, trans. Alan Bass (London: The Athlone Press, 1981), 41.

Index